Over the Line

Over the Line

A History of the
England v Germany
Football Rivalry

Alexander M Gross

First published by Pitch Publishing, 2022

Pitch Publishing
9 Donnington Park,
85 Birdham Road,
Chichester,
West Sussex,
PO20 7AJ
www.pitchpublishing.co.uk
info@pitchpublishing.co.uk

A CIP catalogue record is available for this book
from the British Library.

ISBN 978 1 80150 168 2

Typesetting and origination by Pitch Publishing
Printed and bound in Great Britain by TJ Books, Padstow

Contents

How shall we find the concord of

this discord?

SHAKESPEARE

Das Alte stürzt, es ändert sich die Zeit,

Und neues Leben blüht aus den Ruinen.

SCHILLER

Acknowledgements

MY THANKS go to Jane Camillin, Graham Hales, Gareth Davies and others at Pitch Publishing for helping to bring this book to life. Many thanks to Duncan Olner for the splendid cover design.

I am grateful to my mentor Prof. Dr. José Roberto O'Shea for giving me the skills necessary to write a book such as this.

I am also thankful to Tim Vickery for his guidance and support. As many readers will know, there is simply nobody better.

In early 2022 I undertook an insightful trip around Germany for research. I would like to thank Jonathan Harding for taking the time to meet me and for sharing his experiences.

My thanks also to Jörg Jakob and particularly Manfred Münchrath at *Kicker* magazine in Nuremberg for their help and generosity. The *Kicker* digital archive has been an invaluable resource in my research.

I would also like to thank Malte von Pidoll and staff at the German Football Museum in Dortmund for the kind welcome and the comprehensive tour of the museum. *Danke für die Aufmerksamkeit.*

Most of all I would like to thank my wife, Gabriela, for her patient support, and my parents, who are ultimately the reason for this book's existence. The courage of my mother, Claire, in leaving England for Germany in June 1970 with nothing but a will to discover more of the world and to overcome difference is what lies behind life stories like mine, and an Anglo-German upbringing has in turn resulted in my desire to find answers to questions about cultural relations.

List of Matches

FA†	DFB ††	Date	Home	Score	Away	Venue	Competition; notes
-	-	23 Nov 1899	Germany	2-13	England	Kurfürstendamm, Berlin	FA tour
-	-	24 Nov 1899	Germany	2-10	England	Kurfürstendamm, Berlin	FA tour
-	-	28 Nov 1899	Germany	0-7	England	Exerzierplatz, Karlsruhe	FA tour
-	-	21 Sep 1901	England (amateurs)	12-0	Germany	White Hart Lane, London	German tour
-	-	25 Sep 1901	England (professionals)	10-0	Germany	Hyde Road, Manchester	German tour
-	1	20 Apr 1908	Germany	1-5	England	Viktoria-Platz, Berlin	First DFB home international
-	2	13 Mar 1909	England	9-0	Germany	White House Ground, Oxford	Largest margin of defeat in a DFB international
-	3	14 Apr 1911	Germany	2-2	England	Union-Platz, Berlin	
-	4	21 Mar 1913	Germany	0-3	England	Viktoria-Platz, Berlin	
1	5	10 May 1930	Germany	3-3	England	Deutsches Stadion, Berlin	First official international recognised by both associations
2	6	04 Dec 1935	England	3-0	Germany	White Hart Lane, London	
3	7	14 May 1938	Germany	3-6	England	Olympiastadion, Berlin	
4	8	01 Dec 1954	England	3-1	West Germany	Wembley Stadium	First meeting at Wembley Stadium
5	9	26 May 1956	West Germany	1-3	England	Olympiastadion, Berlin	
6	10	12 May 1965	West Germany	0-1	England	Städtisches Stadion, Nuremberg	
7	11	23 Feb 1966	England	1-0	West Germany	Wembley Stadium	
8	12	30 Jul 1966	England	4-2*	West Germany	Wembley Stadium	FIFA World Cup Final
9	13	01 Jun 1968	West Germany	1-0	England	Niedersachsenstadion, Hanover	

10	14	14 Jun 1970	West Germany	3-2*	England	Estadio Léon, León	FIFA World Cup quarter-final
11	15	29 Apr 1972	England	1-3	West Germany	Wembley Stadium	UEFA European Championship quarter-final, first leg
12	16	13 May 1972	West Germany	0-0	England	Olympiastadion, Berlin	UEFA European Championship quarter-final, second leg
13	17	12 Mar 1975	England	2-0	West Germany	Wembley Stadium	
14	18	22 Feb 1978	West Germany	2-1	England	Olympiastadion, Munich	
15	19	29 Jun 1982	West Germany	0-0	England	Estadio Santiago Bernabéu, Madrid	FIFA World Cup second group stage
16	20	13 Oct 1982	England	1-2	West Germany	Wembley Stadium	
17	21	12 Jun 1985	England	3-0	West Germany	Estadio Azteca, Mexico City	
18	22	09 Sep 1987	West Germany	3-1	England	Rheinstadion, Düsseldorf	
19	23	04 Jul 1990	West Germany	1-1* (4-3)	England	Stadio delle Alpi, Turin	FIFA World Cup semi-final
20	24	11 Sep 1991	England	0-1	Germany	Wembley Stadium	
21	25	19 Jun 1993	Germany	2-1	England	Pontiac Silverdome, Pontiac	
22	26	26 Jun 1996	Germany	1-1* (6-5)	England	Wembley Stadium	UEFA European Championship semi-final
23	27	17 Jun 2000	England	1-0	Germany	Stade du Pays du Charleroi, Charleroi	UEFA European Championship group stage
24	28	07 Oct 2000	England	0-1	Germany	Wembley Stadium	FIFA World Cup qualification
25	29	01 Sep 2001	Germany	1-5	England	Olympiastadion, Munich	FIFA World Cup qualification

26	30	22 Aug 2007	England	1-2	Germany	Wembley Stadium	First meeting at new Wembley Stadium
27	31	19 Nov 2008	Germany	1-2	England	Olympiastadion, Berlin	
28	32	27 Jun 2010	Germany	4-1	England	Free State Stadium, Bloemfontein	FIFA World Cup round of 16
29	33	19 Nov 2013	England	0-1	Germany	Wembley Stadium	FA 150th anniversary
30	34	26 Mar 2016	Germany	2-3	England	Olympiastadion, Berlin	
31	35	22 Mar 2017	Germany	1-0	England	Westfalenstadion, Dortmund	
32	36	10 Nov 2017	England	0-0	Germany	Wembley Stadium	
33	37	29 Jun 2021	England	2-0	Germany	Wembley Stadium	UEFA European Championship round of 16
34	38	07 Jun 2022	Germany	1-1	England	Allianz Arena, Munich	UEFA Nations League group stage

† Matches recognised by the Football Association
†† Matches recognised by the Deutscher Fußball-Bund

1

Rivals

WHILE I hope and trust that this book will be of interest to anyone with a fascination for football and its political and cultural contexts, I expect that many readers will be either English, German or – like me – a bit of both. I was born in Munich in 1985 to a German father and an English mother, neither of whom expressed any interest in football. Yet my earliest memory, to the extent that it is possible to distinguish between my own recollections and those of people around me, is of watching the 1990 FIFA World Cup semi-final between West Germany, as it was known then, and England on a small Blaupunkt television in our home in Hamburg. It was an exciting time for the country, with reunification on the horizon following the fall of the Berlin Wall nine months earlier. My mother had already spent 20 years living in Germany and was well assimilated. Except for a few words here and there, my parents, my older sister and I only spoke German in the house, and the green grass of Wimbledon's centre court, so famous in Germany because of Boris Becker's successes in the 1980s, was the only English sporting institution I knew. As I remember it, this match in Turin was the moment I became aware of another side to my identity, having been told that I had a connection to both teams. I knew that for my football-averse family to gather around the television, and for me to be allowed to stay up late into the evening, something special must be happening.

After they were eliminated from the competition on that dramatic night, I forgot all about the England national team. West Germany beat Argentina four days later to win the country's third World Cup, and I was swept away by the euphoria and positivity, while even my parents understood that Guido Buchwald had done an excellent job in marking Diego Maradona. In the ensuing years, I played football in the street on a daily basis, and I eagerly collected stickers and photographs of the German players in the run-up to the 1992 European Championship. The tournament was held in Sweden, the destination my parents had chosen in their ignorance for a serene family holiday that summer, just as the latter stages were played out. The semi-final, in which Germany beat the hosts 3-2 with two goals from Karl-Heinz Riedle, was probably the first match that I watched with a great sense of hope and expectation, and it was followed four days later by the first crushing disappointment when Denmark sensationally won the final. On our journey back to Hamburg, the ferry from Sweden to Denmark was bedecked with a cornucopia of red shirts, flags and novelty hats that made an indelible impression.

In May 1994 we moved as a family to London, and I was placed in a school where neither the pupils nor the teachers could speak my language, or rather, I could not speak theirs. The new boy from Germany was duly introduced to the class during preparations to mark the 50th anniversary of D-Day. As ever, football was the international language that made the gap between the cultures – even then significantly wider than it is now – more easily passable.

On account of the club's signing of Jürgen Klinsmann that summer, my English uncle pointed me towards Tottenham Hotspur, and my emotional link to English football was irreversibly established. England's absence from the 1994 World Cup in the United States meant that I was all the more surprised to see and feel the excitement and euphoria that spread like waves from Wembley Stadium during the European Championship in the summer of 1996. Like most people in England, I was enthralled by Paul Gascoigne's volley against Scotland, and by those few minutes against the Dutch when everything seemed to click. When England reached the semi-final, however, I was faced with a problem. Germany were the opponents, and seemingly overnight, the nation was gripped by angst, wallowing in anti-German rhetoric. It was a bewildering situation for me to be caught up in at the age of 11, and the high drama of the match that ensued only deepened my fascination.

* * *

At some level, every book addresses a problem, and while this book is primarily about football, it is also about Anglo-German relations. The problem I address – to some extent subliminally – in these pages is one of cultural difference. My interest centres on the question of how two nations, two football teams with long and storied traditions could produce so many dramatic contests and unforgettable moments in a series of matches that now spans 123 years. How could a nation which waited 69 years for a first win against the sporting rival it looked to emulate then come to dominate the rivalry? How did the erstwhile apprentice to the pioneer of the sport come to win seven major championships, six more than the former master? What lies behind England's 56 years of hurt? What are the foundational qualities of Germany's indomitable success? These are the questions that a cursory glance through the record books of international football will throw up, but there is much more that an in-depth study of the history of Anglo-German encounters in football can reveal. Just as the two nations navigated a path on which they were once mortal enemies, at other times close allies, and often keen students of each other's successes and failures, so the two national football teams have passed through periods of enmity, admiration and even co-operation.

This book is entitled *Over the Line* because of the single moment that is emblematic of the whole history of the rivalry between these two nations, an incident of great drama and utmost controversy. England's third goal in the 1966 FIFA World Cup Final at Wembley was scored by Geoff Hurst in the first half of extra time, when the score was 2-2. His shot hit the crossbar, causing the ball to bounce down and *on to* the line. The ball did not cross the line and the goal should not have been given, but this is a fact that must coexist in history with the actuality that the goal was awarded and that the end result was a 4-2 win for England. The salient point is that the moment has been mythologised to such an extent that in the collective memory on one side of the debate, the ball *was* over the line. In this sense, the moment represents not just the broader football rivalry, but relations between the countries. At times, a will to believe is sufficient for facts to become unstable. Mindful that no history is truly objective, my sincere hope is that by examining events from both sides, from both English and German perspectives, I am able at least to produce an even-handed account which eschews such wilful obfuscation of the facts.

* * *

At the beginning of William Shakespeare's *Hamlet*, Bernardo, a sentinel, bids Francisco good night on the battlements of Elsinore Castle with the words, 'If you do meet Horatio and Marcellus, the rivals of my watch, bid them make haste.' The use of the term 'rivals' here to denote 'partners' is exemplary of the variant and changing meanings of words, since Shakespeare frequently uses 'rival' in its modern sense of competition elsewhere. The sporting rivalry between England and Germany should be considered with such variance in mind, since at its inception it was in effect a partnership in the development of international football. Later, it was of course underscored by political differences and military conflict, while later still, and particularly in 1966, it became a direct sporting contest for the highest honours. England's rivalry with Scotland, which began with the very first officially recognised international match in 1872, is distinguished by its historical primacy. Yet the teams have only met twice in FIFA or UEFA competition finals, on both occasions in the group stage. Meanwhile, the Netherlands are often cited as Germany's fiercest football rival, and this holds true in terms of both on-field controversy and off-field enmity, but as we shall see, the football rivalry began in earnest only in 1974 and has simmered somewhat since the 2006 World Cup. For historical scope, socio-political context and sporting significance, it is hard to look beyond England v Germany. Added to these factors is the sheer quality and dramatic intensity of the most famous matches between the two teams. The four most important encounters, discussed in greatest detail in this book, are the 1966 World Cup Final, the 1970 World Cup quarter-final, the 1990 World Cup semi-final, and the 1996 European Championship semi-final. All four of these matches required extra time, and the latter two were settled by means of a penalty shoot-out. With this rich heritage in mind, the German term *Klassiker*, often applied to matches against England, is perhaps more apt than any notions of bitter rivalry. England v Germany is best described as a classic of unmatched historical pedigree in international football.

The list of matches printed in this book indicates that the first five encounters between representative teams from England and Germany, from 1899 to 1901, are not recognised by either the English Football Association (FA) or its German counterpart (DFB), while the four pre-war matches between 1908 and 1913 are recognised only by the DFB. For this reason, there are four more meetings in the German records of the rivalry than in their English equivalents. The first official international recognised by both associations was played on 10 May 1930 in Berlin. This match is discussed at the beginning of chapter three, while the nine previous meetings from 1899 to 1913 are considered together in chapter two. The head-to-head record since 1930 is remarkably close, at 15-14 in favour of Germany from 34 matches, counting the two penalty shoot-outs as victories.

The time periods indicated in chapter headings throughout this book are merely indicative. At times they are chosen for reasons primarily related to football – as for example in chapter ten, 'Football Comes Home' – while on other occasions political and cultural developments take precedence, as in chapter four, 'Triumph and Disaster'. In every case, however, the stated years signal the time period of greatest relevance to the given chapter. The German character 'ß' is pronounced as a sharp 's', elongating the preceding vowel sound. I have retained original spellings for the names of German football clubs, including those where the respective city has an anglicised name, as for example in FC Bayern München and TSV 1860 München, both from Munich. The common appellation '1. FC' denotes the first football club in a given place, such as 1. FC Köln in Cologne and 1. FC Nürnberg in Nuremberg. Hamburg's largest club is called Hamburger SV, or HSV; Borussia Mönchengladbach is often shortened to Gladbach; and Bayern München is most commonly referred to as FC Bayern, since 'Bayern' is also the name of the federal state of Bavaria. The DFB's men's national football team is named *Nationalmannschaft*, and in using this term I consider the team's entire history since 1908, spanning various historical eras and the division and reunification of the country after the Second World War.

* * *

Ultimately, a sporting rivalry of this type requires regular competition for it to thrive and retain significance. England's 2-0 victory over Germany at Wembley on 29 June 2021 came 11 years after the teams' previous competitive encounter, at the 2010 FIFA World Cup in South Africa. In the coming years, however, they are likely to face each other more often with more than just pride at stake. The implementation of the UEFA Nations League increases the number of high-quality matches among European national teams between tournaments, and England and Germany have already been drawn together in the 2022/23 edition of this competition. Both teams have qualified for the 2022 FIFA World Cup in Qatar, and England will also bank on qualification for the 2024 UEFA European Championship, where the prospect of success on German soil is bound to stir excitement among England fans once again. The successful youth team programmes of both nations are also likely to continue to produce regular confrontations at FIFA and UEFA tournaments, such as the final of the 2009 UEFA Under-21 European Championship, discussed in chapter 12.

At the time of writing, England and Germany are among the favourites at the 2022 UEFA European Women's Football Championship. England's first win over Germany in women's football only came at the 21st attempt in 2015, in extra time of the World Cup third-place play-off in Canada, but the rapid growth in quality and exposure of the women's game in England will inevitably lead to more high-profile meetings between the two nations. The English FA's 50-year ban on women's football, which was only lifted in 1972 with the encouragement of UEFA, meant that the first England women's international match took place a century after the earliest FIFA-recognised men's international, the goalless draw between Scotland and England in Glasgow on 30 November 1872. Similarly, the DFB only lifted its ban on women's football in 1970, and the German women's national team was not formally established until 1982.

Yet a cultural breakthrough for women's football in Germany came sooner than for its English counterpart, with a television audience of over 10 million for the 2003 FIFA Women's World Cup Final in the United States, the first of two successive World Cup wins for Germany's women's team. Particularly under the auspices of the supportive Theo Zwanziger, DFB president between 2006 and 2012, the *Nationalelf* enjoyed great success, repeatedly winning the UEFA Women's Championship. England's Lionesses, meanwhile, have reached the semi-finals at the last two World Cups and are now enjoying an unprecedented run of good results under the team's first non-British permanent manager, Dutchwoman Sarina Wiegman. England's historic first win over Germany on home soil, on 23 February 2022 at Molineux, indicates that a previously formidable gap between the two teams has now closed.

England v Germany at whatever level and in whatever mode of competition is now a well-established metaphor for the two nations' relative standing in the world, and the pages that follow constitute an attempt to apprehend how such a signification has been shaped over 123 years of history. Almost 20 years ago, the sports historian Peter Beck wrote, 'British attitudes towards Germany, far from resulting from a balanced and informed assessment of contemporary realities, are often influenced, indeed distorted, by fading memories of British greatness and unity of purpose, alongside mythologies, images, emotions and irrational prejudices moulded principally by Hitler's Germany and the Second World War.'

Public discourse has progressed significantly in the intervening years, yet these words still obstinately hold true for many people, especially in private. If this book can go some way to providing the type of balanced and informed assessment that is lacking elsewhere, it will have achieved its aim.

2

Strange it All Seems
1899–1914

When England took to the field in Berlin in May 1930 for what is now recorded as the first full international between these two great rivals, they brought with them, from nine matches before the First World War, an unbeaten record for English sides against German opposition. Seventeen years had passed since the last meeting, a 3-0 win for the visiting amateur side in Berlin, which was the last of four matches between 1908 and 1913 that are recognised by the German football association but not by its English counterpart.

Overall, the series of pre-war internationals between teams representing the two nations, which began in 1899 and comprises eight handsome English victories and just one draw, represents a formative period for German football. By the time the two European powers, Britain and Germany, declared war in the summer of 1914, German footballers had begun to mitigate the great gulf in quality that favoured the English, the originators of association football whose national team was as old as the unified German state itself.

1899
Football Association tour
Berlin, Prague, Karlsruhe
The earliest English sides to face teams representing Germany were chosen from a 14-man touring group which played four international matches inside six days during November 1899 in Germany and in Prague, then part of the Austrian Empire.

The first of these encounters, played on Thursday, 23 November on the athletics field at Berlin's Kurfürstendamm, was in fact the first international football match played in Germany. Moreover, it was the first match played by a representative English XI outside the British Isles, nearly 30 years after the earliest meetings between England and Scotland. Telegrammed reports relayed news of an easy win for the visitors, by a score of 13-2. The hosts were 'fairly fast but they lacked combination and were quite outmatched'. A rematch played at 10am the following day, ahead of the touring party's train journey to Prague, ended 10-2 in favour of an England side with three changes from the previous day, including Newcastle United centre-forward Joe Rogers, who scored five goals.

After an 8-0 win over an Austrian XI in Prague, the tour continued to the city of Karlsruhe in south-west Germany where, on 28 November, the English won 7-0 against a team made up of local footballers and players from Berlin who had featured in the earlier matches. This first foray abroad was a resounding success for the English FA, ending with 38 goals scored and only four conceded in four matches. The visitors were reportedly 'delighted with their reception in Berlin' and, according to *The Times*'s correspondent on the eve of their return home, 'had an extremely pleasant tour'.

While the tour no doubt consolidated English notions of footballing superiority – and in some quarters, invincibility – its greatest impact was on the fabric of incipient German football, with the formation of a national association following just weeks after the visiting English party had returned home. The tour itself had been the brainchild of Walther Bensemann, one of the most prominent figures in the early development of the German game. Aged just 26 at the time, Bensemann sent a letter to the English FA in August 1899 with an invitation to play three matches against representative German sides and one against an Austrian XI. He even appeared in person at the FA Selection Committee meeting on 9 October to convince the English football authorities of his bold plan, and after the tour he was awarded an FA gold badge in recognition of his efforts to promote international competition. The ignominious scorelines, however, did little to help Bensemann's cause within Germany, where local associations opposed his plans and his self-nomination as representative of the national game.

Bensemann's international outlook and his commitment to growing the game of football had been in evidence since his teenage years, when he founded FC Montreux in Switzerland. In 1889, still aged 16, he founded the International Football Club in Karlsruhe, the city in which he would organise England's final tour match a decade later. There followed several years of abortive study in cities such as Lausanne, Strasbourg and Freiburg, where he was reprimanded for 'having induced pupils of Freiburg secondary schools to play soccer, and to indulge in drinking bouts after matches in pubs and a local brewery'.

When, in 1898, the unathletic Bensemann selected himself as captain of the German team for a match against local amateurs in Paris, he was ridiculed in the country's first illustrated sports paper, *Sport im Bild*. According to sports historian Heiner Gillmeister, the incident was followed by a battle played out in the pages of *Sport im Bild* and its rival publication *Spiel und Sport*. The 'chief antagonists' were Bensemann and Gustav Manning, the English-born secretary of the Federation of South-German Football Clubs, who strongly opposed the visit by the English delegation. At a meeting of German football functionaries in Leipzig on 28 January 1900, Manning's faction pushed through plans for the inauguration of a national association, and Manning himself became First Secretary.

Although Bensemann was frozen out and his attempts to send a German team to the 1900 Paris Olympics were voted down, it was on his suggestion that the new association was named Deutscher Fußball-Bund, or DFB. He is today perhaps best remembered as the founder of *Der Kicker*, a weekly football publication launched in 1920. As the son of a Jewish banker, Bensemann was forced to resign as editor-in-chief when the Nazi party rose to power in 1933, and he died in Switzerland a year later. *Kicker Sportmagazin* lives on, however, recently marking its centenary as an authority on German football.

English newspapers at the time of the FA's historic tour to Germany were dominated by reports from the Second Boer War, which had begun just a month previously in southern Africa. Particularly in the first phase of this costly war for the British Empire, during the English winter of 1899/1900, the Boers scored several tactical victories. In the so-called Black Week of 10–17 December, the British Army suffered devastating defeats at the battles of Stormberg, Magersfontein and Colenso, and in January the Boers also prevailed in the brutal battle on the steep slopes of Spion Kop. Such morale-sapping military defeats at the very end of Queen Victoria's reign and at the start of a new century were emblematic of an all-powerful global empire on the wane, just as Germany, a new nation unified only 30 years prior, was rapidly growing as an industrial, military and colonial power.

It is a striking coincidence that English and German teams first competed with each other on the football field at the same time that the respective nations began to manoeuvre into a geopolitical rivalry destined for war. Tensions had been raised in January 1896 by Kaiser Wilhelm II, who was notorious for a string of personal blunders during his 30-year reign as German emperor.

His telegram to the president of the South African Republic, Paul Kruger, had caused great indignation among the British public because it was interpreted as a German incursion into Britain's colonial sphere of influence, and the Kaiser was forced to clarify his position in a letter to his grandmother, Queen Victoria. Perhaps he was still atoning for this error of judgement when visiting the Queen in November 1899, on the very day, indeed, that 11 footballers representing the imperial black, white and red flag first took to the field against the English masters of the game. One *Times* correspondent summarised the mood from Europe on the Kaiser's visit to Windsor:

'Not only is the event regarded as a public confirmation of German neutrality in regard to the Anglo-Boer war, and hence as precluding European complications, but also as a proof that the Triple Alliance [between Germany, Austria-Hungary and Italy] under German leadership has, by renewing friendship with England, regained that predominance in Europe which is held to constitute the surest guarantee of peace.'

1901
German tour of England
London and Manchester

Bensemann's direct influence on the nascent football rivalry between England and Germany extended to 1901, when a pair of international matches were played in England as the FA reciprocated hosting duties for a German touring party. On this occasion the English fielded separate amateur and professional teams, with the Germans first welcomed to Tottenham Hotspur's White Hart Lane on 21 September for the inaugural match of the England national amateur football team. There was some hope in the English press that the visitors would offer more credible opposition than they had two years earlier, and the significance of the occasion was not overlooked, at least in the *Daily Telegraph*:

'The fact of a team of Germans coming over here to play representative elevens of Englishmen is a notable event in football history, and as such is one to be heartily welcomed ... Whether they win or whether they fail badly, they are to be congratulated upon their enterprise, and they may rest assured of a very hearty welcome.'

But fail badly they did. In what was described in *The Observer* as 'dull weather' in north London, England's amateurs scored five first-half goals and ran out 12-0 winners. The match was given an extensive write-up in the *Daily Telegraph* of 23 September, where seasickness and inappropriate footwear for the heavy ground were offered in mitigation for the travelling Germans' inadequate performance. There was agreement among the English press that the visiting goalkeeper saved his team from further embarrassment, with *The Times* commenting, 'But for Lüdecke in goal the Germans would have had a much more sorry tale to tell.' *The Telegraph* speculated that 'the score would certainly have been nearer 20 goals than 12' were it not for Lüdecke's 'brilliant saves'. *The Times*'s report also offers an assessment of the visitors' play as 'very elementary', noting that the 'Englishmen had the game in their hands from the start and played capital football'. The star performer with six goals was Reginald Foster, better known for his cricket career.

Despite their perhaps sceptical acknowledgement of mitigating circumstances, the English press took the game as an indication of the continual gulf between the two nations on the field, 'When every allowance … is made for our visitors, the conclusion is forced upon us that the day when Germany will be able to engage England at football with an even chance of success is still a long way off.'

Comforted by such glaring superiority, the crowd of over 5,000 at White Hart Lane did indeed offer the Germans a hearty welcome, providing plenty of vocal support and even cheering at an English free kick that sailed over the bar when the scoreline was already damning. There is only the slightest hint of irony in the *Daily Telegraph*'s praise for the home crowd, 'Strictly analysed, all this encouragement of the Germans was perhaps not really flattering, but it betokened a kindly spirit, and it is pleasant to be able to state that, however pronounced the shortcomings of the visitors, there was never any ridiculing of their efforts. Indeed, the manner in which the spectators conducted themselves was truly admirable.'

The *Manchester Guardian* warned that 'the visitors from Germany will either have to play a very superior game or else suffer another rout' on the following Thursday when they would face a professional XI. From a modern perspective it is important to note, as did the same newspaper, that at the start of the 20th century 'an average team of amateurs [was] fractionally stronger than an average team of professional players' and so the Germans had perhaps already endured their biggest trial of this two-match tour.

At Manchester City's Hyde Road ground on 25 September, a German team with just one change from the match at Tottenham lost 10-0 to the English professionals. Among the goalscorers was 'football's first superstar', Steve Bloomer, who scored 28 times in his 23 recognised England internationals between 1895 and 1907, and who remains Derby County's record goalscorer. Again, Lüdecke was praised for his efforts in keeping the score down, and again the German halves and backs were said to have 'failed utterly in their attempts to stop the English forwards'. Any sympathy in the press for the visitors after the match at White Hart Lane had now dissipated, *The Telegraph* making clear its view that the German football challenge to the best players in England was, at present, a waste of time:

'For the moment any idea of Germany seriously challenging England at Association football may be put aside as absurd … the Football Association could scarcely entertain for some time to come any idea of again pitting representative teams against any side that Germany could send over here.'

1908–1913
Official DFB internationals
Berlin and Oxford

In fact, no German side would play another international match against any opposition until 5 April 1908, the date of the first official DFB international, a 5-3 defeat to Switzerland in Basel.

Two weeks later, on 20 April 1908, Germany welcomed an England amateur side to Viktoria-Platz in Berlin for their first official home game. The result that day was a now resonant 5-1 away win for England, but the crowd of around 6,000, reportedly a record at that time for football in Berlin, was seen by the *Daily Telegraph* correspondent as 'fresh proof of the success which has attended the efforts to acclimatise British sports in Germany'. Moreover, the Germans must have improved significantly since 1901 for both *The Times* and the *Manchester Guardian* to report that 'their defence was sound'.

Another major setback, however, came the following year. The 9-0 defeat to England in Oxford on 13 March 1909 remains Germany's heaviest loss in international matches recognised by the DFB. As such, it is still referenced in the modern German media when the *Nationalmannschaft* suffer an embarrassing defeat, such as the 6-0 reverse at the hands of Spain in the UEFA Nations League on 17 November 2020. As with the previous visit to England in 1901, seasickness was again cited by the German players as a particular problem. 'I couldn't bear to take the lift in our luxury hotel on Oxford Street,' said Freiburg full-back Josef Glaser, who captained the German team on his debut. Even during the match at Oxford's White House Ground, he 'thought the ground was floating dizzyingly up and down like the deck of the pounding ship'. The footballers had evidently not yet found their sea legs, despite Germany at this time amassing

Europe's second-largest navy as part of the Anglo-German naval arms race. To Glaser we also owe knowledge of the tantalising detail that only ten players had assembled for the journey to England. The final member of the team would be 18-year-old Willy Baumgärtner, whose record as the youngest player ever to appear for Germany still stands today. Baumgärtner was living in England at the time, and his selection saved the DFB considerable travel expenses.

Glaser talked of confusion and embarrassment at the lack of organisation for this trip and recalled how the German players could only stare in amazement at their English counterparts, 'Their combinations seemed to work naturally, each one of them was far superior to us in terms of speed and ball control. Thank God our goalkeeper, "Adsch" Werner, was on top form; without him it would have been much worse.' Perhaps most telling is his analysis, many years after the fact, of the lessons learnt for German football, 'We recognised that 11 individuals did not make a team, and we began to consider which players would combine most effectively in the national team. More and more, we strived for a cohesive team game.'

A decade after the Boer War and the Kruger telegram, meanwhile, the conduct of Kaiser Wilhelm II was once again a concern, most notably because of a diplomatic incident known as the *Daily Telegraph* affair, which occurred between the 1908 and 1909 England v Germany fixtures. Anglo-German relations took a significant turn on 28 October 1908 with the newspaper's publication of a so-called interview with the German head of state. Despite *The Telegraph*'s claims that this was 'an authentic record of a conversation which recently took place between the Kaiser and a representative Englishman, and should be accepted by our readers as absolutely unprejudiced and perfectly accurate', it was in fact a reworked write-up of a conversation between Wilhelm and an English landowner who had hosted him in November 1907. The newspaper sent the piece to the Kaiser for review, and he in turn forwarded it to his chancellor, Bernhard von Bülow, for approval. Yet, after the document passed through the Foreign Ministry without due scrutiny, it returned to Wilhelm unaltered and was eventually published in the *Daily Telegraph* with his consent.

What followed was a diplomatic and public relations disaster for the Kaiser, particularly domestically. He had expressed his frustration at English perceptions of his intervention in the Boer War, and of Germany's ambitions on the world stage, 'To be for ever misjudged, to have my repeated offers of friendship weighed and scrutinised with jealous, mistrustful eyes, taxes my patience severely.' His impassioned assertions that he was 'a friend of England' and his repeated, uncensored professions of amity towards the English were seen as signs of weakness and indiscretion. He was also quoted as saying that he was in the minority among his people in holding this view, undermining relations further, 'My task is not of the easiest. The prevailing sentiment among large sections of the middle and lower classes of my own people is not friendly to England. I am, therefore, so to speak, in a minority in my own land, but it is a minority of the best elements, just as it is in England with respect to Germany.' As the historian Margaret MacMillan has noted, 'At any other time the British might not have paid much attention to Wilhelm's words but they were published when the naval race was entering an ominous new stage and after a summer of public apprehension about a German invasion.' Such factors conspired to ensure that the most unfortunate words attributed to the Kaiser that day would underscore Anglo-German relations for many years to come, 'You English are mad, mad, mad, as March hares. What has come over you that you are so completely given over to suspicions quite unworthy of a great nation? What more can I do than I have done?'

On England's return to Berlin in 1911, the fledgling DFB side demonstrated significant improvement and earned the first draw for a German XI against their illustrious counterparts. A wired report which appeared in both the *Manchester Guardian* and *The Telegraph* on 15 April 1911 notes that the previous day's game 'was fast and hotly contested' and mentions a large crowd, described in the *Chronicle of German Football* as 'the first five-figure attendance at a football match in Germany'. This game took place at Union-Platz in Mariendorf, which was located just a stone's throw from the site of the 1908 and 1913 fixtures at Viktoria-Platz but was a distinct venue. The report goes on to state that 'a well-known English authority who was present declared that the Germans had improved a hundred percent since they last played in England'.

The outstanding player was forward Ernst Möller of Holstein Kiel, at that time a dominant club in the far north of Germany that went on to win the national championship the following year. Aged just 19 and making his national team debut, Möller scored two quick-fire goals early in the second half. He would win another eight caps for Germany by 1913, but like so many of his generation, his life was cut short by the devastation of the Great War. Möller was killed in battle on 8 November 1916, aged 25. He might have been the scorer of Germany's first winning goal against English opposition were it not for an equaliser that day from Hull City outside-left Gordon Wright, who was part of the Great Britain team, made up entirely of Englishmen, that won the gold medal at the 1912 Olympic Games in Stockholm. Alongside the Hamburg-born striker Adolf Jäger, who was able to continue his career after the war, Möller is regarded as the best German player of the pre-war era. His club and international team-mate 'Adsch' Werner remembered Möller's golden moment against England:

'I can still see him running round four Englishmen in succession. He was always driving forward, and with his powerful shot across goal he was a nightmare for goalkeepers at the time. He was a natural outside-left.'

Pre-war enthusiasm for football in Germany peaked for the England amateurs' second visit to Berlin's Viktoria-Platz on 21 March 1913. Both the 1911 and 1913 games were scheduled on Good Friday, allowing for large holiday attendances, and on this occasion a reported 17,000 people forced the closure of the ground due to overcrowding, with the *Kicker* chronicle describing how 'even the pitch-side barriers were breached as young and old alike were standing, kneeling, and perching on the sidelines'. Yet the home crowd would be disappointed, with England running out 3-0 winners. Among the scorers was Chelsea forward Vivian Woodward, captain of that gold medal-winning side in Stockholm. Woodward had been England's highest goalscorer since overtaking Bloomer in 1911, and his record would stand for some 47 years before it was surpassed by

Preston North End legend Tom Finney. Woodward died on 31 January 1954, prompting warm words, published in *The Times*, from the Labour minister and Nobel laureate Philip Noel-Baker:

'Mr Vivian Woodward was, to many of my generation, the greatest footballer they ever saw, and the living embodiment of the finest spirit of the game. His brilliant play and his outstanding leadership of the victorious British team in the Olympic Games at Stockholm in 1912 will never be forgotten by those who were there; he did much to form the splendid tradition of clean play and sportsmanship which has endured in the Olympic competition ever since.'

1914

The Great War

On 4 August 1914, British Prime Minister Herbert Asquith was forced to declare war on Germany upon the expiration of an ultimatum which demanded the withdrawal of German troops from Belgian soil. Aged 35 at the outbreak of war, Woodward became one of the most high-profile recruits of the so-called Footballers' Battalion, the 17th Battalion of the Middlesex Regiment, which he joined in December 1914. The unit was established in response to growing pressure on footballers to join the war effort, but hostility at this time towards professional players in particular was rooted in the origins of the codified game in English public schools and universities.

The first decade of the FA Cup following its inception in 1871/72 had been dominated by teams made up of former public school pupils and university graduates in the south and south-east of England, such as Wanderers FC, Old Carthusians, Old Etonians and Oxford University AFC. When Blackburn Olympic overcame Old Etonians in extra time of the 1883 final at Kennington Oval, the short-lived Lancashire club became the first from a working-class background to win the trophy. The next three iterations of the FA Cup were won by Blackburn Rovers, a slightly older club from the same northern industrial town, and a founding member of the Football League in 1888 alongside 11 other clubs from the north of England or the Midlands. As a signal of the growing strength of league clubs, the FA Cup trophy would remain in those regions for another decade, until Tottenham Hotspur became the competition's last non-league winners in 1901.

The proliferation and rise of clubs that paid their players was cause for much criticism and concern in the English upper and middle classes, but the FA was forced to legalise professionalism in 1885 to forestall a damaging split in the national game. In their exhaustive study of the Footballers' Battalion, entitled *When the Whistle Blows*, Andrew Riddoch and John Kemp affirm, 'The animosity would continue to simmer through the game in the years leading up to the First World War, as the game's amateur administrators strove to limit the growing commercialisation of football and the perceived erosion of true sporting ideals.'

This socio-cultural fault line in and around the incipient English game explains why professional football, to a far greater extent than cricket, rugby and other sports, became the focus of censure from the press and public during the early months of the war. The prevailing attitude of that period is perhaps best conveyed by the famous *Punch* cartoon of 21 October, entitled 'The Greater Game'. The sketch shows Mr Punch admonishing a 'Professional Association Player' with the words, 'No doubt you can make money in this field, my friend, but there's only one field today where you can get honour.' In response to the FA's commitment to play out the 1914/15 FA Cup season, the magazine's caption below reads, 'The Council of the Football Association proposes to carry out the full programme of the Cup Competition, just as if the country did not need the services of all its athletes for the serious business of War.'

With the armies now entrenched along the Western Front and the First Battle of Ypres raging during late October and November, the FA and its secretary Frederick Wall came under growing pressure to provide recruits, and as Riddoch and Kemp point out, 'The hostility towards professional football was growing by the day, particularly in London and the south-east.' Finally, in early December, a meeting with professional clubs was convened by the FA in London to urge the formation of a Footballers' Battalion. A meeting for the players' enlistment was then set for 15 December at Fulham Town Hall, facilitated by Henry Norris, the mayor of Fulham who in his capacity of club chairman had just the previous year succeeded in relocating the struggling Woolwich Arsenal FC to a new site in Highbury, north London.

The battalion was to be made up of 1,350 men from the amateur and professional football ranks, and players would be given leave by the War Office 'to play their club matches while they are making themselves efficient in Army drill'. Woodward, a high-profile star of the amateur game, had originally enlisted on 8 September 1914, but he transferred to the 17th Middlesex on 29 December and reached France in November 1915. After being wounded in January 1916, he survived further deployments during the course of the war but could not return to football.

On the professional side, perhaps the best-known recruit to the new battalion was Walter Tull, a pioneer in the history of mixed-heritage footballers in Britain. Tull's grandfather was a slave, and his father had immigrated to England from Barbados in 1876. Walter began his football career with the London amateur club Clapton FC, before signing for Tottenham Hotspur in 1909 and then Northampton Town in 1911. On 25 March 1918, aged 29, Tull was killed in action near the village of Favreuil in northern France. A memorial unveiled in the town of Northampton in 1999 bears the following inscription in his honour:

'Through his actions W.D.J. Tull ridiculed the barriers of ignorance that tried to deny the people of colour equality with their contemporaries. His life stands testament to a determination to confront those people and those obstacles that sought to diminish him and the world in which he lived. It reveals a man, though rendered breathless in his prime, whose strong heart still beats loudly.'

It is ironic that the Footballers' Batallion was formed at home so close to the time of one of the most remarkable and mythologised events of the Great War, an event closely associated with football in the cultural consciousness. The Christmas truce of 1914 is, for many people, best represented by the image of British and German soldiers playing football in so-called no man's land, the desolate area between the lines of trenches at the front in Belgium and France. The idea that opposing soldiers, perhaps to the disquiet of their commanding officers, could unite in games of football against this backdrop of death and devastation at once underlines the futility of war and stirs a hope in the permanence of human values and kinship.

But did it really happen? Certainly, the concept of any single, organised game of football between 'England and Germany' at the front is fatuous, but there is ample documentary evidence to indicate that games were played in various locations along the Flanders front and that they did involve sporting confrontations between members of opposing fighting forces. 'On Christmas Day a football match was played between them and us in front of the trench,' wrote a member of the London Rifle Brigade to *The Times* in a letter published on New Year's Day. Another letter in the same newspaper mentions incredulously that a regiment 'actually had a football match with the Saxons, who beat them 3-2'. Stanley Weintraub, in his book on the Christmas truce entitled *Silent Night,* cites evidence from the 133rd Saxon Regiment which corroborates anecdotes of an organised match that ended 3-2 in the Germans' favour. The ceasefire, apparently spontaneously agreed on Christmas Eve, lasted only until midnight on Christmas Day, and the rifleman's account of enemy conduct that day concludes with these poignant lines:

'They were really magnificent in the whole thing and jolly good sorts. I have now a very different opinion of the German. Both sides have started the firing, and are already enemies again. Strange it all seems, doesn't it?'

3

Political Football
1930–1938

It was in the aftermath of the First World War and the Paris
Peace Conference that international football increasingly came
to express the political relations and conflicts between European
powers. In their study of German football in the time of Nazi
rule, Gerhard Fischer and Ulrich Lindner cite the national team's
warm reception in the Dutch city of Zwolle for a match against
Netherlands in March 1912 as an example of the friendly feeling
and sportsmanship that had typified the incipient sport before
the Great War, even at a time of rising nationalist tensions.

By contrast, the circumstances surrounding the first postwar
DFB international, against Switzerland in Zurich in June 1920,
indicate a shift in attitudes within football towards the defeated
and politically isolated Germans. Britain, France and Belgium
threatened the Swiss with a football boycott for granting the
match, but it went ahead with the home side winning 4-1. The
newly formed League of Nations – which excluded Germany and
the other Central Powers of Austria, Hungary, Bulgaria and the
Ottoman Empire – had met for the first time in January that year,
and Belgium also excluded those states from the upcoming 1920
Summer Olympic Games to be held in Antwerp. Britain then
led calls for Germany's exclusion from FIFA, and when this was
denied, the associations of England, Scotland, Northern Ireland
and Wales responded to the impasse by withdrawing from the
governing body, to rejoin only in 1924. It was a conspicuously
political stance to adopt for the British football authorities that
had publicly endeavoured to keep politics out of the sport.

With a view to participation at the 1928 Olympics in Amsterdam, a first appearance at the Games for Germany in 16 years, DFB president Felix Linnemann appointed 33-year-old former teacher Otto Nerz as the national team's first manager, or *Reichstrainer*, in the summer of 1926. A first-time coach at Tennis Borussia Berlin, Nerz had made a name for himself as a tactically astute and principled football theoretician, and he soon introduced the so-called W-M system to German football, a formation pioneered by Herbert Chapman at Arsenal during the 1925/26 season. This system was developed in response to a change to the offside law in 1925, which reduced the number of opposing players required between an attacker and the goal line from three to two. The addition of a centre-back effectively turned the existing pyramid formation into a 3-2-2-3 that resembled the letters 'W' and 'M'. Germany beat Switzerland 4-0 in the first round in Amsterdam before succumbing to a 4-1 defeat to incumbent Olympic champions and eventual gold medallists Uruguay in the quarter-final. In Turin in April 1929, Nerz achieved Germany's first win over Italy in the first German international to be broadcast on the radio, and this was followed in June by a prestigious draw with Scotland in Berlin.

Although German football remained steadfastly committed to preserving the sport's amateur status, the years under Nerz's tenure at the end of the 1920s brought significantly improved results, to the extent that a great sense of excitement grew at the prospect of a first game against England since before the war. This was finally agreed in 1929, in the context of Weimar Germany's thriving culture before the Great Depression, and before the untimely death in October of Foreign Minister and former Chancellor Gustav Stresemann, whose prudent foreign policy had done much to reconcile Germany with Britain and France over the preceding six years.

10 May 1930
Germany 3-3 England
Deutsches Stadion, Berlin

While the pre-war meetings between 1899 and 1913 had featured England amateur teams and touring parties made up of a mixture of amateur and professional players, the 1930 fixture was, according to *The Times*'s correspondent, 'The first in which 11 of England's best had met a German team, and, football having taken a firm hold of the German imagination, it was the biggest sporting event of its kind for years.' Walther Bensemann, the pioneer of German football who had helped to bring about those first meetings between the two nations, wrote in his *Kicker* editorial that this conciliatory sporting occasion represented 'the liquidation of the war psychosis, a gateway to the good relations of old, and a clear indication to all countries that in sport we can no longer work under the arbitrary frameworks and constraints generated by the war'.

Victory against England, the originators of the sport that now so captivated the public, was the elusive milestone which German football longed to reach, even if double Olympic champions Uruguay were acknowledged as the best team in the world ahead of the inaugural FIFA World Cup in that country, later in 1930. The prohibitive costs and impracticalities involved with a two-week sea voyage to South America, at a time when ruinous economic depression began to set in at home, ensured Germany's absence from that tournament. The English FA, meanwhile, had withdrawn again from FIFA at the start of 1928, and this time the rift would not be healed until after the Second World War. On this occasion the British associations had disagreed with a concession by the International Olympic Committee to allow so-called broken-time payments, which compensated players for time spent away from gainful employment, to be given to footballers participating at the Amsterdam Olympics. Yet as historian Peter Beck has noted, 'Although the actual breach was occasioned by their refusal to accept FIFA's definition of amateurism, the fundamental problem proved a function of the British football associations' conservatism and insularity.' The English FA subsequently rejected a direct invitation to the World Cup from its Uruguayan counterpart in November 1929. Instead of joining four other European nations – Belgium, France, Romania and Yugoslavia – on the trip to South America, England opted for an end-of-season tour to Germany and Austria. So it was that England and Germany found themselves on the sidelines ahead of the first World Cup summer, when South American football asserted its global dominance.

On 10 May 1930, an estimated crowd of 50,000 packed into Deutsches Stadion, the Berlin arena that was replaced just a few years later by the monumental new Olympiastadion on the same site. The visitors were in confident mood, just one month after winning the annual British Home Championship for the first time since the Great War with a rousing 5-2 victory over Scotland at Wembley. The England line-up in Berlin featured four players from league champions Sheffield Wednesday, as well as Arsenal's prolific forward David Jack, fresh from an FA Cup Final win over Huddersfield Town two weeks earlier. At inside-left was Joe Bradford, who to this day remains Birmingham City's record goalscorer. Bradford scored two first-half goals, his second described by *The Times* as 'a low, fast shot from 20 yards out, the best shot in the game'. Yet the star of this match would turn out to be German captain Richard Hofmann, of Dresdner Sport-Club. Aged 24 in May 1930, Hofmann had already scored two international hat-tricks, against Switzerland in 1928 and Sweden in 1929. On this famous day he repeated that feat, and he would go on to make it five hat-tricks for Germany in five successive years between 1928 and 1932.

The key incident of the match was an injury to left-half Billy Marsden of Sheffield Wednesday after an early collision, reportedly with a team-mate. Marsden was withdrawn at half-time and taken to hospital, leaving England a goal up but a man down at the start of the second half. *The Times*'s correspondent tells us that the Germans now 'took command of the play, and for 15 minutes were as superior as their opponents had been before. The absence of Marsden had thrown the English defence out of balance, and before it had adjusted itself the Germans had drawn ahead.' The underdogs were also helped by the deteriorating conditions: in the rain, Hofmann scored twice, on 49 and 60 minutes, to add to his first-half goal that had cancelled out Bradford's early opener, and an excitable Berlin crowd savoured the prospect of a historic first win against the illustrious English opposition. According to the Berlin paper *Fußball-Woche*, for his third goal Hofmann 'set off with giant strides and guided the ball at the right moment with fascinating assurance past the English goalkeeper and into the unguarded net. 50,000 celebrated as though they were Italians.'

It was in arrears that England then began to play 'the best football of the afternoon', and the pressure on the German goal finally told just minutes from the end when Jack combined with Derby County's Sammy Crooks on the right flank and headed in the equaliser. The 3-3 draw was nonetheless welcomed as a great achievement for the hosts, and for *The Times*'s correspondent, this near-miss for England was indicative of Germany's arrival at the top table of international football:

'The great crowd, disappointed in its hopes of victory, nevertheless departed jubilant over the unexpected draw. The result has given great pleasure in Germany and is one with which all concerned may very well be satisfied. England was unlucky to lose Marsden, but the German side proved itself to belong to the highest class.'

Marsden had suffered a serious spinal injury and remained in hospital in Berlin for over a month, never to play top-level football again. An insight into the impact of Marsden's injury on his team-mates comes from Sheffield Wednesday's Ernie Blenkinsop, who played at left-back that day and was quoted in the German press:

'The loss of Marsden meant everything in this game, not just because of his absence but because I saw straight away, as did the others, that he was completely absent-minded when he fell for the second time. The sight of Marsden in the dressing room was devastating. We know him as such a hard man that we knew he must be in a bad way.'

Centre-forward Bradford, Middlesbrough's Maurice Webster, and West Ham United's Victor Watson were all quoted as saying that England would have won the game with 11 men, but Bradford and Blenkinsop both offered words of praise for their opponents, stating that Germany had played better than the French, Belgian and Spanish teams England had faced on the previous year's tour.

Hofmann, who had been signed by English manager Jimmy Hogan at Dresden two years prior, became the most popular footballer in Germany, lauded by his adversary Jack as the best centre-forward in the world. He would be known as König Richard, the king, and would lead his beloved Dresdner SC to its greatest successes in the early 1940s. Yet despite his immense popularity, he was suspended from the national team by the DFB for breaking the rules of amateur status, and duly missed the 1934 World Cup in Italy where Germany reached the semi-finals. Frozen out by the authorities, Hofmann's greatest game in German colours would remain that famous draw with England in 1930, in which his three goals pushed Germany to the brink of victory.

4 December 1935
England 3-0 Germany
White Hart Lane, London

By late 1935, and the occasion of the first visit to England by a German XI since 1909, the social and political landscape in Germany had changed dramatically, to say the least. Amid the economic ravages of the Great Depression, Adolf Hitler's National Socialists had seized power between 1931 and 1933, with Hitler installed as chancellor on 30 January 1933. Football was used as a Nazi propaganda tool from the very beginning of the regime. An international match against France scheduled in Berlin for 5 March 1933, the very day of the federal elections in which Hitler sought to legitimise his power by terrorising voters and opponents, was in doubt because the French feared for their safety. The game ultimately went ahead two weeks later, on 19 March, after the intervention of Jules Rimet, president of FIFA and the French FA. The Nazi party's newspaper, *Völkischer Beobachter*, was used to peddle quotes from Rimet in which he praised the 'exemplary peace and order' on show in Berlin that day, which 'provided the best possible evidence of the German people's highly civilised culture'. This in a city that had a week earlier witnessed the tumult of the Reichstag fire, a pretext for Nazi claims about communist conspiracies against the government.

The visit of the *Nationalmannschaft* to London in December 1935 was similarly a carefully calculated propaganda exercise, and one which, despite defeat on the football field, seems to have been a great success for Nazi Germany. For in the English press reports of the fixture, there is conspicuous mention of the 'pleasant and sporting' spirit of the occasion and 'perfect peace in all London'. The regime in Berlin certainly stood to gain from such positive international exposure before hosting the 1936 Olympic Games. Now just eight months away, the Olympics represented a major opportunity for Hitler to promote his government and promulgate his ideology on an international stage. Notable members of the visiting party in London were Hans von Tschammer und Osten, the *Reichssportführer,* or leader of the Nazi sports authority, and Theodor Lewald and Carl Diem, the president and secretary of the Berlin Olympic organising committee, respectively. The dignitaries were anxious to head off any talk of relocating the Games for political reasons, as had been suggested by the American Olympic Association earlier in 1935.

Most startlingly from a modern perspective, the special report on the game in *The Times* of 5 December, a rare instance of newspaper coverage for a football fixture outside the sports pages at this time, betrays palpable relief at the absence of meaningful protest against the German regime:

'All that could be observed of anti-Nazi feeling was the attempted distribution of literature, a few scuffles as the police took possession of the pamphlets, and one or two protests – "Stop the Nazi match" – scrawled on walls. There was otherwise no exhibition of anything but good will towards the Germans.'

Such anodyne press reports overlook the contentious build-up to the match and the repeated attempts to force its cancellation. The FA's dunderheaded decision to host England's controversial opponents at White Hart Lane, home to Tottenham Hotspur and its sizeable Jewish following, precipitated a lengthy and bitter public debate between trade unionists, anti-fascists and the Jewish community on one side, and the football authorities and British government on the other. Especially pertinent was the fact that in September 1935 – after the match had been agreed between the respective associations in late August but before word had reached the press – the Nazi party had enacted the Nuremberg Laws, which amounted to the state-sanctioned persecution and denigration of Jews as second-class citizens.

Opposition to the fixture grew yet further when it became clear that an enormous cohort of German supporters would accompany the *Nationalmannschaft* to London. Efforts were clearly made on both sides to allow the visit to run as smoothly as possible, with reports of special trains laid on from the ports in Dover and Southampton to London's Victoria and Waterloo stations, respectively, and sealed orders for coach drivers to take German fans on agreed sightseeing routes. Yet while the major national newspapers shamefully assisted the government and the FA in playing down the significance of politics in sport, the *Jewish Chronicle* opined:

'It is idle to suppose that the great German descent on London has been organised and encouraged – even to the extent of providing cheap travel – out of pure love of the game … there can be little doubt that the ulterior purposes in the present instance is to present to the world the spectacle of mass Anglo-Nazi fraternisation … and to create the impression that this country is reconciled with Nazism and all that it implies.'

The left-wing *Daily Worker* newspaper also published trenchant criticism of the authorities involved, but in *The Times* of the day before the match, a contemptuous editorial under the title 'Sport and Politics' presages the injudicious policy of appeasement adopted by Prime Minister Neville Chamberlain between 1937 and 1939. Reporting on the latest appeals to the Home Office by the General Council of the Trades Union Congress to cancel the match, the piece ridicules the idea that 'a large number of Germans should be interpreted as an expression of sympathy by our Government with Nazism and its excesses' with a curt remark, 'Imagination so extreme has the hallmark of hallucination.' In summarising the home secretary's response to those calling for better judgement, the same report states, 'The event he was asked to ban is a game of football, and a sporting fixture in this country has no political implications. So says every one.'

The editorial was published alongside a letter to the editor which exhibits conveniently similar sentiments, 'Sir, with enthusiasm for the Berlin Orchestra in London and the Provinces and an almost sold-out house for their last concert on Sunday, why should we treat our friendly visitors any differently upon the football field?' It was this prevailing stance of obeisance on the part of the English governing bodies and press towards the delegation representing the totalitarian Nazi regime which shamefully caused the swastika flag to fly from the roof of White Hart Lane on 4 December 1935. Furthermore, an extensive report on the occasion in *Der Kicker* informs us that the ceremonial band played three verses of the so-called Horst Wessel song, the Nazi party anthem between 1930 and 1945, 'The Germans sing along, standing with outstretched arms. Spontaneous applause tells us that the English sports fan wants nothing to do with the protests called for by the trade unions.'

Besides propaganda, the Germans were also not without hope of on-field success on this occasion. *Reichstrainer* Nerz had overseen an upturn in results since the beginning of his tenure in 1926, but especially since 1933. The *Nationalmannschaft* won seven of eight internationals in 1934, finishing third in the FIFA World Cup in Italy, and 1935 had so far brought maiden victories over France and Czechoslovakia. With a 3-2 success over Netherlands in Amsterdam in February, a winning overall record was established that has never been relinquished since.

The team featured the legendary Schalke 04 inside-forward Friedrich 'Fritz' Szepan, and Karl Hohmann of VfL Benrath, scorer of both German goals in the previous year's World Cup quarter-final win over Sweden. On the English side, this match came just over a year after the controversial visit to London of new world champions Italy for a tempestuous game since known as the Battle of Highbury. The two sides had drawn 1-1 in Rome in May 1933, and the Italians had since suffered only one defeat, to the formidable Austrians in February 1934. Manager Vittorio Pozzo, already involved with the national team for over two decades, included in his side foreign-born Italians such as Raimundo Orsi and Luis Monti, both 1930 World Cup finalists with Argentina, and capitalised on home advantage and Benito Mussolini's enthusiastic support to win the 1934 edition for the *Azzurri*. The match with England at Arsenal's stadium on 14 November thus came to represent somewhat of a summit meeting for international football. For fascist Italy, its significance went far beyond the sporting, and Beck notes that the game was 'characterised by a range of unsavoury incidents assumed to be a function of the high political and footballing stakes attached to the result'.

Italy were a man down almost from the beginning, with Monti forced off injured after a challenge with Arsenal forward

Ted Drake, an England debutant that night. The home side subsequently raced into a three-goal lead, and Italian aggression boiled over. Among many other incidents, England captain Eddie Hapgood suffered a broken nose from the elbow of Juventus midfielder Luigi Bertolini. In the second half, the great Internazionale striker Giuseppe Meazza pulled two goals back for Italy, but England's ten men held on to win 3-2.

In the *Daily Telegraph* the following day, Frank Coles reported that the occasion had served up 'more thrills ... than in any international ever played in this country', but that 'as a spectacle of how football should be played the match failed almost completely'. In the news pages of the same edition, he informed readers that five England players had been seriously injured, while Monti had suffered a broken foot. According to Coles, the brutality of this high-profile international match could have significant consequences, 'A prominent member of the Football Association told me last night that, in all probability, a resolution will be tabled next year urging the abandonment of matches with Continental nations.'

Germany in December 1935 were the first such continental opponents to visit England since the Battle of Highbury, so it comes as no surprise that there was much scrutiny in the English press of the on-field behaviour of the two teams on this occasion. Five members of the England team at Highbury that evening also played in the match at White Hart Lane, including Hapgood and the young Arsenal outside-left Cliff Bastin. A report in *The Times* of 3 December 1935 informed readers of an injury to Middlesbrough's Ralph Birkett, who had made his England debut in the previous international, and that 'his place will be taken by Matthews, the Stoke City right-winger, who has been showing splendid form lately'. This was a young Stanley Matthews, aged 20 and with hitherto only two England appearances under his belt. He would play in three matches against Germany in an international career that lasted over 20 years, and from a perspective which rightly venerates Matthews as one of the greatest players of the English game, it is surprising to read the criticism of his performance in this early outing, 'Twice in the opening quarter of an hour Matthews had scoring chances and shot badly. One could excuse shooting errors on a pitch that reminded us of a gluepot, but he had other failings. The worst of them was complete inability to lift the ball into the air when making his centres.' His duel on the right flank that day with Alemannia Aachen full-back Reinhold Münzenberg would stick in Matthews's craw for some years to come.

The match itself was a disappointment not just for Matthews, perhaps because of the persistent morning rain that had brought about that characterisation of the pitch as a gluepot. England, in royal blue jerseys and white shorts, laboured through a first half for which even the star of the match, George Camsell, would not escape censure in the press. Camsell, Middlesbrough's record goalscorer, won only nine caps for England between 1929 and 1936, but his remarkable tally of 18 goals from those games leaves him with the highest goals-to-games ratio of any England international to have played more than a single match. In the *Daily Telegraph*, Coles wrote, 'I had become resigned to a goalless first half when Camsell scored three minutes before the interval.' On this occasion he eluded the Bayern München centre-half Ludwig Goldbrunner, who had, alongside full-backs Münzenberg and Sigmund Haringer, otherwise frustrated England's attacking trio of Camsell, Matthews and Bastin. 'The goal was long overdue, as the play had gone,' wrote Coles, 'and when the second half started we settled down in expectation of a runaway England win. Not a bit of it. Germany, though handicapped by an injury to [Ernst] Lehner, fought back with splendid spirit and determination.'

Indeed, the Germans had the ball in the opposition net early in the second half, only to see the goal ruled out for offside. 'In the next ten minutes Germany were playing so well together that an equalising goal might have arrived at any moment,' observed Coles. Yet Camsell doubled England's lead midway through the second half, heading home a Bastin cross. Just three minutes later, Bastin got his reward for a fine performance, with Camsell providing the opportunity. Both the *Daily Telegraph*'s and *The Times*'s correspondents afforded England debutant at right-half Jack Crayston special praise, with Coles especially effusive, 'Rarely have I seen such a display of perfect tackling, sound positioning, and discreet attacking as that given by Crayston.' Among the visitors, it was Szepan who caught the eye, his blond hair and crisp white shirt earning him the nickname 'Mr Snowball'. Coles remarked that 'were he an Englishman', and thereby able to play the game professionally, 'his transfer value would be considerable'.

The dismissive tone of the press towards those concerned about politics and protests was again in evidence after the match, in a report entitled 'Football Supporters' Day in London: A Sporting Occasion', which appeared in *The Times*:

'London was visited yesterday by 10,000 German tourists who had come to see a team of their countrymen play England at football on the Tottenham Hotspur ground. Here and there traffic was temporarily dislocated, and at one time Leicester Square might almost have been mistaken for a Berlin *Platz*, but of demonstrations and counter-demonstrations feared by imaginative people there was none.'

Perhaps the most damning indication of moral vacuity on the part of the English governing bodies and press surrounding this fixture comes in *The Telegraph* of 5 December, under the headline 'Honour to Nazi Footballers'. The report begins with details of a toast to Hitler given in honour of the visitors during an FA dinner at the Hotel Victoria on the evening of the game. The president of the FA, Charles Clegg, then addressed the audience, 'We, as English sportsmen, desire to express our regret at the annoyance to which our visitors have been subjected. I may say that it is annoyance over which we, as the ruling body of English football, had no control.' Clegg continued in ebullient form, directing his criticism 'amid thunderous applause' at the Trades Union Congress, 'These T.U.C. people seem to forget that football is a sport. It is a great sport, free of all political influences, and, as far as I know, they will never succeed in dragging politics into the great game of football.'

It is satisfying to note how the British intent to depoliticise sport is directly undermined in a short missive from the *Daily Telegraph*'s Berlin correspondent, published directly below the reportage of Clegg's speech. The piece quotes Dr Kurt Stutterheim, the London correspondent of the *Berliner Tageblatt*:

'England regards sport as a factor which binds the nations together. Although she eliminates politics from her mind altogether today, she yet lays great value on the psychological effect of the visit of so many thousands of Germans to London. For on this occasion it is just the people who do not usually travel who are coming together. To this extent today is more than a merely sporting event.'

Among those arrested at White Hart Lane that day was Ernie Wooley, aged 24, who reportedly scaled the roof of the main stand and cut the lanyard that secured the Nazi flag flying above. The charge of malicious and wilful damage was dismissed on account of a lack of evidence.

* * *

The political significance in Germany of the final meeting with England before the Second World War, on 14 May 1938, was magnified by the fact that the Olympic football tournament two years prior had not gone to plan for the Nazi regime. After an easy 9-0 win over Luxembourg, the German XI was knocked out by Norway in the quarter-final. Both these games took place at the smaller Poststadion in Berlin's Moabit district, and the hosts were thus denied the chance to appear at the new Olympic stadium, the gleaming venue for both semi-finals and the final. The match against Norway was attended by Nazi party leaders Hermann Göring, Joseph Goebbels, deputy leader Rudolf Heß, and Hitler himself. Expectations were high, with over 50,000 spectators crammed into the venue, and with a potential semi-final against world champions Italy just three days away.

Germany were unsettled by an early goal from Magnar Isaksen after just seven minutes and never recovered. Minutes from time, Isaksen added a second goal to complete the upset. As propaganda minister, Goebbels had done much to promote the German team as favourites for the Olympic football tournament, and his diary reveals just what an impact this occasion had on the Nazi leadership, 'The Führer is very upset, and I can hardly control myself. It was a real test for the nerves. The spectators went berserk. A battle never seen before. A game as a piece of mass suggestion.' The term *Massensuggestion* carries connotations of influence by suggestion, indicating the positive impression that the spectacle made on Goebbels despite Germany's defeat.

Nerz would lose his job in the wake of this embarrassing defeat, but it was DFB president Linnemann who had insisted on resting numerous established players with the showpiece games at the Olympiastadion in mind. After the painful defeat under the watchful eye of Hitler, Linnemann diverted the heavy criticism to Nerz, an injustice that caused Eintracht Frankfurt midfielder Rudolf Gramlich to withdraw from the national team.

The following year, in June 1937, an invitation from the DFB, with the approval of von Tschammer und Osten, was sent to the English FA. By November, an agreement on reciprocal international fixtures in Berlin and London had been reached. Each association would retain the gate receipts from their home fixture in place of a profit-sharing model but, of course, the return fixture scheduled for the 1939/40 season would never take place. Foreign Office records indicate that its diplomats only found out about the Berlin fixture on 4 May 1938, ten days before it was due to kick off, and while this is barely believable given the press coverage in both countries, it perhaps serves as an indication of the FA's relative autonomy in arranging international matches. Moreover, the little time now available precluded any government-led withdrawal from the commitment, as such a decision would unavoidably be seen by German authorities as a hostile political intervention. The prevailing policy towards Germany at this time was that of Prime Minister Chamberlain's appeasement, and the perceived advantages that the football match held for Anglo-German relations were considered as much as the disadvantages of a cancellation. On 11 May, the England party, led by FA secretary Stanley Rous, duly set off on their post-season tour, with a first commitment in Berlin three days later.

The match against England was the DFB side's final international before the 1938 FIFA World Cup, which began in France just three weeks later with the British associations once again on the sidelines. Between November 1936 and this latest visit by England, the *Nationalmannschaft* had played 16 matches without defeat, and that series included the famous 8-0 win over Denmark in Breslau, Lower Silesia, now Wrocław in Poland. Yet failure at the Olympic Games had resulted in a power struggle between Nerz and his good friend and assistant Josef 'Sepp' Herberger. Although Herberger was named *Reichstrainer* as early as September 1936 for the first international after the Olympics, the complex and protracted working relationship between the two men from Mannheim was only definitively resolved when Nerz stepped down from his post as DFB committee chairman on 12 May 1938, two days before the England game.

The star of the team during this period was Schalke's Szepan, while defender Münzenberg and outside-right Ernst Lehner, who had both played at White Hart Lane, jointly held the international appearance record. Lehner had already scored 19 goals for Germany and would go on to become the country's record goalscorer, overhauling Richard Hofmann and ending his career with 31 goals in 65 international games. Goalkeeper Hans Jakob of SSV Jahn Regensburg had been in the side since 1934 when he replaced Willibald Kreß, whose errors had cost Germany the World Cup semi-final against Czechoslovakia in Rome. In all, nine members of that team at Breslau, with an average of 30 caps between them, took to the field at the Olympiastadion on 14 May, constituting the most experienced international team England had yet faced.

It is the appearance in the German side of the Austrian forward Johann Pesser, however, which signals the complex political backdrop to the DFB's preparations for the 1938 World Cup. The so-called *Breslau-Elf*, or Breslau XI, still considered one of Germany's best-ever sides, ought to have gone on to a strong showing at the tournament in France but was broken up by the fulfilment in March that year of Hitler's long-standing objective of *Anschluss*, the annexation of Austria by Nazi Germany. This caused the Austrian national team to be discontinued and subsumed into a composite *großdeutsche Nationalmannschaft*. At a time when both Germany and Austria should have challenged the likes of Italy and Brazil for the World Cup, what transpired instead was another footballing embarrassment on the global stage for Hitler and the Nazis, as Germany failed to progress past Switzerland in the first round of the tournament.

Anschluss with Austrian football

Football in Germany and in neighbouring Austria had developed in markedly different ways during the inter-war period before *Anschluss*. Although both countries in the early years after the Great War had to make do with international opponents from a small pool of fellow defeated powers, neutral nations, or Mussolini's Italy after 1922, Austrian football was the quicker to modernise. Most notably, Austria in 1924 became the first country on the continent to introduce a professional league, whereas it would be almost 40 more years before a fully professional national league was implemented in German football with the formation of the Bundesliga in 1963. Long-serving Austrian national team coach Hugo Meisl, also president of FK Austria Wien, was largely responsible for this progressive step, and he subsequently oversaw the initiative of the Mitropa Cup, a knockout tournament for central European clubs first staged in 1927. He also pioneered a central European international tournament comprising Austria, Hungary, Italy, Switzerland and Czechoslovakia in a league format that was first played out between 1927 and 1930.

Meisl was a polyglot with a commitment to the technical development and interconnectedness of football, acknowledged by football historian David Goldblatt as Europe's 'first significant football thinker and bureaucrat'. His Austrian team grew to be one of the leading sides in international football during the early 1930s, earning the moniker *Wunderteam*. In Vienna in May 1930, this team achieved a draw against England which signalled what was to come. Between April 1931 and December 1932, the *Wunderteam* compiled a 14-match unbeaten run that included a 6-0 win over Germany in Berlin's Deutsches Stadion. The extraordinary sequence ended only with a 4-3 defeat to England at Stamford Bridge on 7 December 1932, a game in which the Austrians' fast and precise play was noted by the English press. Under the headline 'Austrians Astonish England' the following day, the *Daily Telegraph*'s Frank Coles reflected, 'Continental football takes on a new aspect in an Englishman's eyes after yesterday's happenings at Stamford Bridge.'

Another winning streak followed in the run-up to the 1934 FIFA World Cup in Italy, for which, particularly because of the absence of holders Uruguay, Austria were considered favourites alongside the hosts. Yet the team was significantly undermined at the tournament, which took place between late May and mid-June, by the fallout of the Austrian February Uprising. Engelbert Dollfuss, chancellor since May 1932, had aligned himself with

Mussolini in developing Austrofascism to counter the threats of German Nazism and domestic communism, and his government's erosion of Austrian democracy culminated in February 1934 with a brief civil war against the Social Democrats. Dollfuss was later assassinated as part of a Nazi *Putsch*, but not before the World Cup, in which a discomfited *Wunderteam* laboured to narrow wins over France and Hungary before losing to Italy in the Milan semi-final.

Worse still, the subsequent play-off for third place in Naples ended in a 3-2 defeat to Germany. The game began inauspiciously for the Austrians, who lost the right to wear their traditional white shirts in a drawing of lots after the teams arrived in near-identical kits. At the height of tensions between Dollfuss's Austria and Nazi Germany, the irony of both teams potentially playing in white was not lost on the reporter for the Austrian newspaper *Reichspost*, who quipped, 'An *Anschluss* on the sports field would be absurd, just as it would be in the political arena.' The Austrians ultimately played in the sky-blue jerseys of local side SSC Napoli, further endearing themselves to an Italian public that was politically aligned with Austria. Yet the already beaten and disconsolate *Wunderteam*, without injured talisman Matthias Sindelar, were no match for a German side that here reached 'an unprecedented level' according to Fischer and Lindner. Austria would lose again to Italy in the final of the 1936 Olympic football tournament in Berlin, and Meisl remained in post until his death in February 1937. His involvement with the national team spanned three decades and ended just over a year before the demise of Austrian football as part of *Anschluss*.

The larger German national team came into being directly after the sham plebiscite of 10 April 1938 that legally confirmed the Nazi annexation of Austria. A month had already passed since the *Wehrmacht* moved into Austrian territory unopposed, and on 3 April an unofficial football match had been staged in Vienna as part of a propaganda campaign. Known in German as *Anschlussspiel* or *Versöhnungsspiel* (reconciliation match), the game ended in a 2-0 win for the hosts, although of course the entire exercise was designed to show that neither side was now playing away from home. In Austria, star player Sindelar's legacy is in part founded on his refusal to play for the new national team after *Anschluss*, and this match in front of around 60,000 people in Vienna would be his last international. The lore around his demands for his team to play in red and white, his passionate celebration in front of visiting German dignitaries, and his valedictory goal for Austria that day has grown and grown. Sindelar's death on 23 January 1939, ostensibly due to carbon monoxide poisoning in his home, remains a ground for widespread speculation.

As an emblem of solidarity and with a view to the international exposure afforded by the upcoming World Cup in France, the Nazi leadership now demanded the inclusion of at least five Austrian players in the new German national team. DFB president Linnemann reportedly responded to the *Reichstrainer*'s misgivings with the words, 'Don't you know what has happened here? The *Führer* wants a 6:5 or a 5:6 split. That is what history expects from us.' Herberger was thus presented with a formidable predicament, as the two in-form teams embodied differing qualities. For the Germans, the emphasis lay on fitness, speed and mental discipline, while the *Wunderteam* exhibited a more offensive, intuitive and technically proficient style.

Quite apart from Sindelar's withdrawal, there were interpersonal problems too, in part because the German players still officially held amateur status in opposition to their professional counterparts. 'The mood among the players was marked by mistrust and mutual dislike,' note Fischer and Lindner, 'with the players from the old empire in particular seeing their Austrian colleagues as arrogant.' With reference to the coffee-house traditions of Vienna, Herberger later reflected, 'A Viennese blend with a Prussian twist – it couldn't have gone well.' The World Cup training camp in the Black Forest began on 2 May, and preparations for the visit of England on 14 May added to the disruption, since Herberger was expected to field a team of German players for that match, before completing preparations for a combined German and Austrian XI to appear at the tournament in June. Fischer and Lindner suggest that the 'banal motive' of higher gate receipts in Berlin for a team of home-grown players was behind a DFB decision to field the nine members of the *Breslau-Elf* against England, but it is more likely to reflect an agreement between the respective associations that England would play a German team which did not benefit from the politics of *Anschluss*. On the following day in the same stadium, Aston Villa would face a team of former Austrian internationals, and if *The Times*'s correspondent in Berlin, displaying that publication's then-customary intent to downplay the role of politics in sport, is to be believed, high gate receipts from either fixture were seemingly not in doubt:

'The international football match between England and Germany, which will be played here to-morrow at the Olympic Stadium, and the match on Sunday between Aston Villa and an Austrian XI, have for the German public thrust politics into the background. Tickets for both games have been sold out for many weeks, and each will be watched by 100,000 spectators from all parts of Germany.'

14 May 1938
Germany 3-6 England
Olympiastadion, Berlin

The final meeting between England and Germany before the Second World War was thus the best attended football match between these two nations in history. This was the first England side to play at the famous Olympiastadion that still stands today in Berlin's Westend district, and which is the German venue that has hosted the most iterations of this fixture. *Der Kicker*, at this time announcing itself on its cover page as the 'official outlet of the Reich Office for Football in the German Reich League for Physical Exercise', reported on the great excitement generated by the match, stating that 410,000 tickets had been requested with only 105,000 available.

Ultimately, however, this politically charged encounter – perhaps one of England's greatest-ever sporting victories given the circumstances – will be remembered for a momentary but consequential gesture made before a ball was kicked in anger. In the days following the match, the photograph showing the England team performing the Nazi salute in the Olympiastadion was printed in newspapers around the world. England's salute followed calls in the *Daily Worker* during the preceding week 'not to have anything to do with efforts to embrace them in a political stunt designed especially for the consumption of the German masses, thus kidding them that we in this country are in support of Hitler'. On the advice of the British ambassador to Berlin, Nevile Henderson, FA officials agreed that the gesture, proffered in front of Nazi leaders Heß, Goebbels, von Tschammer und Osten, and Foreign Minister Joachim von Ribbentrop, was the correct course of action. Indeed, in reviewing the post-season tour, the FA later concluded that the players' salute 'did much to ensure a friendly reception by the huge crowd present' and created 'the right atmosphere'. Accounts from those involved in this regrettable episode vary greatly, with FA secretary Rous claiming that he faced little objection from the players, while Eddie Hapgood described 'much muttering in the ranks' upon the instruction. Matthews, meanwhile, presented a very different scene in his autobiography *The Way It Was*:

'The dressing room erupted. There was bedlam. All the England players were livid and totally opposed to this, myself included. Everyone was shouting at once. Eddie Hapgood, normally a respectful and devoted captain, wagged his finger at the official and told him what he could do with the Nazi salute, which involved putting it where the sun doesn't shine.'

This account, in a book professing to record 'the way it was', was published in 2000 and written at a great historical distance, having been omitted from Matthews's earlier memoirs. As such, it should be considered with caution, although as Beck has noted, some contemporary press reports do offer corroboration for players resisting the FA's directive. For these reasons, I am inclined to subscribe to David Downing's conclusion on the matter:

'It seems most likely that the players held a variety of views, that some objected to giving the salute because they despised the Nazis, that others demurred because they hated the idea of being involved in any political act, and that others again had no strong feelings one way or the other.'

After dutifully saluting before kick-off on the following day, Jimmy Hogan's Aston Villa side reneged on an agreement to repeat the gesture at the end of the game against the former Austrian internationals. *Daily Express* correspondent Henry Rose described what transpired after an ill-tempered contest, 'The

German players lined up to give the Nazi salute but the Villa team, with the exception of [Jimmy] Allen, the captain and one or two others, ran off the field. Allen tried to call the players back but they refused to return.' Probably overstating the significance of an episode that went unreported in the German press, Rose added, 'The view of the Football Association officials who watched the game was that all the good work of the previous day, when England had defeated Germany 6-3 in the international in a friendly atmosphere, had been completely destroyed.'

Overshadowed in the modern consciousness by our judgements of the politics of appeasement and the shameful salute, England's win in the cauldron of Hitler's Olympiastadion, in stiflingly hot sunshine, was in footballing terms a great success. A relatively inexperienced side, with only Hapgood and Bastin on double figures in terms of international appearances, had barely two days in Berlin to prepare for this encounter with a disciplined German XI that had just completed a ten-day training camp in the Black Forest, albeit with the organisational difficulties outlined above. In his eighth international, Matthews at outside-right again lined up against Münzenberg, his adversary at White Hart Lane two and a half years prior. On this occasion England's 'Wizard of the Dribble' tormented his opponent in a performance he still remembered fondly some 60 years later, 'My confidence soared as time and again I got the better of Münzenberg. I was pulling out all the stops, he returned again and again but never once did he win the ball from me.'

England took the lead after a quarter of an hour when West Ham United's Len Goulden had his shot parried by Jakob, only for Bastin to score. After an equaliser from Rudolf Gellesch, England raced into a 3-1 lead with quick-fire goals from Jackie Robinson of Sheffield Wednesday and Aston Villa's Frank Broome, who was singled out for effusive praise in the *Daily Telegraph*, 'Not for a long time has an England forward line been so well led as by Broome.' Shortly before the interval, Matthews got his name on the scoresheet with a virtuoso solo effort from the right wing, but the German centre-forward Josef Gauchel, the only player in the team besides the Austrian Pesser not to have appeared at Breslau, headed in from a corner to reduce the arrears still before half-time.

The second half began with another England goal, Robinson's second putting the visitors 5-2 ahead, before Pesser added a third for Germany 15 minutes from time. It just remained for Goulden to add the crowning touch to a thrilling and dominant England performance with an effort described by Matthews as 'probably the greatest goal I ever saw in football'. Matthews had again left Münzenberg in his wake on the right flank before dispatching a cross that Jakob was just able to palm away. The ball then fell to Goulden on the left side of the penalty area, only to be returned to goal by means of a fierce right-footed volley. Description of Goulden's finish is best left for Matthews, notwithstanding his embellishment of the distance involved:

'To use modern parlance, his shot was like an Exocet missile. The German goalkeeper may well have seen it coming, but he could do nothing about it. From 25 yards the ball screamed into the roof of the net with such power that the netting was ripped from two of the pegs by which it was tied to the crossbar. The terraces of the packed Olympic Stadium were as lifeless as a string of dead fish.'

The German press were similarly impressed with England's spectacular sixth goal, as may be seen in this example from the special 22-page section dedicated to the game in *Der Kicker*:

'Goulden made himself into a footballing immortal in Berlin with his missile of a shot. People will talk about his ferocious finish, which no one saw but which Jakob felt with all the more pain, for many years to come. It was a drastic demonstration of the confidence and power of the English in their shooting.'

England's 6-3 win in Berlin was called 'a splendid exhibition' in *The Times* of 16 May, while the *Manchester Guardian* of the same day reported, 'Words apparently almost fail German sports writers today in their descriptions of the English team.' The German publication *Fußball-Woche* concluded, 'They are the world champions of football after all, these English. If a proof has been necessary it was shown in the wonderful game of the English national 11 [who] showed how football should be played.' However, the symbolic Nazi propaganda victory in footballing defeat is underlined by a quotation from the party newspaper, *Völkischer Beobachter*, that was printed in the *Daily Telegraph* two days after the match:

'The action of the Englishmen in raising their right arms in greeting during the playing of the German National Anthems and in taking leave of the spectators with the German greeting at the end of the game was particularly well received. In itself probably only a gesture of politeness; but when one knows the disinclination of English footballers for every kind of formality, this proof of esteem of comradely feeling should be particularly emphasised.'

It is difficult today to eschew the conclusion that a contest which was accented by one of England's best-ever performances against Germany on the football field was effectively over before it began.

* * *

Hans Jakob suffered personal tragedy when his four-year-old daughter was taken ill shortly before the game, and coach Herberger denied his goalkeeper's request to leave the team. Jakob's daughter died soon after, causing him to withdraw from the World Cup squad. 'I could never have played in my condition at the time, grieving for our child,' he was quoted as saying years later. Jakob later returned to the national team for three more games but was forced to retire after the 5-1 defeat to Hungary in September 1939, due to a severe lung infection. With his status as Jahn Regensburg's greatest-ever player secured, Hans Jakob died on 24 March 1994, aged 85. One of his most memorable quotes is now displayed on the wall outside the dressing room at the club's Jahnstadion Regensburg:

'A footballer's first responsibility is to be a good team-mate. No matter how great a player may be, if he does not possess this virtue, he will do more harm than good to his club. A team can be made up of the best individuals, but if there is no cohesion, it will never achieve the same success as a team with less talented players who resolutely stick together.'

4

Triumph and Disaster

1949–1958

On 8 May 1945, almost six years after Britain declared war on Nazi Germany, Prime Minister Winston Churchill stood on the balcony at Whitehall and waved to the jubilant crowds that amassed to celebrate the enemy's unconditional surrender. It would become known as Victory in Europe Day, or VE Day. Its 75th anniversary was celebrated in Britain in poignant circumstances in 2020, just weeks after the beginning of the Covid-19 pandemic and during a full national lockdown. A two-minute silence at 11am was followed at 3pm by the BBC broadcast of Churchill's words from the same moment 75 years earlier, 'We may allow ourselves a brief period of rejoicing, but let us not forget for a moment the toils and efforts that lie ahead.'

Just two months after he had delivered this message, Churchill was voted out of office and replaced by Clement Attlee, whose Labour government faced the formidable task of rehabilitating the country's postwar economy. Rationing would become the most important issue of the next general election in 1950, as the Conservatives campaigned to put an end to the austerity measures that marked the first five years of recovery. Europe experienced a harsh winter in 1946/47, with particularly adverse weather conditions affecting Britain from the end of January 1947. Disruptions to the energy supply necessitated many restrictions, and fuel and food shortages quickly followed. These problems came at a time when resources were already stretched, as large sums were diverted to sustain destitute German citizens in the British sector of occupied Germany. Moreover, at the start of that same winter, on 6 November, the government passed the National Health Service Act 1946. This established one of the first universal health care systems in the world, building upon the innovations of Otto von Bismarck in the German empire of the late 19th century.

In Germany, meanwhile, 8 May 1945 was for many years known as *Stunde Null*, or zero hour. This disputed term was initially used to designate the critical transfer of power from the *Wehrmacht* and SS to the Allies on the day of surrender, but it later came to be applied to the four-year period of Allied occupation in Germany between the end of the war and the formation of the Federal Republic of Germany (*Bundesrepublik Deutschland*, or BRD) on 23 May 1949. In this sense, *Stunde Null* signified not only the unconditional surrender and conclusive dissolution of the national socialist state, but also the notion that the widespread destruction of cities, businesses and infrastructure brought about a comprehensive rupture with the past in German society, meaning that there was no continuity between the BRD and its predecessors.

It was a period of intense hardship, with the winter of 1946/47 remembered as the self-evidently named *Hungerwinter*. The demand for basic necessities grew with a circa ten per cent increase in the population immediately after the war as between eight to ten million displaced persons, including foreign prisoners of war and concentration camp inmates, began to be integrated in society. The desperate conditions and everyday focus on survival meant that for many in postwar Germany the spectre of the Nazi regime receded quickly into the distance, as exemplified by one British officer's impressions of Berlin in 1946, 'It was simply impossible to harbour any feelings of enmity towards these unhappy creatures.'

The Allied initiative of denazification (*Entnazifizierung*) also assisted in this but was undermined by mutual mistrust and growing tensions between the Western Allies and the Soviet Union. Deteriorating relationships also caused plans to dismember and deindustrialise the German state to be shelved in favour of a system in which each Allied power would receive reparation payments from its respective occupation zone. The division of Germany into four zones had been agreed at the

Yalta Conference in February 1945 and was then ratified at Potsdam in August of the same year, but the vexatious question of war reparations contributed to the widening rift with the Soviets during 1945 and 1946 that brought about the start of the Cold War and, eventually, the formation of two separate German states by 1949: the BRD in the west and the German Democratic Republic (*Deutsche Demokratische Republik*, or DDR) in the east.

The twin economic measures of the United States' Marshall Plan and the introduction of the Deutsche Mark in 1948 provided the conditions to revitalise the country and signalled America's intent to establish a separate West German state geared towards free market capitalism. In response, the Soviets blockaded West Berlin with a view to preventing the new currency's introduction into the city. All road and rail links with West Germany were severed, prompting the remarkable joint American and British enterprise of the Berlin airlift, which saw food and supplies delivered to the citizens of West Berlin between June 1948 and May 1949. It was a crucial turning point in the relationship between Germany and the Western Allies, and thereby in Anglo-German relations. In his authoritative volume *A History of 20th-Century Germany*, Ulrich Herbert writes, 'Probably no other event of the postwar period had a greater effect in strengthening the emotional bond between the West Germans and the Western world than this one.'

For the inhabitants of West Berlin and those watching in the rest of West Germany, 'The aggressiveness and brutality of the Soviet Union was contrasted with the daring assistance of the British and American pilots.' Meanwhile, the city of Berlin at this time became a symbol of the free world in the context of a growing preoccupation on the part of British and American politicians to stop western Europe, specifically Germany, from falling into the Soviet sphere of influence. Herbert's explanation of the impact of this geopolitical development on the German people bears quoting at length:

'For the Germans, and particularly for the West Germans, this was a remarkable piece of good fortune, as would soon become clear. For, in this way, the conflict between Nazi Germany and the Allies, the catastrophic impact of Germany's policies of war and annihilation, and the resulting consequences for the Germans, were overlain and supplanted ... by the new world conflict between the western democracies and the Soviet dictatorship. As a result, Germany's role and importance altered quite miraculously. The country was rehabilitated "with unnatural rapidity" and transferred from the role of beaten and ostracised foe to that of "partner on probation".'

Among reasons for the, at times, spirited contestation of the term *Stunde Null* in German cultural and intellectual life is the problematic notion of starting 'from zero' and forgetting, as opposed to processing, the past. A more scrupulous public discourse around the nation's relationship with its past is seen to have begun in earnest only during the 1960s and 70s, and in some institutions much later still. By the end of the 20th century, this process had earned the suitably convoluted denomination of *Vergangenheitsbewältigung*, a word perhaps necessarily particular to the German language but which may be translated as 'the struggle to come to terms with the past'. A pointedly apposite example of a high-level German institution that experienced significant problems in this struggle is the country's football association, the DFB. In an essay published at the turn of this century, the renowned football writer Dietrich Schulze-Marmeling was particularly critical of the political history of the DFB:

'The political side of its history is far less glorious than the sporting. It is marked by the dominance of hard-line conservative officials, who repeatedly showed themselves to be susceptible to making contacts and arrangements with right-wing extremist dictators and ideologues.'

Schulze-Marmeling goes on to explain that after 1945, 'democratisation and denazification largely passed the DFB by' as the association sought to insulate itself from politics. An illustrative example is the infamous speech made by DFB president Peco Bauwens during the reception for the 1954 FIFA World Cup winners at the Löwenbräukeller beer hall in Munich. The radio transmission of the event was cut when Bauwens invoked rhetoric that recalled the national socialist era, giving rise to much debate within politics and the press. Gerhard Fischer and Ulrich Lindner, meanwhile, note with heavy sarcasm the tendency of former players and officials to claim that they were uninterested in politics and had resisted Nazi party influence between 1933 and 1945, 'The accumulation of politically blinkered people, who claim to have been so removed from politics and the outside world, is somewhat astonishing.' Despite the high-profile failures the Nazis experienced with football during the 1930s, as outlined in the previous chapter, there is no question that the regime nonetheless instrumentalised the sport to achieve its foreign policy goals. The authors of *Stürmer für Hitler* conclude that football was utilised in this way, even if it was never again the direct focus for ideological fomentation after the calamity of the 1936 Olympic Games.

Perhaps the most troublesome question for German football to address is that of individual responsibility. To this end, Fischer and Lindner employed the categories used by the *Spruchkammerverfahren* (a word which designates the special denazification tribunals held in the western Allied-occupied zones primarily during 1945 and 1946) to differentiate between active Nazis; *Mitläufer*, or passive followers; and *Widerständler*, or resisters. Among the first group of most serious offenders are Guido von Mengden, DFB press attaché from 1933; Felix Linnemann, president of the DFB from 1925 to 1945; and Otto Nerz, Germany's first national team manager from 1926. In the case of Nerz, a series of articles he published in 1943 point to his virulent antisemitism, allowing for the conclusion that he 'appears as a thoroughly politically minded person who openly professed national socialism and was politically active'. It is perhaps this definition for Nerz's grievous transgressions which in part exonerated his successor, Sepp Herberger, who remained in his post as national team manager for almost two decades after 1945. Herberger is classed by Fischer and Lindner as a *Mitläufer*, a term used for passive followers of the Nazi regime, and to which category the majority of respondents during the denazification process were assigned. His extensive notebooks famously contain no mention of politics or indeed anything outside football, and the suggestion is that he cleverly prioritised his football career and avoided political engagement, but as Fischer and Lindner rightly note, 'From today's perspective, it is difficult to understand how someone could maintain such disinterest in view of the clearly evident radicalisation of the regime.' Indeed, David Goldblatt ascribes to Herberger an 'emotional autism and narrowness of vision' that was paradoxically necessary for him to survive in his post and rebuild German football in the context of *Stunde Null*. What cannot be questioned from a football perspective is that the retention of Herberger as national team manager led to the German national team's greatest triumph less than a decade after the end of the Second World War, and with it a sporting zero hour for the German psyche.

Following a request from the English FA in 1949, FIFA lifted the postwar ban on German clubs facing international opposition, still before the establishment of a new federal government and thus initially under the auspices of the occupying powers. The DFB was then formally re-established on 21 January 1950, just a week before the 50th anniversary of its initial foundation in Leipzig. On 22 September of the same year, albeit too late to allow for participation in the first postwar World Cup, the association was formally readmitted by FIFA. Two months later still, on 22 November, it was time for the first official German international match since 1942. The immense crowd of 115,000 in Stuttgart for the match against Switzerland is indicative of the collective will to forge a new national identity through football. Yet since the new federal republic did not yet have a national anthem, the stadium fell silent for one minute ahead of the game. This peculiarity must also have given pause to reflect, and to remember the international players that had been lost to the conflict, since nine of the 12 players used that day were debutants. As Alex Raack mindfully put it in an article for the 60th anniversary of the occasion:

'Herberger could not even invite many of his protégés from the past as guests of honour to the Neckarstadion – they being dead or still in captivity, robbed of their youth by their own war-hungry nation, by blind fanaticism, and by the weapons of the enemy.'

Herberger's young side delighted the great crowd with a victory by means of a first-half penalty from Herbert Brudenski of Werder Bremen. The team would play another 18 matches, suffering just three defeats, before taking to the field at the 1954 FIFA World Cup in Switzerland. Of particular note was the

3-2 defeat to Ireland at Dalymount Park on 17 October 1951, in which an apparent last-minute equaliser from a corner was discounted when the referee claimed to have previously blown the final whistle. Alongside its report on what it called a 'moral victory' in Dublin, the German paper *Sport-Magazin* gave details of a mischievous suggestion from among the DFB delegation to present the referee with a stopwatch at the post-match banquet, on account of his failure to allow for the requisite amount of additional time to be played after an earlier pitch invasion by Irish fans. The referee in question was the Englishman William Ling, with whom the *Nationalmannschaft* would again have significant dealings some years hence.

* * *

In the same year as the rebirth of the DFB and the *Nationalmannschaft*, the English FA finally sent its national team to participate in a FIFA World Cup for the first time, having rejoined the federation in 1946. The fourth edition of the tournament was held in Brazil in 1950 and is forever remembered for its final match, the *Maracanaço*, in which the host nation succumbed to a shock 2-1 defeat at the hands of Uruguay in front of almost 200,000 people at the Maracanã Stadium in Rio de Janeiro. By that point, two weeks had already passed since England were eliminated from the tournament in discreditable fashion. The premature exit came as an awakening jolt for English football after four postwar seasons in which its presumed superiority had gone largely unquestioned. Indeed, the 10-0 win over Portugal in Lisbon on 25 May 1947 and the 4-0 success in Turin against the Italians on 16 May 1948, with Stanley Matthews and Tom Finney together in the side on both occasions, are counted among England's finest away performances.

The FA had, in 1946/47, taken the step of appointing a national team manager, the educator and former Manchester United player Walter Winterbottom. Aged just 33 at the time of his initial appointment as the FA's director of coaching, Winterbottom, together with secretary Stanley Rous, represented a modernising arm of the governing body, with team selection remaining the responsibility of what author

David Goldblatt has called a 'cumbersome, arcane, secretive, and often incompetent selection board'. An unwelcome milestone was passed in September 1949 at Everton's Goodison Park, when the Irish inflicted England's first defeat to a non-British team on home soil. The 2-0 loss ought to have alerted the English football authorities to the growing strength of rival nations and a possible decline in fortunes, but it was ascribed in the press to 'an extraordinary sequence of escapes for Eire' in the second half, while the FA's own report on the match blamed an 'experimental forward line' that 'persistently missed chances'. Moreover, the fact that the Irish XI included nine players from English Football League clubs meant that England's proud unbeaten home record against foreign opposition was seen by many as remaining intact.

After winning the 1949/50 British Home Championship, England travelled to the World Cup in Brazil with every intention of demonstrating their footballing pre-eminence on the global stage, but the weaknesses of Winterbottom's side were memorably exposed. Matthews had fallen out of favour in the 18 months leading up to the tournament and was only a late inclusion in the squad, while Finney and captain Billy Wright were the only other members of the squad with more than 20 caps to their name.

England's first World Cup finals match was an unremarkable 2-0 win over Chile at a rainy Maracanã on 25 June 1950, and this was followed four days later by the meeting in Belo Horizonte with the inexperienced and unfancied United States team. England were beaten by a first-half goal from Haitian-born forward Joe Gaetjens, and although newspaper coverage of the distant competition was relatively sparse, the team faced sharp criticism at home for what was described as 'probably the worst display ever by an England side'. Early elimination from the World Cup was confirmed three days later back in Rio de Janeiro, when England lost their final group game against Spain, also 1-0. The wing partnership of Matthews and Finney was restored and a much-improved performance ensued, but 'in spite of the good football England were frequently baulked by the obstruction tactics of their opponents which went unpunished by the Italian referee'.

Another significant member of the squad was Tottenham Hotspur's Alf Ramsey, who played at right-back in all three matches in Brazil. He was an integral part of Arthur Rowe's 'push and run' Tottenham side that won the Second Division title in 1949/50 and would go on to claim the First Division title the following season. Ramsey was deeply affected by the humiliation at the hands of the United States, with one journalist noting that 'his face creased and he looked like a man who had been jabbed in an unhealed wound' when asked about the match years later. He finished his England playing career in 1953 with 32 caps and was chosen to succeed Winterbottom as manager nine years later. In the interim, attempts by Winterbottom and Rous to modernise the national team saw the FA undertake a first American tour at the end of the 1952/53 season, during which an England team struck by illness and fatigue lost 2-1 to World Cup holders Uruguay at Estadio Centenario in Montevideo. Later that same year, on 25 November, a game that became known as the 'Match of the Century' heralded the start of a chastening eight-month period for England in which the nation's century-old pretensions to footballing supremacy were finally – and comprehensively – extinguished.

Hungary's 'Magical Magyars' had come to the world's attention at the 1952 Summer Olympic Games in Helsinki, where they scored 20 goals across five matches to win gold. By the time of their visit to Wembley for the match against England, Hungary had not lost for over three years, and their star players, including Ferenc Puskás and Sándor Kocsis, had attained worldwide notoriety. In a stunning performance that commanded international praise, the Magyars swept England aside in front of a spellbound crowd of over 100,000 and won 6-3. The *Daily Telegraph*'s Frank Coles called it 'the most brilliant display of football ever seen in this country', while Geoffrey Green in *The Times* noted the visitors' impressive 'mixture of exquisite short passing and the long English game'. A recognition of the significance of the result and its implications for the football world order is evident across the English press, 'The England team was competent by British standards ... but on the evidence of this afternoon this standard will not long be good enough for England to retain her position in the high places of the football world.' More poetically, Green noted how 'here, on Wembley's velvet turf, [England] found themselves strangers in a strange world, a world of flitting red spirits, for such did the Hungarians seem as they moved at devastating pace with superb skill and powerful finish in their cherry bright shirts'.

If there were any lingering doubts, they were summarily dispelled six months later in Budapest, where England were again outclassed. Hungary's 7-1 win against the former masters of the game on 23 May 1954 confirmed the 'Golden Team' as outstanding favourites for the upcoming FIFA World Cup, and it remains the England national team's record defeat to this day. For Coles, it brought back memories of 1950:

'We now have the prospect of a repetition of the failure in the World Cup in Switzerland next month as happened in South America four years ago. English football flags almost incredibly behind the highest Continental standard.'

The esteemed football writer Brian Glanville perhaps put it best when it comes to anatomising the hubris that brought England to this point, 'The myth of supremacy rested on the fact that neither England nor Scotland had been beaten on home ground by a foreign team. They had failed time and again, away; in the great amorphous never-never land known vaguely as abroad, where defeats, obscurely, somehow didn't count, because one get-them-in-our-British-mud and we would kill them.'

1954 FIFA World Cup
Switzerland

On the uppermost of three levels at the German Football Museum in Dortmund, the history of the DFB and the *Nationalmannschaft* is meticulously told, with areas reserved for the story of the East German team and the development of women's football. At the far end of the space is a spectacular multimedia display commemorating the national team's triumph at the 2014 FIFA World Cup in Brazil, from which guests are directed downstairs to marvel at the *Schatzkammer*, or trophy room.

Although the early history of the DFB and football's complex relationship with the Nazi regime are conscientiously recounted as part of the exhibition, the narrative experience begins precisely 60 years before glory in Rio de Janeiro. As visitors step off the escalator that has whisked them from the main entrance directly to the third floor, they are met with an imposing, reverential rotunda dedicated to the 1954 world champions. At its centre is the ball used in the World Cup Final played at Wankdorfstadion in Bern on 4 July 1954, a date which now represents the starting point of the modern history of German football. Above life-sized photographic representations of the 11 players there is a quote from outside-left Hans Schäfer, 'For me, it's not a miracle. It was simply a great performance from a great team, who also had a lot of luck.' Schäfer's denial that a miracle had taken place is a nod to the phrase that has been attached to this match in German football lore ever since it happened: *Das Wunder von Bern* (The Miracle of Bern).

The many stories told about the final are underpinned by what had happened earlier in the competition. After overcoming Turkey 4-1 in their first of only two group games within a unique World Cup format, Germany faced Hungary in Basel on 20 June. The Magical Magyars had scored nine goals in their opening game and added eight more here, with the great marksman Kocsis already on a tally of seven for the tournament after two matches. Yet despite losing 8-3, Germany still looked forward to a chance to progress to the quarter-finals via a tie-breaking play-off with Turkey three days later. Indeed, Herberger may have had this in mind when he made seven changes from the opening game in preparing his team to face the formidable Hungarians. For *Kicker* at least, which referred to this line-up as a 'B team' in its report, it was an uncontroversial consideration:

'The chances of avoiding the play-off with Turkey by means of a win or a draw against Hungary were so slim that it would have been an unforgivable tactical error from Herberger to field the same team against Hungary that had played against Turkey. They would have run themselves into the ground in the sweltering heat, and they would have been physically weakened for a renewed battle with the Turks.'

Hungary's talisman Puskás was injured in a tackle by Kaiserslautern defender Werner Liebrich, forcing him to sit out the quarter-final and semi-final, and even *Kicker* admitted that the referee had been lenient when it came to Liebrich's 'very rough' fouls. This was the English official William Ling, whose blunder in Dublin was by no means forgotten, 'Today his half-time whistle again came noticeably too early, despite stoppages! Perhaps he should buy himself a proper stopwatch. He is in the country of clocks, Switzerland, after all!' Puskás would return for the final just 14 days after the injury and reportedly played with a hairline fracture of the ankle. A restored German first XI won the play-off match with Turkey 7-2, with the Swiss World Cup already well on its way to establishing the record goals-per-game average of 5.38 that still stands today.

Another idiosyncrasy of the 1954 tournament meant that group winners advanced to a separate half of the quarter-final draw from the runners-up. Hungary would thus have to face the much-fancied South American powers Brazil and Uruguay in the quarter-final and semi-final, respectively, while Germany played Yugoslavia and Austria. The semi-final brought Germany's record result against Austria, a 6-1 win in the border town of Basel that provided much-needed confidence before a rematch against the Magyars with the Jules Rimet Trophy at stake.

The final started in ominous fashion for Herberger's men. Within the first ten minutes, Hungary had taken a 2-0 lead and their coronation as world champions after 32 games without defeat seemed a mere formality. Another ten minutes later, however, Germany were level through goals from the prolific Nürnberg forward Max Morlock and Rot-Weiss Essen winger Helmut Rahn. The Hungarians assailed the opposition goal throughout the second half but to no avail, thwarted in part by the heroic goal-line clearances of Kaiserslautern left-back Werner Kohlmeyer.

Six minutes from time, the comeback was complete. Rahn received the ball in space just outside the penalty area, dragged it to his left with his right foot, and then drilled a low left-footed shot through a narrow gap between two defenders into the bottom corner of Gyula Grosics's net. Much like the dénouement of the previous World Cup in Brazil, the unthinkable had happened with just minutes remaining. When Puskás subsequently latched on to a through ball from Mihály Tóth and finished past Toni Turek in the German goal, the Hungarian players celebrated a deserved and timely equaliser, only for it to be ruled out for offside. Once again, the referee was

William Ling, who on this occasion provided Germany with an almighty reprieve upon consultation with his Welsh linesman Sandy Griffiths. The television footage was inconclusive, just as it would be 12 years later, when another World Cup Final was apparently decided by a referee and his assistant in conference, although not in Germany's favour.

West Germany thus became only the third nation to win the FIFA World Cup, after Uruguay and Italy. The improbable journey from international pariahs to world champions had taken less than a decade, far quicker than anyone would have dared to dream. Mythologies have continued to grow around not just the final in Bern but also around Fritz Walter and his team-mates, Herberger's ingenuity, and even the role of Adolf Dassler, the team's equipment manager and founder of the Adidas sports footwear business. Dassler's lightweight 'Argentinia' boots and innovative screw-in studs do by many accounts seem to have made a significant difference to the final, which was played out during constant rainfall. The use of longer studs in the second half gave the Germans a firmer foothold on the rapidly deteriorating pitch, and Dassler's design allowed the change to be made quickly and efficiently. The rain also helped to popularise throughout Germany the phrase *Fritz-Walter-Wetter* to designate the cold and wet conditions in which the team's popular leader thrived ever since he had contracted malaria during the Second World War. Particularly around the start of this century, there was an efflorescence of cultural production around *Das Wunder von Bern*, with Sönke Wortmann's feature film of that title released in 2003, ahead of the 50th anniversary. Arguably the two biggest stars of the team, captain Fritz Walter and winning goalscorer Helmut Rahn, passed away in 2002 and 2003, respectively, prompting countless tributes and recollections.

The extent to which the Miracle of Bern can be seen as a foundational moment for a new West German national identity remains a topic of vigorous cultural and intellectual debate. The influential and divisive historian Joachim Fest was among those who saw the 1954 World Cup win as the true birth of the BRD, more than five years after the republic had come into nominal existence. Weekly news magazine *Der Spiegel* reflected as much in the days following the final, using Churchill's recent speech on 'the century of the common man' as a touchpoint to consider how ordinary Germans collectively had responded, 'Before the eyes of the whole world, they acted as if they had now, at the end of June 1954, after 2,000 years of historical meanderings, finally found the only auspicious meaning and true purpose of their national existence.' The mood is more pithily conveyed by the saying which became a commonplace across Germany in the aftermath of the World Cup, *'wir sind wieder wer!'* – 'we're somebody again!' Likewise, the famously emphatic words of commentator Herbert Zimmermann which greeted the final whistle – *'Aus, aus, aus – aus! – Das Spiel ist aus! – Deutschland ist Weltmeister'* – are taken by some to represent the end point of Germany's postwar period of abnegation. They are every bit as integral to the cultural fabric in Germany as Kenneth Wolstenholme's phrase 'They think it's all over; it is now!' is in England. The national team's victory gave rise to an unprecedented wave of euphoria and helped to stabilise a new and divided nation that had lain in ruins less than a decade earlier. From a broader historical perspective, however, its impact must be weighed along with that of the contemporaneous *Wirtschaftswunder* – Germany's economic miracle.

While many western European nations – with the notable exception of the United Kingdom – enjoyed a significant economic upturn during the 1950s and 60s, this was particularly important in West Germany in terms of rebuilding self-esteem and promoting self-determination. Between 1949 and 1954, the Gross Domestic Product of the BRD grew by an average of 8.8 per cent per year, and in 1955 the growth rate reached 12 per cent. Of the various international factors cited as causes of the postwar economic boom, the surge in arms production during the Korean War of 1950–1953 is only indirectly applicable to the BRD. In view of a prohibition on armaments production, West German industry reorientated towards the manufacture of durable consumer goods. This resulted in 'an unprecedented export boom, stimulated particularly after 1951 by the classical German export industries of mechanical engineering, electro-technology, chemicals, optical instruments and precision mechanics'. The great increase in the postwar population meanwhile ensured that housing became a priority for the first BRD chancellor, Konrad Adenauer, and his economics minister and eventual successor, Ludwig Erhard. Herbert thus identifies 'a vibrant domestic market, energetic house building, and strong demand from abroad' as the main factors behind the statistics that gave rise to that widespread *Wirtschaftswunder* moniker, 'Between 1950 and 1960, West German industrial production grew by 150 per cent, unemployment fell from 10.3 per cent to 1.2 per cent, the number of people in employment rose by almost 6 million, and gross wages doubled.' As Herbert is also careful to point out, the trio of steps taken by the Allied powers in integrating West Germany into the western sphere of influence – the Marshall Plan, the introduction of the Deutsche Mark, and the foundation of the BRD – were also essential factors in bringing about the economic recovery which followed.

Taken together, the sporting and economic *Wunder* of the postwar period had profound and transformative effects on the psychology, culture and living standards of the German people, and not least the young men who grew up to form the next generation of the *Nationalmannschaft*. When Fritz Walter received the World Cup from Jules Rimet himself in Bern, Sepp Maier and Wolfgang Overath were ten years old; Franz Beckenbauer and Gerd Müller just nine.

* * *

England fared somewhat better in their second World Cup appearance than they had in Brazil, where they set an admittedly low bar. With Matthews and Finney on the wings and prolific Bolton Wanderers goalscorer Nat Lofthouse, who scored 30 goals in 33 England appearances, at centre-forward, the team possessed plenty of firepower, but defensive frailties were again exposed. Leading 3-1 with barely 20 minutes to play in the opening match against Belgium on 17 June, England conceded twice and then once more in extra time – used for the 1954 tournament's group games – to draw 4-4. With Matthews and Lofthouse absent through injury for the second group fixture three days later, England overcame hosts Switzerland in Bern with goals from two Wolverhampton Wanderers forwards, Jimmy Mullen and Dennis Wilshaw.

The victory set up a quarter-final in Basel against incumbent world champions Uruguay, who had won their group with a resounding 7-0 win over Scotland the previous day. England's performance in the subsequent 4-2 defeat to the South American masters should be viewed from a perspective which considers the impact of those two chastening defeats by Hungary in the run-up to the tournament. Moreover, the esteem in which the opponents were held at this time is evident in a report published in the *Manchester Guardian* on the morning of the match, 'It is as well that television has given Britons at home some idea of the strength, speed, and brilliance of the Uruguayans. It would be difficult, otherwise, to paint a true picture, for there is no team of comparable quality and style in the British Isles.' As such, news of England's defeat was relayed in the press under headlines such as 'England's Football Pride Regained' or 'England's Splendid Fight in Vain'.

Matthews and Lofthouse had returned to the England line-up, and after 16 minutes the latter cancelled out Uruguay's early opening goal. World Cup-winning captain Obdulio 'Papa' Varela, who would sadly miss the semi-final against Hungary because of an injury sustained in this match, put his team ahead late in the first half, and shortly after the interval England found themselves 3-1 behind. Finney scored from the rebound off a Lofthouse shot, but another goal for Uruguay with six minutes remaining sealed England's exit. Match reports in the English press combined praise for the beaten side's determination with great admiration for Uruguay, 'They love this ball, and they want to keep it, often withdrawing it from a tackle with the sole of the foot as if they were rolling a pat of butter.' Yet the palpable concern for England's place in the football world after this latest sobering experience is best summarised by a rhetorical question in the *Manchester Guardian*:

'Can England go on using what her Continental critics with such surprising unanimity call stereotyped, conservative, primitive methods against opponents whose tactical ingenuity has evolved a system which enables them to attack with five forwards in line and a roving centre half-back [Varela] who is ever ready either to hover on the fringe of an attack or get back and form part of a solid defensive phalanx on whatever flank an attack may develop?'

It is a comment which may be seen unknowingly to anticipate the versatile talents displayed in the half-back position by Duncan Edwards, who would make his England debut the following year at the age of 18.

1 December 1954
England 3-1 West Germany
Wembley Stadium, London

In England, the Germans' unexpected triumph in Bern was greeted with surprise and praise, as well as the perhaps impertinent observation that 'they did it in the English style, with quick, long passes through the middle'. Geoffrey Green lauded 'their tremendous enthusiasm, drive, stamina, strength, and their willpower', and reserved special praise for goalkeeper Turek's 'four saves that bordered on the miraculous'. On the *Daily Telegraph*'s front page from 5 July, meanwhile, a short article entitled 'Germany wins World Cup' ends with the following remark:

'From the English point of view the result is welcome. England play Germany at Wembley on Dec. 1. The fact that their opponents will now come as World Cup holders will greatly add to the appeal of the match.'

England's first postwar meeting with Germany, the first game between the two nations at Wembley, was indeed highly anticipated. The Empire Stadium had been the venue for the FA Cup Final ever since its inauguration in 1923 amid preparations for the British Empire Exhibition, but it played host to international matches against Scotland exclusively until 1951, when Argentina came close to ending England's proud record on home soil. Now it was the Germans' honour to play at Wembley, and as *Kicker* declared on its cover page in the week before the game, London continued to represent '*Endstation Sehnsucht*' for all footballing nations. This phrase was the German title given to Tennessee Williams's Pulitzer Prize-winning 1948 play *A Streetcar Named Desire*, conveying the idea of a final destination for aspiration or desire. For the magazine's publisher Friedebert Becker, this was no ordinary international match, but 'a football pilgrimage to the promised land' where Wembley 'awaits us like a Mecca'. *The Times* of 1 December could not ignore the wider significance of this great occasion, notwithstanding the publication's time-honoured principle of downplaying the role of politics in sport:

'The appearance of Germany's international football side against England at Wembley Stadium this afternoon adds its bit to Anglo-German relations. It is true that sport in these islands – though not by any means always oversea – holds no political significance, but there could be no more appropriate guest of honour at this particular match than the Foreign Secretary. If the presence of 12,000 and more Germans, transplanted across the Channel to the Wembley terraces, may have no particular import, it at least shows that sport and time can be great healers.'

The next day's edition included a photograph of Foreign Secretary Anthony Eden, who succeeded Churchill as prime minister the following year, shaking hands with members of the German team before kick-off. The image represents an important milestone in postwar relations between the two nations, within but also beyond the context of football.

Lamentably, only three players from the starting XI in Bern, and one other from the World Cup squad, were available to be selected for the Wembley test. Besides Josef Posipal, Werner Kohlmeyer, Werner Liebrich and Herbert Erhardt, no member of the team to face England had played more than twice for Germany. The reasons for Herberger's severe limitations in selection at this time went unreported in the press but have since come to light: by October 1954, three months after the World Cup triumph, several of the heroes of Bern had fallen ill with symptoms of jaundice. On 27 October, 13 players were examined by specialists in Düsseldorf at the request of the DFB, and many were found to have liver damage. The DFB publicly attributed this to a supposed oral infection that had been transmitted in the close-knit, high-performance conditions of the World Cup camp, but it also admitted that the players had been given vitamin C injections during the tournament. A study published in the medical journal *Deutsches Ärzteblatt* in 2010 concluded that the players' symptoms may be explained by 'an acute parenteral transmission of viral hepatitis', which is to say, the virus was likely passed on through the use of unsterilised needles. This was probably hepatitis C, which was unknown in 1954, around 35 years before its identification.

Among the players who were given their debuts at Wembley in the absence of the first-team stars was Fortuna Düsseldorf forward Josef 'Jupp' Derwall, who only featured in two internationals as a player but who later served as national team manager between 1978 and 1984. Winning his second cap at centre-forward, meanwhile, was the Hamburg starlet Uwe Seeler, just turned 18. This match thus has the noteworthy distinction of featuring both Stanley Matthews, in his last of three appearances against Germany, and Seeler, who would go on to win 72 caps and whose last international appearance came in 1970, 36 years after Matthews's first. Indeed, Seeler was born on 5 November 1934, a month after a 19-year-old Matthews scored on his England debut in Cardiff on 29 September.

The unfortunate absence of many of Germany's world champions meant that the English press expected the home side to prevail with relative ease. Green's special report ahead of the game under the headline 'Taking Stock of English Football' provides valuable insights into efforts to modernise and support the national team in the 12 months that had passed since its historic defeat against Hungary in the Match of the Century. The FA's selection committee had been reduced from nine to three – Winterbottom and two others – and match preparation was also taken more seriously, 'The England team is beginning to have periods of training and tactical planning together, of longer duration than ever before.' This development was seen as 'a beginning within the limits of the British system, where the requirements of club have always taken precedence over country in the past'. The article also weighs up the roles of two types of footballer in the contemporary game – 'the ball player' and 'the runner'. The success of 1953/54 First Division champions and current league leaders Wolverhampton Wanderers is attributed to 'a style of headlong speed, long first-time passing, and hard tackling' but Green 'doubts very much if the salvation of English football, in the long run and in the international comparison, lies in that direction'. Instead, the grounds for England's success in international football are seen to lie in 'the more intelligent, patterned approach ... offered by thoughtful sides such as Preston North End, Blackpool [the teams of Finney and Matthews, respectively], Manchester United, Tottenham Hotspur, and West Bromwich Albion'. In summary, the demands of the arduous English football league season were at odds with those of top-level postwar international football, and the skilful ball players of yesteryear were considered better suited to the latter.

For the match against West Germany, the selectors duly turned to experience, with the average age of the XI exceeding 30. Captain Billy Wright had already amassed 63 caps, and the partnership of Matthews and Finney was restored for the first time since the World Cup. Alongside these mercurial wingers in the forward line, Roy Bentley, Ronnie Allen and Len Shackleton had all recently returned to the England fold after missing out on the World Cup squad. Previewing the match in the *Daily Telegraph*, Frank Coles suggested, 'After many experiments and disappointing responses from younger players … the selectors may be proved right on this occasion in voting for ball-playing wingers.' The following day's headline for Coles's match report – 'Matthews' Magic Wrecks German Defence' – indicates how this assessment was proved correct in thrilling style on the Wembley turf.

Playing in red Umbro shirts, white shorts and red socks, England dazzled on the wings in front of a crowd of around 100,000 beneath a cloudless winter sky. The opening goal came just short of the half-hour mark with direct involvement from Matthews. After Derwall was penalised for handball on the edge of the penalty area, Matthews was alert to a loose ball from the resultant free kick and crossed for Bentley at the far post to head home. Shortly after half-time Finney combined smartly with Shackleton and advanced on goal, only to be denied by Friedrich Herkenrath, the goalkeeper and outstanding German player on the day. Herkenrath's parry fell to Allen on the penalty spot and the centre-forward extended England's lead.

The second half saw no further goals until England were awoken, 13 minutes from time, by a goal from the debutant Alfred Beck of St. Pauli. Prior to this moment, according to Coles, 'liberties were taken by the [England] forwards which, while delightful to watch, were destroying the thrust and purpose of the team'. After Beck's goal, the many thousands of visiting supporters sensed the possibility of snatching a famous draw, with BBC commentator Kenneth Wolstenholme remarking, 'Now the German supporters are really going to town.' It was left for Sunderland inside-left Shackleton to settle the contest with the best goal of the day, a well-timed chip over the advancing Herkenrath from just inside the penalty area.

For his ageless skill and physical prowess on the wing, however, the star of the match was indubitably Matthews. 'He tantalised at walking pace one moment, then daringly darted through the next,' wrote Coles. 'One opponent, two, or even three made no difference. It was exquisite artistry.' More often than not, the opponent was the experienced left-back Kohlmeyer, a world champion with no answers to Matthews's perplexing riddles. It was an individual performance that inspired artful turns of phrase, such as Green's observation that 'to contain Matthews in this vein was like trying to imprison a shaft of light in a matchbox'. The man himself later recalled, 'I was delighted to receive such write-ups. I had been up against a good full-back in Kohlmeyer and had led him a merry dance.'

On the final whistle, Wolstenholme rightly predicted that Matthews's name would 'always be associated with this game'. In Germany too, the legendary Blackpool winger was the focus of much press attention, as for example in Willy Meisl's special *Kicker* column under the subtitle 'The defender who can stop the "Wing Wizard" has not yet been invented!' Meisl called Matthews 'the Churchill of football', explaining that 'both get better and better the older they become, like fine wine'. Most significant, perhaps, is the same writer's aphoristic assertion, '*Vor solcher Kunst vergißt man Trennendes.*' This charming phrase conveys the idea that when we are faced with such sublime art, we forget what separates us.

Another German admirer was a young Franz Beckenbauer, who was born just months after the end of the Second World War and watched Matthews's later career on television. Paying tribute upon Matthews's death on 23 February 2000, Beckenbauer remarked:

'He was a fantastic player. Respected throughout the entire world of football. Wherever you went in the world, they knew the name Stanley Matthews. He stood for everything that is good about the game. Football has lost its greatest player.'

Alongside bold claims that 'our World Cup-winning XI would have won in London', *Kicker* focussed on matters beyond the purely sporting in determining Germany's first visit to Wembley a great success. Across the extensive reportage of the occasion, much is made of the warm welcome enjoyed by German fans in England, and of the visitors' good behaviour. The match was reportedly one of exemplary sportsmanship, decency and fairness, and the young German players had impressed their hosts with their manners and attitude. The positive impact on Anglo-German relations of this first postwar meeting on the football field was a significant consideration as for example in *Kicker*:

'The uncommonly strong impression left by the young German players made us particularly happy because of the presence of distinguished guests in the royal box, where not only the leading men of FIFA were seated, but also Sir Anthony Eden, England's Foreign Minister who is wholeheartedly committed to the German cause.'

This comment came less than two months after Eden had undertaken a tour of western Europe to advocate for West Germany to be granted sovereignty and admission to NATO. To a large extent, these objectives were achieved by the subsequent Paris Accords signed in October 1954.

26 May 1956
West Germany 1-3 England
Olympiastadion, Berlin

The return fixture in Berlin came shortly after England's first meeting with Brazil. Matthews, captain Billy Wright, and the Manchester United duo Roger Byrne and Tommy Taylor had all featured in the World Cup, but the other seven players chosen to face the much-admired South Americans at Wembley on 9 May 1956 were fresh blood. Sheffield United outside-left Colin Grainger made his debut, while Manchester United prodigy Duncan Edwards, now 19, won his sixth cap, and Fulham's talented inside-left Johnny Haynes made his fifth international appearance.

England took on a Brazil side at the end of its seven-match tour of Europe; a team led by the great Nílton Santos of Botafogo and which featured several other players that would go on to lift the World Cup in Sweden two years later. The hosts were 2-0 up inside just five minutes with goals from Taylor and Grainger, but Brazil struck back twice after half-time to level the score. Taylor and Grainger both scored again from chances created by the irrepressible Matthews to seal a famous 4-2 win for England. The significance of the occasion as part of the exciting development of the international football landscape during the 1950s is encapsulated by the headline above the match report in *The Times* of the following day, 'Triumph of Old World Over New'. The *Daily Telegraph*'s Frank Coles noted with some relief that the result 'sends a message to all those who are writing off English football as beyond quick recovery in an age of carefully prepared national teams'.

The *Nationalmannschaft* made rather less grandiose experiences in the run-up to England's visit, enduring a difficult 1955/56 season of four defeats in five international matches. The return of several World Cup winners, however, made for an intriguing fixture against an England side regaining its confidence. Apart from Herkenrath in goal, here winning his tenth cap, the German line-up was entirely changed from that which had lost at Wembley 18 months earlier. Captain Fritz Walter was back in the side alongside his younger brother and fellow Kaiserslautern star Ottmar, while Karl Mai, Max Morlock and Hans Schäfer were the other returning heroes from Bern. Yet their presence was not enough to withstand another excellent England performance in Berlin, 18 years on from the last.

The city was of course a very different place, now split into four occupying zones and with access to the eastern sector beginning to be restricted as part of Cold War tensions that would lead to the construction of the Berlin Wall in 1961. The Olympiastadion is situated in the Westend district of the borough of Charlottenburg, which was included in the British sector of Berlin after 1945. Consequently, a significant number of British servicemen were among the crowd of around 95,000 people on 26 May 1956 cheering on the England team. The

Daily Telegraph reported ahead of the game that 'carpenters have been working overtime to meet the soldiers' demands for rattles with which to spur on their countrymen', and indeed, the Pathé News footage of the game shows numerous men in uniform supporting their team with such ratchet instruments.

The same footage includes the outstanding goal of the game, a solo effort from Edwards that encapsulated the young half-back's versatility and skill. Fresh from winning the First Division title with Matt Busby's Manchester United, Edwards gave perhaps his finest performance in an England shirt on that day in Berlin, and the opening goal was its crowning moment. Collecting the loose ball from a robust challenge between Ronnie Clayton and Fritz Walter in the German half, Edwards turned swiftly, proceeded to 'crash his way past three opponents as if he were flicking a speck of dust from his sleeve, and let loose a rocket that hurtled low past Herkenrath's right hand'. Although still only 19, his performance against Brazil had already alerted the German manager to his talent, 'Hadn't Herberger warned of Edwards as a sixth forward after seeing the bullish, acrobatic "English Kupfer" threaten Brazil's goal?' *Kicker*'s comparison to Andreas Kupfer, a member of the acclaimed *Breslau-Elf* from 1937, was high praise indeed.

In the second half, Grainger latched on to a long pass from Haynes and doubled England's lead, while at the other end Schäfer could only direct a powerful shot from the left wing on to the crossbar. Haynes then settled the contest with a neat finish from 12 yards following a goalmouth scramble. Fritz Walter, now aged 35, was again the starting point for much of Germany's best play, and the goal that his performance deserved came just minutes from the end, when he turned Schäfer's cross past Reg Matthews in the England goal to give the frustrated German fans a consolation goal to cheer. The 3-1 result was cause for greater cheer still in the English press, with Green acknowledging that it represented 'a gift in itself in a world where, for better or worse, sport has come to play a part of much significance in wider affairs'. The final word, however, must be for Edwards, memorably extolled by his captain Billy Wright:

'The name of Duncan Edwards was on the lips of everybody who saw this match. He was phenomenal. There have been few individual performances to match what he produced in Germany that day. He tackled like a lion, attacked at every opportunity and topped it all off with a cracker of a goal. He was still only 20 [in fact, 19] and was already a world-class player. Many of the thousands of British soldiers in the crowd surrounded him at the final whistle and carried him off. It was fantastic to be a part of it. We had beaten the world champions in their own back yard.'

In Germany, much was made of the home side's strong start to the game, but in the context of a poor run of results as world champions and pre-existing anxieties about the future of German football, this result caused considerable hand-wringing. In an emotive *Kicker* editorial following the match, Friedebert Becker pointed to the players' physical condition as a major weakness when compared to the English but also to other teams, such as the Dutch, who had won on German soil earlier that year. Restating the case for the sport's professionalisation, Becker wrote:

'We hardly need once again to explain to our readers the deeper reasons behind Germany's inability to compete at international level while there is no small, focussed top division that can provide the same conditions for daily training that are offered to England's professional footballers.'

The formation of Germany's professional football league, the Bundesliga, was still seven years away, but these were precisely the considerations that would eventually help to bring that about. Becker's piece ends on a sober, though encouraging note, 'We must have patience. Let us not be under any illusions! Let's stop thinking that "German football" is the world champion. There was only ever one team of world champions.'

* * *

One man whose words appeared in the pages of *Kicker* at this time deserves attention in any discussion of Anglo-German relations within and beyond football. Born in the Hanseatic city of Bremen in 1923, Bernhard 'Bert' Trautmann was an unknown prisoner of war who became the hero of the 1956 FA Cup Final just three weeks before England's visit to Berlin. On 14 May, the magazine began a special three-part series of articles entitled 'The Trautmann Story', in which the famous goalkeeper told his remarkable life story. After first enlisting with the *Luftwaffe* in 1941, Trautmann was sent to the eastern front as a mechanic. The following year he retrained as a paratrooper and was one of only 90 of 1,000 volunteers for his regiment to survive the rest of the war. In May 1944 he was transferred to France to help repel the Allied invasion and narrowly escaped death when he was buried in rubble for three days after a bombing. During the war, he was captured on separate occasions by the French, Russians and Americans, but finally fell into British hands in Belgium in March 1945.

Trautmann was moved to a prison camp in Lancashire, to be released three years later. He had started playing football while still a prisoner and joined local club St Helens Town upon release. Having garnered much attention for his talents in goal, Trautmann signed for First Division club Manchester City in late 1949, causing great controversy. Manchester's outraged Jewish community was mollified by the local rabbi Alexander Altmann, himself an émigré from Nazi Germany in 1938, but Trautmann still suffered abuse around the country as he began his long but ultimately successful journey to win over the public. In 1955 he appeared on the losing side in the FA Cup Final against Jackie Milburn's Newcastle United, but the following year Manchester City returned to Wembley, this time to face Birmingham City. A few weeks before the final, Trautmann was voted the Football Writers' Association Footballer of the Year for 1955/56, an honour which earned him a prominent front-page photograph on *Kicker*'s 9 April issue.

With just over a quarter of an hour of the final remaining and his side leading 3-1, Trautmann rushed to the feet of oncoming Birmingham forward Peter Murphy and collided head first with Murphy's outstretched leg. With no substitutions permitted, Trautmann played through the pain that was evident to all those watching, and a short while later he lifted the cup in front of the Queen. The story of his bravery and commitment that day was assured its place in English football lore when it was revealed, five days after the game, that the goalkeeper had suffered a broken neck in the incident with Murphy.

After some time spent in Manchester Royal Infirmary, he flew to Germany as guest of honour of the DFB for the

England international. On 25 May, the eve of the match, he was welcomed by the German press in Düsseldorf, still visibly weakened and jaded from his time in hospital. Yet he talked of his excitement at the upcoming occasion in Berlin and reiterated his desire to one day play for the German national team, even if he understood that his career in England meant that this was an unlikely prospect. That same evening, he received the tragic news that his five-year-old son John had been struck by a car in Bramhall, south of Manchester. Trautmann immediately returned to England but sadly arrived to find that his son had died from his injuries. The heartbreaking story recalls that of another German goalkeeper, Hans Jakob, who found out about his daughter's sudden illness shortly before the match against England in 1938. All the more poignant is Bert's dedication of his article 'Trautmann's story' in the pages of *Kicker* to his young son just ten days before the accident, 'I also dedicate my story to my young son, John, and I hope that he will one day follow in my footsteps to show the world that football is the best means to overcome prejudice and politics.'

* * *

If the England football team reached a nadir with those two defeats to Hungary, a political embarrassment of similar magnitude would stop Anthony Eden's ostensibly prosperous premiership in its tracks at the end of 1956. Determined not to repeat Neville Chamberlain's mistakes, and convinced of the threat posed by a foreign actor, Eden resolved to launch a military attack on Egypt in response to President Gamal Abdel Nasser's seizure in July of the strategically vital Suez Canal. After a costly delay, and in collusion with the Israelis, Britain planned for an invasion of Egypt that would require French involvement but which British politicians at first kept secret from their French counterparts. American support for the operation was vital, meanwhile, because of Britain's economic dependence on the United States at this time, and chancellor Harold Macmillan mistakenly assured his prime minister that he could count on American backing for his plan to retake control of the Suez Canal.

What transpired was a military and political blunder with far-reaching repercussions. US President Dwight Eisenhower was stunned by news of the operation on 30 October, with the presidential election just a week away. When Nasser rejected the terms of a cynically prearranged Anglo-French ultimatum, British attacks on Egypt began, but by 2 November the UN General Assembly approved an American resolution calling for a ceasefire and Britain was left diplomatically isolated. Under increasing political and economic pressure, Eden was forced, on 6 November, unilaterally to announce a ceasefire. The climbdown was abrupt and, to many observers, misguided. Not least to Eden's predecessor Winston Churchill, who remarked, 'I am not sure I should have dared to start, but I am sure I should not have dared to stop.' Eden resigned on 9 January 1957 on grounds of ill health and was succeeded by Macmillan. Britain had been economically hamstrung since 1945 and had now, by colluding with Israel and double-crossing the Americans, lost all claims to moral superiority too. On the wider significance of the Suez crisis, historian Dominic Sandbrook concludes:

'The symbolic importance of the crisis was that it marked a confrontation between the old ambitions of British imperialism and the new realities of post-imperial retrenchment. Indeed, the Suez affair illustrated with striking clarity the decline of British imperial power. It was not … a cause of that decline; rather, it was a reflection of Britain's changed role in the world, partly as a result of two ruinously expensive global wars.'

In global politics, as in international football, complacency and mismanagement had led to failures that signalled an end to the age of empire.

6 February 1958
Munich air disaster

Just over a year after Eden's resignation, a tragedy of unprecedented proportions befell British football. The aircraft transporting the Manchester United squad, staff and journalists from a European Cup tie in Belgrade back to Manchester crashed on take-off at Munich-Riem airport following a refuelling stop. Of the 44 people on board, 20 died at the scene, and another three lost their lives subsequently. The 23 fatalities comprised eight Manchester United players, eight journalists, four club staff, two crew members and a travel agent. Among the journalists who lost their lives was the former goalkeeper Frank Swift, working for the *News of the World*, who was the player whom Bert Trautmann replaced when he signed for Manchester City in 1949.

After two failed take-off attempts due to mechanical problems and with weather conditions deteriorating, captain James Thain and his co-pilot Ken Rayment resolved to make another bid to get airborne just after 3pm. The plane failed to reach the requisite speed to get off the ground and skidded off the end of the runway, crashing into surrounding dwellings and bursting into lethal flames. The harrowing monochrome photographs from the aftermath are dappled with large falling snowflakes illuminated by flashbulbs on the dark background of the evening sky. In the centre lies the mangled silvery wreckage of the Airspeed Ambassador aircraft. It remains difficult – perhaps impossible – to comprehend the well-documented acts of bravery such as that of Northern Ireland goalkeeper Harry Gregg, who saved himself and returned inside the fuselage to rescue four others, including his team-mates Bobby Charlton and Dennis Viollet.

Manchester United were returning from the second leg of their European Cup quarter-final against Red Star Belgrade, in which a 3-3 draw had secured progress to the semi-final. It was the third season of organised continental competition after the inaugural UEFA Congress in March 1955 had ratified proposals for a European club championship. Chelsea withdrew from the first edition of the tournament under pressure from the Football League, but Busby's Manchester United side then entered the 1956/57 European Cup, overcoming German opposition in the first round. Indeed, the tie with Borussia Dortmund represents the first Anglo-German confrontation in UEFA club competition, with the first leg played in front of a large crowd at Manchester City's Maine Road stadium because of a lack of adequate floodlighting at Old Trafford. The German champions were three goals behind at half-time but rallied in the second half to reduce the deficit to a single goal. *The Times*'s match report hints at the European Cup's inauspicious start in England as well as the ramifications for English football of those humbling failures of the mid-1950s:

'The Football League have frowned upon this competition. More than 75,000 people watched and enjoyed a tense match in which there was a lot of hard and elegant football. Surely this is what is wanted to revive the fading English interest in football.'

Busby's promising young side, nicknamed the Busby Babes, progressed to a semi-final against the illustrious Real Madrid team of Alfredo Di Stéfano, Francisco Gento and Raymond Copa, which proved a bridge too far. Yet, after retaining the league title and reaching the FA Cup Final in 1957, the team returned to European competition the following season and were counted among the favourites for the trophy. The 3-3 draw in Belgrade on 5 February, the night before the accident, secured a 5-4 win on aggregate and set up a semi-final with AC Milan two months later. The fact that a devastated Manchester United team was able to win the first leg against the Italians 2-1, with survivor Viollet on the scoresheet, points to what the press called 'the unbounding spirit' of the club at this time.

Busby was seriously injured in the crash and suffered with feelings of guilt in the aftermath. He had pushed for Manchester United to play in the European Cup against the wishes of the Football League, and he also wondered if he might have persuaded Thain and Rayment to abort that fatal third take-off attempt. His wife Jean helped to rehabilitate him and convinced him to continue as manager, and by the time of that season's FA Cup Final, which the new threadbare side remarkably reached by beating Sheffield Wednesday, West Bromwich Albion and Fulham in the six weeks after Munich, Busby was able to attend Wembley. He would resume his duties the following season and lead the club to yet more success in the 1960s, building another great team around the surviving young players, such as Charlton and Bill Foulkes, as well as the likes of Denis Law.

The Munich air disaster unquestionably had a profound impact on Winterbottom's national team, meanwhile. Three key members of the England team, who had amassed 70 caps between them, were lost: left-back Roger Byrne, centre-forward Tommy Taylor, and the bright star Duncan Edwards, who was just 21. Also among the fatalities was outside-left David Pegg, who was tipped to succeed Tom Finney in the position and had made one appearance for the senior team.

Of the survivors, the experienced outside-right Johnny Berry had won four England caps deputising for Stanley Matthews but would sadly never play football again due to the injuries he sustained in the crash. Bobby Charlton was only 20 years old at the time and found himself thrust into a position of great responsibility in rebuilding the Manchester United team. He then won his first England cap in the first post-Munich international match, a 4-0 win over Scotland at Hampden Park. 'Charlton did enough on his debut for England to make it clear that he has come to stay,' remarked James Wilson in the *Sunday Times*. Although included in the squad, however, Charlton would not get an opportunity to play at the 1958 FIFA World Cup in Sweden, where England failed to win a game in a group with the Soviet Union, Austria and eventual winners Brazil.

Veteran captain Billy Wright was still at the heart of defence and approaching his 100th cap, and Finney equalled Nat Lofthouse's England goalscoring record with a late penalty in the opening game, but he sadly sustained a knee injury that kept him out of the rest of the tournament. Fulham's Johnny Haynes and Blackburn's Ronnie Clayton were the only other players with significant experience, and the young England side were eliminated in a group play-off match against the Soviet Union in Gothenburg. It was a result which seemed to confirm the extent to which England had fallen behind in international football, but the tragic loss of Byrne, Taylor and Edwards so soon before the tournament, not to mention the injury to Finney, surely played a significant role.

The airfield of Munich-Riem has long since been redeveloped into a sprawling complex for international trade fairs, but at the south-west corner of the site, beside an inconspicuous and quiet road in the Trudering-Riem district of Munich, there is now a memorial to those who lost their lives on 6 February 1958. This was unveiled in 2004, and for the 50th anniversary four years later, the locality was renamed Manchesterplatz. Ahead of their UEFA Champions League quarter-final second leg against Bayern München in April 2014, the Manchester United squad, accompanied by Bobby Charlton, visited the site to pay their respects. The following year, Charlton joined FC Bayern chairman Karl-Heinz Rummenigge to unveil a new permanent commemorative exhibit in the club's museum at the Allianz Arena. 'I'm very happy and ever so proud of the association between Bayern Munich and Manchester United,' Charlton said. 'Our club had an awful, awful experience but we have been helped enormously by Bayern Munich and the people of Germany.'

5

White Heat
1962–1966

At the 1960 FIFA Congress in Rome on the eve of the Olympic Games, England won the right to host the 1966 World Cup. The vote was close, and the runner-up was West Germany. The England delegation had secured the co-operation of their Spanish counterparts in advance by emphasising the significance of the FA's centenary in 1963. The arrangement was known to observers in Germany, such as *Kicker* publisher Friedebert Becker, who criticised the DFB's denials that the vote was a foregone conclusion. Moreover, he expressed relief that a desperate attempt by controversial DFB president Peco Bauwens to win late votes from eastern European associations fell on deaf ears, 'His bow to the eastern bloc, offering the world the stadiums of the Soviet zone (!) for a world championship in the Federal Republic, did not catch on.' Becker's parenthetical exclamation mark gives some indication of the diplomatic folly of this idea at the height of the Cold War.

Football, then, was to come home. The eighth edition of the FIFA World Cup would be played in the country where the game began, and this offered England the best possible conditions to finally excel in the championship that they had at first not deigned to enter and in which they subsequently, under Walter Winterbottom in the 1950s, won only two out of ten matches. Yet, at this time, there was still relatively little excitement at the prospect, with domestic league football, the FA Cup, and the early phases of organised European club competition constituting English supporters' clear priorities. The

1953 FA Cup Final between Blackpool and Bolton Wanderers, dubbed the 'Matthews Final', was, according to John Hughson, 'the first FA Cup Final to receive a mass television audience, largely due to the widespread sale of television sets ahead of the Queen's Coronation on 2 June 1953'. An equivalent milestone in Germany was the 1954 World Cup Final.

As far as international football was concerned, supremacy in the British Home Championship, which England had not won outright for three seasons, was the immediate concern. England enjoyed one of their best Home Championship campaigns in 1960/61, winning 5-2 in Belfast and then beating Wales 5-1 and Scotland 9-3, both at Wembley. That scoreline against the Scots on 15 April 1961 caused the English press some problems in containing their excitement. David Miller in the *Sunday Telegraph* wrote, 'How to be truthful, but not exaggerate? How to speculate for the future, while keeping the present in perspective? It is almost impossible, after a fabulous afternoon in this sun-strewn stadium.' Brian Glanville in the *Sunday Times* was similarly effusive, 'After Flodden and Culloden Moor, one must inscribe, in the blackest annals of Scottish History: Wembley, 1961. It would take a very Pacific of whisky to drown and wash away the humiliation; a very Highland Division of pipers to proclaim the wake of Scottish football.' The *Sunday Telegraph*'s headline in response to the rout – 'Masterly Display by Forwards Boosts World Cup Hopes' – reminds us that the 1962 tournament in Chile was also beginning to loom large.

As it turned out, disappointing performances at FIFA's third South American World Cup led to changes of the utmost significance in both English and German football, and no fan of the game needs reminding that the two nations met four years later at Wembley to contest the biggest prize of all. In this period of accelerated transition, Winterbottom's 16-year tenure as England manager came to an end, and Sepp Herberger stepped down after more than three decades of involvement with the German national team. Beyond football, Konrad Adenauer's foundational chancellorship of West Germany ended after 14 years, and Labour regained power in Britain after 13 years of Conservative rule.

In Berlin, the escalation of Cold War tensions was keenly felt. Walter Ulbricht, the head of the DDR state council, had proclaimed on 15 June 1961 that 'no one has the intention of building a wall', but construction began less than two months later. The Berlin Wall became a physical manifestation of the ideological divide between two very different worlds: the capitalist west and the communist east.

These were also the years of the Beatles' first six studio albums and the 'Beatlemania' period as the Liverpudlian band reached worldwide fame following an earlier series of residencies in Hamburg. In October 1963, the Labour leader Harold Wilson sought to harness the sense of possibility occasioned by postwar developments in technology. In his landmark speech at the party conference in Scarborough, Wilson advocated for science and technology to be integral to any prospective socialist revolution. Such a revolution, Wilson affirmed, could not 'become a reality unless we are prepared to make far-reaching changes in economic and social attitudes which permeate our whole system of society'. He then laid out the blueprint for a modern, technocratic nation, 'The Britain that is going to be forged in the white heat of this revolution will be no place for restrictive practises or for outdated methods.'

Wilson became prime minister a year later, albeit with a minimal majority. Much like Anthony Eden before Suez, he enjoyed an unruffled start to his premiership, winning by a landslide in a snap election called to consolidate his position in March 1966. This was Wilson's 'high tide of authority and self-esteem'. However, the month of July that year marked the 'clear break point in Wilson's premiership', after which his reputation suffered and relationships soured. Ultimately, he was unable to deliver on the promises of his Scarborough oration and lost the 1970 election to Edward Heath.

At that critical moment for Britain in the summer of 1966, English football did finally fulfil its promise, and the gleaming Jules Rimet Trophy found its way into an Englishman's hands. The team was forged in the white heat of Alf Ramsey's footballing revolution, which put paid to the restrictive practises and outdated methods of the Football Association in the Winterbottom era.

1962 FIFA World Cup
Chile

Herberger's side had performed better than expected at the 1958 World Cup in Sweden, reaching a semi-final against the hosts – Fritz Walter's last international match – before losing 6-3 to Just Fontaine's France in the third-place play-off. The defeat to Sweden in Gothenburg would rankle for years to come and is still known in Germany by all sorts of evocative epithets. The blue touchpaper of strained relations between the two nations – among players, fans and press alike – was lit after 58 minutes of the match, when West German defender Erich Juskowiak lashed out at Swedish forward Kurt Hamrin in retaliation for a foul. Juskowiak was sent off by the Hungarian referee István Zsolt, whose impartiality had been questioned in the German press ahead of the game because of the ramifications for Hungarian football of the 1954 World Cup Final. During extensive pleas from Juskowiak, photographers rushed on to the field of play and captured what are now otherwise barely recoverable moments in time. Eventually, the inconsolable defender was escorted off the field by the experienced Walter and the captain Hans Schäfer. Walter was then badly hurt by a foul from Sigvard Parling and West Germany were effectively reduced to nine men, while Hamrin and Parling both went unpunished. Sweden scored twice in the final ten minutes to progress to the final, to the delight of a fervent Gothenburg crowd. DFB president Peco Bauwens vowed that his team would never again set foot in Sweden.

West Germany's qualification for the 1962 tournament in Chile was secured with four victories from four matches against Northern Ireland and Greece. The Hamburg striker Uwe Seeler was now established in the side and was joined in attack by the Augsburg forward Helmut Haller, three years Seeler's junior. At the World Cup itself, West Germany were drawn in a group with Switzerland, hosts Chile, and an Italian side in transition between the tragedy of Superga in 1949 and the great team under Ferruccio Valcareggi that lost just six games in eight years between 1966 and 1974.

Winning the group was a priority for Herberger, since the team could then remain in the capital Santiago for the quarter-final, instead of playing in the port city of Arica in the far north of the country. Five points from wins over Switzerland and Chile and a goalless draw against the Italian defensive masters were enough to achieve just that, and West Germany progressed to face Yugoslavia on 10 June in a repeat of the 1954 and 1958 quarter-finals in Geneva and Malmö, respectively. With just five minutes of the match remaining, Yugoslav captain Milan Galić eluded Willi Schulz and Karl-Heinz Schnellinger on the right flank before crossing into the penalty area, where Petar Radaković came to meet the ball with a thunderous right-footed shot into the top corner. Yugoslavia, who had won Olympic gold in Rome two years prior, thus consigned *Angstgegner* West Germany to elimination from the tournament.

The immediate reaction to the defeat was measured, with Becker arguing in his *Kicker* editorial that West Germany would not fear playing any of the sides that had progressed to the semi-finals. An impressive 3-0 win over Uruguay in Hamburg two months before the World Cup had given cause to believe in Herberger's system, which moved Gladbach outside-right Albert Brülls to inside-left to combine with Schäfer on the left flank. The outside-right position meanwhile passed from player to player for each match in Chile, and for the Yugoslavia game Brülls was moved back there, sacrificing his effective interplay with Schäfer. In an effort to address this problem, Herberger had, in January that year, even paid a visit to Helmut Rahn, the hero of Bern who had played his last international match in April 1960, but he found him to be overweight and unfit. Becker identified the lack of attacking impetus on the wings as a key problem, 'In all four games we could have done with a Rahn from the years 1954 and 1958.'

In the ensuing weeks, Herberger faced growing criticism for his adherence to the now outdated W-M system. The fact that the World Cup Final in Chile was contested by Brazil and Czechoslovakia, who employed the more modern 4-2-4 and 4-3-3 formations, did not help his cause. Brazil, the pioneers of the back four, won a second successive World Cup with two centre-forwards, Pelé (replaced by Amarildo in 1962) and Vavá, flanked by Mario Zagallo on the left and the outstanding Garrincha on the right. On the losing side that day, the Czechoslovak coach

Rudolf Vytlačil later affirmed, 'The W-M system is dead. All players now have to be able to defend and attack. The forwards are the first line in a team's defence.' Two national teams who had not yet apprehended this development, but were soon prompted to react, were England and West Germany.

England's appearance in Chile was their first in South America since a disastrous end-of-season tour in 1959, when they were beaten handsomely by Brazil and Peru. In the interim, Winterbottom's side also lost in Madrid, Budapest and Vienna. Bill Nicholson's double-winning Tottenham Hotspur team emulated the Busby Babes in reaching the semi-finals of the European Cup just weeks before the 1962 World Cup, but Winterbottom could not benefit from the talents of Belfast-born Danny Blanchflower, Scotsman Dave Mackay, or the Welsh wing wizard Cliff Jones. In fact, only two Spurs players, Jimmy Greaves and Maurice Norman, were included in England's World Cup squad.

While still a Chelsea player, Greaves had enjoyed a prolific 1960/61 season in England colours, scoring 13 goals in eight appearances including a hat-trick on that famous day against Scotland. During a short and unhappy stint at AC Milan at the beginning of the following season, Greaves was not selected for England, and in December, Nicholson brought him back to London. He was still only 21, and over the next decade he would become Tottenham's record goalscorer with 266 goals.

Greaves returned to the England fold in April 1962 and scored a hat-trick in a World Cup warm-up match in Lima to help England avenge the heavy defeat by Peru three years before. His club-mate Norman was a debutant that day, as was a young West Ham United defender named Bobby Moore. They joined the more experienced Ron Flowers of Wolverhampton Wanderers in defence and gave cause for optimism among observers. 'Walter Winterbottom is well satisfied with the re-shaped half-back line,' reported Donald Saunders in the *Daily Telegraph*. 'To him this was the best feature of the match. Certainly Norman and Moore fitted in well with Flowers and Moore's tackling gave extra bite to the line.' The same XI found the Hungarians to be a more difficult proposition in the first World Cup group match ten days later, however. The Magyars' 2-1 win was their fourth successive victory over England, and it left Winterbottom's team desperate for a result against Argentina just two days later. An impressive 3-1 win with goals from Flowers, Bobby Charlton and Greaves ensued. Glanville's succinct analysis in his report from Rancagua elucidates how England prevailed in a compelling clash of styles, 'They surprised the ball-playing Argentinians by their direct methods.' Miller in the *Sunday Telegraph*, meanwhile, reserved special praise for England's emerging star, 'The defence was again unshakable. What a find is young Moore. A superb athlete in the best British tradition.'

A lacklustre performance in 'a feeble, insipid match' against outsiders Bulgaria then put paid to any hopes of winning the group and avoiding world champions Brazil in the quarter-finals. Correspondents for the English press made little attempt across the three group games to hide their disdain for the poor attendance figures, facilities and weather conditions at the small venue in Rancagua, a short journey south of Santiago. More importantly, however, it was 'the formlessness and unpredictability of England's football' in this final group match that exasperated onlookers; something which will ring true to many fans from subsequent generations also.

A fourth meeting with the formidable Brazilians now beckoned, with the sequence of previous results tending only one way. The memorable 4-2 win for England at Wembley in 1956 had been followed by a goalless draw in Gothenburg at the 1958 World Cup, and then a 4-1 defeat in Rio de Janeiro on that unsuccessful tour in 1959. The 20-year-old Pelé was now well established in the side and feared by all, but his enforced absence from the rest of the tournament because of an injury sustained in the group-stage encounter with Yugoslavia ostensibly improved England's chances.

In Viña del Mar on Chile's Pacific coastline, the brilliant Brazilians gave England a footballing masterclass. On the right flank where Stanley Matthews had terrorised defenders from all the world in days gone by, the bandy-legged genius Garrincha now put England to the sword. He was a threat from all over the pitch, as evidenced by his curling long-range shot from left of centre for Brazil's third goal in a 3-1 win. The available footage of the game shows how Garrincha repeatedly occupied several

England players with his dazzling runs, tormenting not only his opposing left-back Ray Wilson but also Moore, Norman, Flowers and, at times, Charlton. The virtuoso individual performance from the Botafogo winger helped to ensure that, as with West Germany's simultaneous elimination, the immediate press reaction was measured and accepting. The *Daily Telegraph*'s Donald Saunders called it 'a fighting exit, indeed one of which they need never be ashamed'. Geoffrey Green opted for a tone of admiration for the opposition instead of examining England's tactical shortcomings, remarking that towards the end of the contest 'we were finding that courage and determination were insufficient against the superior ball skill, easy rhythm, and smooth movements of the Brazilians'.

* * *

Winterbottom remained in charge of England for just three more games. News of his resignation, to come into effect at the end of the year, emerged soon after the World Cup. While he did come under scrutiny in the press for England's failure to progress past the last eight, he had already been left disaffected months before the tournament, when he was passed over for the role of FA secretary to replace Stanley Rous, now president of the world governing body. As the new secretary Dennis Follows made clear, the manager's departure 'was entirely at Mr Winterbottom's seeking'. Glanville had earlier characterised Winterbottom as 'altogether too detached, too tightly cocooned in terminology to rouse his players as a great team manager should', and had again called for the end of the England selection committee when bemoaning that 'so long as the team manager's job remains institutionalised one will be playing the same old record'.

The FA was keen to find a new man for the job without delay, given the impending anniversary in 1963 and the home World Cup three years later. By October 1962 the organisation had alighted on Alf Ramsey, who won promotion to the First Division with Ipswich Town in 1961 and then led the club to the league title in its debut season in the top flight, a feat that he had also achieved as a player with Tottenham Hotspur a decade before. Ramsey accepted the job on the condition that the selection committee would be discontinued and that he would be in sole charge, and he agreed to begin full-time work with England at the end of the 1962/63 season, for which he remained with Ipswich. He took the club into the European Cup, losing in the first round to eventual winners AC Milan.

Some of the differences between Winterbottom and Ramsey are worth noting at this point. While the outgoing manager, to give him his due, had made attempts to modernise the England team and was not quite an Oxbridge graduate in the mould of the denizens of the FA, Winterbottom was nonetheless a well-educated former lecturer who attained the rank of wing commander in the Royal Air Force during the Second World War. Ramsey was born in 1920 in semi-rural Dagenham, Essex, and worked at a grocery shop upon leaving school at the age of 14. After joining the army in 1940 he became a quartermaster sergeant in an anti-aircraft unit, serving only on the home front. In short, Ramsey was a very different man to those who employed him. Crucially, however, he took the FA's antiquated workings head on, forcing the abandonment of the selection committee and demanding respect as a senior member of the organisation in his capacity of England manager.

Ramsey's social anxiety, his cumbersome attempts to disguise his Essex accent, and his antipathy towards the press all combined over time to construct an unfavourable caricature. Yet as the academic John Hughson has pointed out, 'The change Ramsey effectively brought to the organisational role of England manager and the upsetting of class presumption this involved has not been regarded carefully enough by those preoccupied with his parodied image.' Moreover, Winterbottom's playing career at Manchester United was curtailed by a back complaint diagnosed as ankylosing spondylitis, and he never played for England. By contrast, Ramsey's international career of 32 caps under Winterbottom, including the 1950 World Cup in Brazil, not to mention his exploits for Arthur Rowe's Tottenham, commanded the players' respect.

A setback came before Ramsey officially took the helm. After FA isolationism had kept the England team away from the first European Nations' Cup (later the UEFA European Championship) in 1960, England did now enter the qualification tournament for the 1964 edition, which whittled 28 entrants down to four qualifiers. West Germany, meanwhile, declined to enter both the 1960 and 1964 editions because Herberger saw the new tournament as an unnecessary distraction. England had won the first leg of their first-round qualification tie against France at Hillsborough in October 1962 but went down to a 5-2 defeat at the Parc des Princes in Paris on 27 February 1963. The match counts as Ramsey's first as England manager, albeit in a part-time capacity and with the team still picked by the selection committee. It was an inauspicious start, with Saunders remarking, 'Ramsey could scarcely have chosen a worse night on which to make his debut as England's manager.'

Unlike Herberger, Ramsey had hoped to use the European Championship campaign as an important part of England's preparations for the 1966 World Cup. When the final stages were played out in June 1964, England travelled instead to Brazil to participate in the Taça das Nações, a four-team tournament celebrating the 50th anniversary of the foundation of the Brazilian Football Confederation. The invited teams were Argentina, Portugal and England, meaning that the event convened many of the game's biggest stars, including Pelé, Eusébio and Bobby Charlton. England had yet another unhappy experience in South America, however, failing to win any of their three games in the round-robin format, and only drawing against fellow Europeans Portugal. As an experience for the new manager in facing South American opposition, the venture proved to be a rude but effective awakening. From that point on, Ramsey's England lost just two matches in four years.

* * *

On 28 July 1962 in Dortmund, the general assembly of the DFB overwhelmingly approved a motion for the formation of a national football league in West Germany. The idea had been debated to various extents throughout the 1950s and was rejected at the extraordinary session of the assembly in Frankfurt in 1958, despite national team manager Herberger's appeal, 'We need this elite division if we want to compete internationally.' Friedebert Becker was present when the proposal finally passed and reported the news with exuberance to his *Kicker* readership, 'Germany has caught up with the world game in the organisation of its football and in the administration of its games, overcoming its provincial backwardness.' Becker and his publication had been advocating for this development for over a decade, and now it had finally come. It was heartily welcomed even if the revolution was still incomplete, since in a separate vote the full professionalisation of German football was rejected in favour of a system with capped wages and maximum transfer fees.

The Bundesliga, as it was called, would begin in August 1963 with 16 clubs selected from among 46 applicants in the five regional leagues (Oberligen) that were established after the Second World War. A convoluted and somewhat controversial system was devised to determine the teams that would participate in the first Bundesliga season, and by May 1963 the field of 16 was complete. A notable omission was FC Bayern München, with cross-town rivals TSV 1860 chosen on the strength of winning the final edition of the Oberliga Süd that year. As an exhibit, simply entitled 'Rejection' (*Ablehnung*), informs visitors to the club's Allianz Arena museum, the last-minute decision hit the club hard and has never quite been forgiven, much less forgotten. FC Bayern had been confident of inclusion as one of the five founding teams from the South German FA, but the DFB would not admit two teams from the same city.

TSV 1860 München went on to achieve great success during the 1960s, winning the DFB-Pokal in 1964 and the Bundesliga title in 1966, as well as reaching the 1965 UEFA Cup Winners' Cup Final against West Ham United. In the long term, however, it is self-evident which of the two Munich clubs has fared better, and another exhibit in the same museum affirms that the perceived 'gross injustice' of 1963 ultimately worked in Bayern's favour, since the club was forced to foster talent from its youth team and the surrounding provinces. Players such as Sepp Maier, Franz Beckenbauer and Gerd Müller soon came to the fore, and in 1965 Bayern reached the Bundesliga via promotion from the regional league. The 1964/65 season was Müller's first with the club, and he signalled what was to come with 39 goals in 32 games.

After overseeing the inception of the Bundesliga, Herberger announced on 23 November 1963 that he would step down from the role of national team manager at the end of that season.

His tenure was to end some 28 years after he took charge of his first international match in the aftermath of the 1936 Berlin Olympic Games.

Herberger's reputation and relationship with the German press had transformed almost overnight after the World Cup in Chile, much to his surprise and dismay. He was blamed for the team's poor morale and a negative playing style orientated towards stopping opposition attacks. Yet the 1962 tournament as a whole was marked by defensive football, yielding a goal average of 2.78 per game, by far the lowest of any FIFA World Cup up to that point.

Another key factor that pushed Herberger towards the exit was a change at the top of the DFB hierarchy. At the same general assembly in Dortmund where the formation of the Bundesliga was agreed, long-time president Peco Bauwens was succeeded by Hermann Gösmann, and the previously invulnerable position of the manager began to weaken somewhat. Yet Herberger would not leave the post before digging his heels in once more. 'The preparations for the 1966 World Cup are still in my hands,' he was quoted as saying in late 1962. 'I decide when I resign. The DFB has given me a completely free hand.' A year later, differences with the DFB could no longer be reconciled. Herberger left the stage in June 1964 after a 4-1 win in Helsinki and was succeeded by his assistant Helmut Schön. The former Dresdner SC forward played in 16 international matches between 1937 and 1941, scoring 17 goals. His first international goal came in World Cup qualification, but he missed out on the 1938 tournament because of the Nazis' ill-judged *Anschluss* policy that saw nine Austrians incorporated into Herberger's squad.

As a coach, Schön had already been closely involved with the national team for a period of eight years that spanned the 1958 and 1962 World Cups. Schön's immediate task was to qualify for 1966, a challenge which his counterpart Ramsey of course did not have to face, as the hosts qualified automatically. The first match of West Germany's new era was thus a crucial encounter with Sweden in Berlin, in which the home side led until just five minutes from time, when the prolific Fiorentina winger – and perceived villain of Gothenburg 1958 – Kurt Hamrin equalised.

Joining the experienced Uwe Seeler, Horst Szymaniak and Karl-Heinz Schnellinger – the outstanding German player in all four games in Chile – were new talents from the incipient Bundesliga. Wolfgang Overath of 1. FC Köln won his seventh cap, while his younger club-mate Wolfgang Weber made only his fourth international appearance.

12 May 1965
West Germany 0-1 England
Städtisches Stadion, Nuremberg

West Germany welcomed England to Nuremberg for the fourth international match under Schön's management in May 1965. This first encounter between the two nations for nine years was part of an end-of-season tour that England undertook just before the first Anglo-German final in UEFA club competition. A mere three days after finishing the tour in Sweden, West Ham's Bobby Moore lifted the Cup Winners' Cup at Wembley, following his club's 2-0 win over TSV 1860 München. The team also included Martin Peters and Geoff Hurst, both as yet untried by Ramsey.

West Ham were the second English club to win a European trophy, following Tottenham's 5-1 win over Atlético Madrid in the final of the same competition in 1963. Since the Busby Babes' trailblazing tie with Borussia Dortmund in 1956, there had also been confrontations in the European Cup between Wolverhampton Wanderers and Schalke 04 in 1958/59; Burnley and Hamburger SV in 1960/61; and, earlier in this 1964/65 season, Liverpool and 1. FC Köln.

On their first foray in European competition, Bill Shankly's Liverpool met the 1964 Bundesliga champions at the quarter-final stage and were forced into a replay at a neutral venue after two goalless draws. Future World Cup winner Roger Hunt scored Liverpool's second goal in a 2-2 draw in Rotterdam that brought about the unlikely scenario of a coin toss after extra time to decide who would progress. Luck was on the side of the English champions. Liverpool went on to lose 4-3 on aggregate in the semi-final to Helenio Herrera's *Grande Inter*, the eventual winners of a second successive European Cup.

The steady accumulation of experience among English and German clubs in formal European competition during the late

1950s and early 60s began to change the football landscape, and high-profile Anglo-German encounters at club level now formed an important backdrop to international matches between the two countries. Indeed, in previewing the Germans' latest attempt to achieve a first victory against England, *Kicker* magazine conceded that the Cup Winners' Cup Final had taken precedence over the international match in terms of significance for the German football enthusiast.

There was nonetheless still great demand for tickets to see England play at the home of 1. FC Nürnberg. Schön was hampered by the absences of Seeler and Weber through injury, and Brülls, Haller, and the outstanding left-back Schnellinger were also unavailable. These three players had given up waiting for the full professionalisation of German football and were now under contract with Italian clubs. Borussia Dortmund goalkeeper Hans Tilkowski was at last the first choice for the position under Schön and played with one eye on the DFB-Pokal Final against Alemannia Aachen ten days later. Gladbach defender Horst-Dieter Höttges made only his third appearance in the senior team, while Overath, still only 21, was beginning to conduct forward play. Both were future world champions in the making.

Ramsey, meanwhile, had to make do without the injured Greaves as well as the Liverpool and Manchester United players who were still involved in the European Cup and Inter-Cities Fairs Cup, respectively. The line-up in Nuremberg was best described by Saunders as a 'patchwork team of reserves and new caps, bolstered by a nucleus of experienced players'. Joining Moore at the heart of a new four-man defence was Bobby Charlton's older brother Jack Charlton, who had made his international debut against Scotland a month before at the senior age of 29. Although perhaps not the most gifted player, the tall Leeds United defender was the perfect foil for the elegant, ball-playing Moore, and Ramsey told him as much. The experienced Wilson was a fixture at left-back, and Fulham's George Cohen had by now superseded Blackpool's Jimmy Armfield on the right side of defence. This back line was here described as 'one of the soundest defensive systems in Europe', with Moore again praised for his calm leadership.

The only goal of the game came towards the end of the first half, when debutant Derek Temple pulled the ball back from the bye-line for Southampton forward Terry Paine to finish past Tilkowski from close range. The West Germans suffered a fair amount of misfortune in searching for an equaliser, with Karl-Heinz Thielen a particular threat. Having hit the crossbar immediately after Paine's opener, Thielen later had a goal disallowed for handball. A photograph of the incident shows the Köln forward with a raised elbow contesting the ball with Jack Charlton and the great Gordon Banks, who made his first of six appearances in goal against West Germany that day.

After the match, an astute analysis of the visitors' development under Ramsey came from Fritz Walter in the pages of *Kicker*:

'England's football has modernised. Every player mastered attack and defence. They were so agile that their actions, whether offensive or defensive, flowed smoothly into one another. In the past, the English players stubbornly drilled the W-M system and hardly knew a thing about positional change.'

Ramsey offered his counterpart Schön a word of encouragement, telling him that he would now go to Gothenburg (for the final match of England's tour) and show him how to beat the Swedes. West Germany's crucial return qualifier away to Sweden was slated for the autumn, and it would decide who would travel to England the following summer, since both teams could bank on beating group minnows Cyprus. With the likes of Seeler and Schnellinger restored to the line-up, Schön's team delivered in Stockholm's Råsundastadion on 26 September, winning 2-1 and securing qualification to the 1966 World Cup. It is testament to Schön's uncertainty and difficult circumstances in this period that no player appeared in all four of the qualifying matches against Sweden and Cyprus.

One young man from Munich who made his debut in the crucial game in Sweden, two weeks after his 20th birthday, would go on to become probably the best-known German footballer in history, winning over 100 caps and both the FIFA World Cup and UEFA European Championship titles as captain. Franz Beckenbauer first played for the FC Bayern senior team in June 1964, and a year later the club was promoted to the Bundesliga. After just six appearances in the top flight he took his place in the *Nationalmannschaft* in Stockholm and never looked back. The words for Beckenbauer in *Kicker* magazine's individual appraisals point the way towards an illustrious career, 'Not a hint of stage-fright in his first international. In the second half, there was even an almost supreme composure to his game. Players of his ability don't grow into the national team, they're right at the heart of it.'

23 February 1966
England 1-0 West Germany
Wembley Stadium, London

Both England and West Germany now looked forward to numerous friendly internationals in preparation for the 1966 World Cup. Schön's side took care of the formalities of qualification with a 6-0 win in Cyprus in November, and then a trip to Wembley – the first since that *tour de force* from Stanley Matthews in 1954 – beckoned in February. Ramsey's England suffered a rare defeat at home to Austria in October, but the result did not weaken his conviction, pronounced publicly in 1963, when he claimed, 'England will win the World Cup.' His 'unshakable optimism showed no trace of flagging', wrote the *Daily Telegraph*'s David Miller.

Against Spain in their final game of 1965, England won 2-0 in Madrid's Santiago Bernabéu Stadium with goals from Joe Baker and Roger Hunt. While this may not have been an especially eye-catching result in the context of the team's good form overall, the game was of great significance to Ramsey, for this was when England's modernised playing system first clicked. As Geoffrey Green revealed in *The Times* in the glorious aftermath of England's triumph half a year later, the austere, emotionally reserved Ramsey appeared to apprehend the significance of the moment:

'The night England beat Spain 2-0 in the bitter temperature of a freezing Madrid, I believed momentarily to have penetrated behind his mask of bland reserve. It was the night the new Ramsey style, carefully planned, of perpetual motion on the field, at last emerged. His 4-3-3 plan really worked; every player clicked together in a way that is often hard to explain in football;

everything went right. He talked of "this precious gem", shaping his hands in front of him as if around an imaginary football. For once there was a momentary gleam of sensitive satisfaction behind his wary eyes.'

The England XI in Madrid was close to that which Ramsey would field at the World Cup; only Greaves, sidelined for three months with hepatitis, and Peters were missing. This was still the case when England welcomed West Germany, as Greaves did not return to international duty until the match against Yugoslavia at Wembley on 4 May, which was also Peters's debut. Against the Germans on 23 February, Ramsey gave a first England cap to the man who would be in the right place at the right time – on a fair few occasions – to become a national hero that summer and forever more. It was on this day that the West Ham striker Geoff Hurst, already an FA Cup and Cup Winners' Cup winner at the age of 24, got a first close look at Franz Beckenbauer, Willi Schulz and Wolfgang Weber.

At the heart of Ramsey's system for the encounter with Germany were two of the toughest tacklers in the game, Nobby Stiles and Norman Hunter, a team-mate of Jack Charlton at Don Revie's Leeds. Three minutes before half-time, Stiles scored the only goal of the game, indeed the only goal of his England career, and he later fondly recalled this match because it was the only occasion on which the Manchester United midfielder wore the number nine shirt. This in itself points to the increased flexibility of Ramsey's 4-3-3 system. While Banks and the back four were now a tried and tested unit, the six men in front of them were still unfixed in terms of name, number and position.

The English press, however, were far from impressed by Ramsey's tinkering on this dreary February night at Wembley. 'One is all in favour of free thinking and free movement,' wrote Green in *The Times*. 'Yet these new methods, which started so well in Madrid in December, seemed to get nowhere. It was almost as if the match was an exercise in confused anonymity, where numbers on the shirts mattered not.' That hint of reproach about a disregard for shirt numbers is presumably the sort of thing that football writer Norman Giller had in mind when he observed, 'Little had been learned since back in the 1950s when [Hungarian midfielder] Nándor Hidegkuti completely baffled England's defence by playing a withdrawn role in the number nine jersey.' Green's report continued in its disgruntlement, 'There were pretensions of cleverness between players who tried to be too clever by half, and for much of the time one longed for something old-fashioned – some fast movement along longitudinal rather than lateral lines ... Little or no use was made of the width of the field.' The negative appraisals were far from exclusive to the press box, as evidenced by the loud jeers ringing round Wembley stadium at the end of the match. These were not – not yet at least – 'wingless wonders'.

Bearing in mind what happened five months later, one incident from this game deserves special mention. Substitute Alfred Heiß's disallowed goal with 15 minutes remaining received short shrift in the English press, but the German perspective is worth noting. Heiß thought he had scored when he met a cross from Sigfried Held with a splendid volley, but Jack Charlton immediately led English appeals. The Dutch referee Piet Roomer had given the goal but now resolved to consult with his linesman on the far side, and the decision was duly reversed on account of the ball having gone over the bye-line before Held could dispatch his cross. The German correspondent Karl-Heinz Heimann did not hide his frustration at the incident:

'Whether the ball was out, we could no more determine from the press box than the television footage allows for conclusions ... This much is certain: in reversing his decision, Roomer allowed himself to be influenced by a linesman who was twice as far away from the scene. He should have trusted his own eyes more!'

Both the English and German accounts concur that the visitors were growing into the game at this late stage, with the characteristic positive play and incisive passing already on show from a young Günter Netzer in only his third senior international. For England, this may only have been an underwhelming and insipid friendly on a rainy night, but as far as West Germany were concerned, the prospect of a precious draw at Wembley – perhaps even the chance to push for that elusive first win over

England – had been snatched away. Roomer's decision rankled with West Germany in the moment, as evidenced by the footage of the players' impassioned protests, and probably for some time afterwards also. Rather pertinently in hindsight, the controversy centred around the question, 'Was it over the line?'

6

Going the Distance
July 1966

The German Football Museum in Dortmund features an expansive area where each year of the DFB's existence is marked with a relevant exhibit. A rugby ball from 1902, Helmut Rahn's shirt from the 1954 World Cup, and Manuel Neuer's rainbow armband from Euro 2020 are notable examples. The chosen exhibit for the year 1966 is among the more curious. It is a football, although no ordinary football in the modern sense. This is a decorated Royal Shrovetide ball from the town of Ashbourne in Derbyshire, presented to the West German national team 'in recognition of their on-field performance and fairness during the World Cup in England'. Of course, the World Cup Final and its attendant controversies are addressed elsewhere in the museum – not without an element of dark humour – but here the focus is on the good relations between the *Nationalmannschaft* and the English public.

The West German squad arrived at the Peveril of the Peak Hotel, three miles outside Ashbourne, on Friday, 8 July after flying from Hamburg to Manchester, via London. The German press informed readers of the origin of the hotel's name in the novel by Walter Scott, set in the famous Peak District national park. Among the many autograph requests that had already accumulated at the hotel, one envelope meant for the Dortmund forward Sigfried Held was simply addressed 'Siggi Held, Peak Nationalpark England'.

Ashbourne is famous for the Shrovetide football game that has been played out on its streets annually for hundreds of years.

The ball used in this extraordinary ritual is filled with cork to allow it to float, since the game is played along a waterway running through the town. The balls are decoratively painted and displayed in pubs and shops around Ashbourne, and the one that was given to the German guests is inscribed with the words, 'Presented to the West Germany World Cup team by the Citizens of Ashbourne, July 1966.' The local people took the team to their hearts after observing training sessions and encountering star players strolling around their town's humble streets, and this was unquestionably important to the DFB. In the case of Helmut Schön, who played for his hometown club Dresdner SC alongside the great Richard Hofmann during the war, good relations with the host country were a priority, as the German football writer Uli Hesse explains:

'The man who had lost his home and many other, less tangible, things to the war was very well aware that his team represented a country which only 26 years previously had reduced London to rubble. Again and again he drummed the idea into his players that the most important thing, more important than winning, was to behave like gentlemen and sportsmen.'

The choice of this quiet and bucolic location in the heart of England is explained by the first televised World Cup draw, conducted on 6 January 1966 at the Royal Garden Hotel in Kensington, London. West Germany were seeded alongside England, Brazil and Italy, and were drawn into group two with Switzerland, Argentina and Spain. The stadia allocated to this group were Sheffield Wednesday's Hillsborough and Villa Park in Birmingham, and the group winners would also play the quarter-final in Sheffield. The town of Ashbourne on the southern fringes of the Peak District was the perfect fit, as it was roughly equidistant between the two venues. In fact, while the administrative effort that went into the selection of an appropriate team base is astounding, the final choice was rather serendipitous.

DFB secretary Hermann Joch had made provisional reservations for the team all over the country, not knowing where they would be allocated. *Kicker* magazine revealed that on the day of the draw, the DFB placed English liaison officers in each of the prospective bases who could watch the draw on television and confirm the reservation with the respective hotel manager at any moment. The first preference, geographically advantageous for games in the Midlands as well as the north-west, was the Stanneylands Hotel in Wilmslow, south of Manchester. Schön and Joch were ready to fly north on the morning after the draw to sign the contract with the hotel, and even brought their trip forward when they heard that Portugal had expressed an interest. What they had not been told by the English organising committee, however, was that the team allocated to group three, with games in Manchester and Liverpool, would be given preference for the Manchester base. A whole host of German journalists and broadcast representatives thus found themselves on the morning after the draw at what was to be Portugal's team hotel for the World Cup.

Later that same day, *Kicker* editor Robert Becker travelled on with Schön and Joch to a remote hotel that had been recommended by Joch's relative living in England. This was the Peveril of the Peak Hotel, and it fulfilled all requirements, including the availability of the football pitch at Ashbourne for training sessions. Concerns about English food were also allayed, 'Even the question of cuisine can possibly be solved without a cook travelling with the team, since the chef at the Peveril of the Peak is Italian, and he can of course, as the hotel management proudly assured us, cook "continental".'

1966 FIFA World Cup
England

In the week of the team's arrival for the tournament in July, there was cause for the DFB to celebrate at the FIFA Congress in London, where the 1974 World Cup was awarded to West Germany. With this decision coming just three months after the 1972 Olympic Games were awarded to the city of Munich, it was clear that a significant moment in the country's rehabilitation had been reached. As the German football writer Dietrich Schulze-Marmeling explains, 'The year 1966 signified a breakthrough for German sports diplomacy. 21 years after the end of the Second World War and National Socialist rule, the Federal Republic was deemed worthy of hosting the two most important international sporting events.'

West Germany's World Cup then began with a resounding 5-0 win over Switzerland at Hillsborough. Held scored the opening goal, followed by two apiece from Helmut Haller and Franz Beckenbauer, who announced his prodigious talent on the world stage at the earliest opportunity. The display drastically shortened the team's pre-tournament price of 25/1 at the bookmakers, who made Brazil and England favourites for the trophy. The German press proudly collated and printed the views of their English counterparts, such as those of Derek Wallis in the *Daily Mirror*:

'If the Swiss could have packed the Alps among their World Cup baggage, they might have had a chance of stopping the remorseless, ruthless German advance at Hillsborough last night ... The skill of linkmen Franz Beckenbauer and Helmut Haller and the power of Uwe Seeler, "Siggy" Held and Wolfgang Overath, are obviously going to make the Germans a feared team. Beckenbauer – "Fabulous Franz" is tall, dark and handsome, just 20, and destined to become a great star of this World Cup.'

In a 2006 television documentary, Bobby Charlton stated that he and his team-mates watched as many games as they could in between their own matches, keenly observing rival teams' progress in the tournament. They will have had an eye especially on West Germany's group, as they knew it would yield a quarter-final opponent. The scoreless draw played out between Schön's men and Argentina at Villa Park on 16 July pointed to the difficult task England would face in the next round and anticipated some unsavoury incidents. The *Kicker* headline – 'Five Minutes of Argentinian Theatre!' – refers to an incident just after the hour mark when Yugoslav referee Konstantin Zečević sent off José Rafael Albrecht for a foul on Wolfgang Weber, and the San Lorenzo defender refused to leave the field. Pictures of the 'palaver' across two pages show Albrecht, the Argentina physios and captain Antonio Rattín, who was later the villain at Wembley, involved in the controversy. The defensive football on show meant that the admiration for the West German team in the English press dissipated every bit as readily as it had shown itself four days earlier.

Few people will now remember that when England and West Germany simultaneously played France and Spain, respectively, in their final group matches on the evening of 20 July, only six minutes of play remained when a quarter-final meeting between the two teams was averted. Schön's side knew that failure to beat Spain would in all likelihood mean finishing as group runners-up and a premature trip to Wembley to face the hosts. With England winning 2-0 late on, and Argentina ahead against Switzerland by the same score, this was indeed the scenario. At Villa Park, a magnificent strike from a tight angle by Borussia Dortmund forward Lothar Emmerich had restored parity after the Spaniards opened the scoring in the first half. With only a few minutes remaining, it was time for Uwe Seeler to score his first goal of the tournament, steering Held's cross past the goalkeeper from six yards after the Dortmund man had made the latest of his bursting runs down the left flank. While being mobbed by his team-mates who understood the importance of that goal, captain Seeler ran back to his own half and ensured that all were alert for the restart. A quarter-final against Uruguay in Sheffield was all but secure.

England, meanwhile, would play the fiercely combative Argentinians at Wembley. Alf Ramsey's side had not set the tournament alight in topping their group with wins over Mexico and France after an opening-day goalless draw with Uruguay that disappointed fans and journalists alike. That was only the second time England had failed to score on the Wembley turf, and the *Daily Mirror*'s Ken Jones lamented afterwards, 'This is obviously going to be the dourest, most defensively dominated championship of them all.' Bobby Charlton's opening goal against Mexico, from a long-distance shot described in the *Sunday Mirror* as 'a royal right-foot thunderball', thus brought great relief. The press remained far from convinced by the 2-0 win, however, with Brian Glanville noting, 'England's deficiencies in attack are seriously comprehensive.' After England won 2-0 again against France, with two goals from Roger Hunt, there was some cautious optimism. Nobody questioned England's unbreached defence, and indeed Geoffrey Green reserved special praise for the 'completely masterful' Bobby Moore.

Yet the tone across the press box was one of concern at the challenge the Argentinians would pose to England's attackers in a quarter-final that was expected to resemble the Uruguay match. Another worry was that Jimmy Greaves, who had been out of sorts during the group stage and still had not scored, was now injured after a vicious challenge from the French midfielder Joseph Bonnel. The anxiety about England's prospects was in part attributable to the fact that the personnel, shape and playing style of the team was still not settled during the group phase. In each of the three matches, Ramsey fielded a different winger to play wide on the right, much like Sepp Herberger had done in Chile four years earlier. These players were Manchester United's John Connelly against Uruguay, Southampton's Terry Paine against Mexico, and Liverpool's Ian Callaghan against France. The young Blackpool midfielder Alan Ball played on the left side in the first of these games but was then replaced by Martin Peters. Ball later recalled that he felt sure that his World Cup was finished, since England won well in the two games he missed, but then the injury sustained by Greaves and the specific challenges posed by Argentina prompted a reshuffle.

Remembering that important experiment in Madrid, Nobby Stiles explained why the notion that Ramsey changed to a 'new' formation at this point was flawed, 'They all said that we changed our system after the first couple of games and played a 4-3-3, but we had actually done that in Spain about eight months before, and they were a good side ... we beat them 2-0 but we could have beaten them six or seven. But he kept it under wraps, and in the three opening games we played a 4-2-4; it was only in the quarter-finals that he changed it.'

For the Argentina game, Ramsey reinstated Ball and asked him to play on the right of the midfield three in order to stifle the Boca Juniors left-back Silvio Marzolini. The England line-up did not change again until the trophy had been won. Ball-winner Stiles played in front of the trusted defensive unit of Gordon Banks, George Cohen, Ray Wilson, Bobby Moore and Jack Charlton. Peters and Ball were now together in midfield, with Bobby Charlton supporting Roger Hunt and Geoff Hurst in attack. Hurst was the beneficiary of the injury suffered by Greaves, and he would have to endure growing calls for the Tottenham striker's recall in the build-up to the final as Greaves did his best to regain fitness in time.

All the while, the other two groups played out in the north-west and north-east of the country turned up the shocks of the tournament, leaving England and West Germany as the only seeded teams in the quarter-finals. Double world champions Brazil were deposed in dramatic fashion at Everton's Goodison Park, where they lost 3-1 to both Hungary and Portugal in the space of five days. Pelé was absent for the match against the Magyars, recovering from the brutal treatment he received in an opening 2-0 win against Bulgaria. He returned to the side against Portugal with a still-injured knee and was then 'butchered' by a cynical tackle from João Morais. Pelé limped on through the remainder of the match but was unable to prevent Brazil's defeat and early elimination.

On the final matchday in group four, North Korea pulled off one of the biggest upsets in World Cup history, beating Italy 1-0 at Middlesbrough's Ayresome Park to progress alongside the Soviet Union to the quarter-finals. An Italian side stocked with talented players, such as double European Cup champions Giacinto Fachetti and Sandro Mazzola of Internazionale and the young AC Milan forward Gianni Rivera, were knocked out in humiliating fashion, having also lost to the Soviet Union in Sunderland three days earlier.

With Brazil and Italy thus eliminated, a path to the final appeared to open for both England and West Germany, even if the Portuguese were still much respected because of the presence of 1965 Ballon d'Or winner Eusébio. The four quarter-finals were played out simultaneously at the traditional time of 3pm on Saturday, 23 July. At Wembley and Hillsborough, the European powers overcame their respective tough-tackling, ill-disciplined opponents from South America. Three were sent off – Argentina's Rattín by West German referee Rudolf Kreitlein, and Uruguayans Horacio Troche and Héctor Silva by Englishman Jim Finney. Together with what had already happened to Brazil in the group phase, these events gave rise to feelings of injustice across South America, and later caused the disgraced former president of FIFA, João Havelange, to allege in an interview with *Folha de São Paulo* that both the 1966 and 1974 World Cups were fixed in favour of the host countries.

There was little sympathy for the 'bad losers' in the English and German press, however. 'As for the two incidents in Sheffield,' wrote Robert Becker, 'they were crystal clear. Finney really exploited every opportunity to spare the Uruguayans having a man sent off. He admonished and he warned. Troche struck Emmerich to the ground behind his back. Silva, already cautioned, committed another rough foul on Haller.' Footage of the match also shows Troche slapping Seeler in the face as he is manhandled by Finney in an attempt to get him off the field, while a minimum of four police officers are later involved in keeping Silva away from the playing surface. The indiscipline is frankly extraordinary. West Germany ran out 4-0 winners with two goals from Haller and one apiece from Beckenbauer and Seeler. The captain's goal was the pick of the four, a right-footed shot into the top corner from the edge of the penalty area.

At Wembley, meanwhile, there were fewer goals but similar levels of controversy. In the English press, the reportage on the England v Argentina quarter-final was the apex of a wave of criticism and anxiety about the negative and violent play on show at the tournament. Most of this censure was levelled at Uruguay and Argentina, but Brazil's European opponents, and in particular their treatment of Pelé, were also in focus. Events had now reached a crisis point, such that the *Sunday Mirror*'s front page urgently asked, 'Can this really be football?' The illustrative photograph below this headline was of referee Kreitlein and his police escort to safety following the match. The *Sunday Telegraph* ran with the headline 'The butchers of Buenos Aires make football a farce'; the *Sunday Times* with 'England subdue the rebels'. The key incident had been the dismissal of Argentina captain Rattín in the first half. He had already been cautioned by Kreitlein and continued harassing the referee to such an extent that he was suddenly sent off while nowhere near the play at the time. Notably, the confusion surrounding the referee's decisions in this game was a major factor that led Ken Aston, chairman of the FIFA Referees' Committee at the 1966 World Cup, subsequently to introduce yellow and red cards into football. Rattín's version of events was as follows, 'I saw the referee give a foul against us which I did not believe was a foul. I asked for an interpreter so that I could explain my protest to him. The referee said "play on" but I insisted that an interpreter should be brought and he sent me off. I did not insult him.' Much like the Uruguyans in Sheffield, Rattín refused to leave the field, delaying the restart by eight minutes.

The ill feeling was compounded when Ramsey was interviewed by the BBC's Kenneth Wolstenholme after the match. The England manager had already rushed on to the pitch to stop his right-back Cohen swapping shirts with his opponent Alberto Gonzáles, and now he added verbal fuel to the fire, 'We have still to produce our best and this best is not possible until we meet the right type of opposition and that is a team that comes out to play football and not act as animals.' Ramsey's insult was picked up and disseminated by at least some members of the press, such as the *Sunday Mirror*'s Sam Leitch, who wrote, 'At Wembley Stadium yesterday I saw Argentine captain Antonio Rattín and his football *animals* disgrace the World Cup before 400 million TV viewers and 88,000 shocked spectators.'

Somewhere amid all the controversy, Hurst had made his mark in the striker's role with a magnificent header 12 minutes from time to send England through to the semi-finals. The goal is memorable also for Martin Peters's celebratory somersault after supplying the pinpoint cross for Hurst.

Just one match now remained for both England and West Germany to negotiate in order to reach the much-anticipated World Cup Final. The Germans faced the Soviet Union at Goodison Park on 25 July, and a day later England took on Eusébio's Portugal at Wembley. Both teams won 2-1 after taking a 2-0 lead. West Germany once again played against ten men in a dour match, after Dynamo Moscow forward Igor Chislenko was sent off shortly before half-time for a foul on Held. Moments earlier, two of the players based in Italy had combined to give West Germany the lead. The great Russian goalkeeper Lev Yashin spared his team's blushes with a series of fine saves, but he was beaten by Haller's neat first-time finish after a through ball from Karl-Heinz Schnellinger. In the second half, the all-important second goal came from Beckenbauer. The young midfielder this time hit a left-footed shot past Yashin into the corner of the Gwladys Street net. A late rally from the Soviet Union, including a goal from Valeriy Porkuyan, proved insufficient, and West Germany took their place in the showpiece final.

The next evening, England overcame Portugal thanks in large part to a brilliant defensive performance in midfield from Stiles. The diminutive Mancunian was given the task of nullifying Eusébio, and he did so to great effect, earning rare individual praise from his manager. 'His shepherding of the Portuguese star was not only beyond reproach but, in the estimation of his colleague George Cohen, "technically and morally brilliant",' wrote Glanville when Stiles passed away at the age of 78 in October 2020.

Once more, European club competition played a significant role. The spectacular European Cup quarter-final between Manchester United and Benfica in the spring of 1966 had yielded ten goals over two legs, with Busby's side progressing 6-4 on aggregate. Five members of the Portugal team at Wembley, including the entire front four in a 4-2-4 system, were Benfica players who had played in that tie against Bobby Charlton and Stiles, where Eusébio had already been left frustrated. The use of Stiles in what we would today call a holding role meant that Ramsey's system evolved from a 4-3-3 into a 4-1-3-2, with Charlton, Peters and Ball playing ahead of Stiles. At the other end of the pitch, the star man was his club-mate Charlton, who added to his fine strike against Mexico with two more goals here. The first was a smart, opportunistic finish from a rebound after José Pereira had beaten Hunt to the ball, and the second, ten minutes from time, was a fine first-time hit of a ball pulled back by Hurst within the penalty area. If 'West Ham won the World Cup', as the proud saying goes in London's East End, it was Manchester United who gave them the opportunity to do so.

The second semi-final was seen to restore football's reputation after the unsavoury events of the quarter-finals. For the *Daily Telegraph*'s Donald Saunders, it 'lifted a great competition out of the rut of mediocrity into which it had sunk' in the preceding days. Portugal received high praise for both their play and their conduct, with Green noting after the second goal how José Augusto 'put out his hand warmly to congratulate Charlton on his merciless finishing stroke'. 'If the final, against the well balanced but rugged Germans … is half as good as this,' wrote Albert Barham in *The Guardian*, 'the 100,000 crowd should be well satisfied.' Even more prophetically, Saunders concluded his description of the tense final minutes after Eusébio's goal from the penalty spot with a warning, 'It was left to Portugal to remind them that no match is won until the final whistle – a thought that England may well take with them on to the pitch against West Germany on Saturday.'

Bobby Charlton recalled a significant visitor to England's team hotel after the semi-final, namely Fritz Walter, who had of course contested a World Cup Final alongside his brother, just as Bobby would now do with Jack. 'In one sense at least I would be walking in his footsteps and sharing some of the emotion he still remembered so vividly 12 years later,' Charlton wrote about his meeting with Walter. 'He had played against Hungary in the company of his brother Ottmar. Jack and I could only hope we enjoyed the same result.'

30 July 1966
FIFA World Cup Final
England 4-2 West Germany (after extra time)
Wembley Stadium, London

The 1966 World Cup Final is the most important match in which England and Germany have ever faced each other, and this will always remain the case. Its significance may one day be emulated, if the two countries meet in another final, but it can never be exceeded. Even if such an occasion does come to pass, that match would have to go some way to approximate the lasting impact of 1966, within football but also in social and cultural terms.

It is also the most significant single match in English football history, and while the same cannot be said for its standing in Germany, its controversial dénouement in extra time meant that even Beckenbauer, speaking almost 30 years later, could call it the most memorable game for Germans. In the annals of German football, the 1966 World Cup Final primarily represents two things: a costly and unjust refereeing decision, and the point of origin of a golden generation's journey towards its successful destiny. In England, a chart-topping song about the national team's lack of success since that day lamented '30 years of hurt' in 1996, and a leading journalist covering the team published the volume *Fifty Years of Hurt* in 2016. So 1966 is thus defined as much by what has followed it as what it signified at the time, if not much more so. Many of these mythologies and ramifications will be discussed later in this book, but at this point the focus is on the match itself as a historical event. I attempt in these pages to synthesise various contemporary descriptions and appraisals of the match from both English and German perspectives. The first objective is always to ascertain with precision what happened that day, in an effort to eschew the obscurantism of later memoirs and national mythologies.

Facing Ramsey's 4-2-3-1 as described above was Schön's 4-2-4, which boasted a front line of Uwe Seeler and Helmut Haller alongside the Dortmund pair Sigfried Held and Lothar Emmerich. Wolfgang Overath and Franz Beckenbauer were the versatile midfielders who played ahead of Willi Schulz and Wolfgang Weber, and the full-backs Horst-Dieter Höttges and Karl-Heinz Schnellinger. Hans Tilkowski made his penultimate appearance in goal for Germany in a match that he would never be allowed to forget. The only change from the semi-final at Goodison Park was the recall of Höttges at right-back, replacing Friedel Lutz, a veteran of Eintracht Frankfurt's 1960 European Cup Final defeat against Real Madrid.

Tilkowski thought that Lutz was a better direct opponent for Hurst, after seeing the West Ham striker at close quarters when playing for Borussia Dortmund in the Cup Winners' Cup semi-final in April 1966. Dortmund won that tie 5-2 on aggregate, with four goals from Emmerich across the two legs. At Hampden Park on 5 May, they faced Bill Shankly's Liverpool in both clubs' first European final. Tilkowski, Held and Emmerich all lined up against Hunt, with Held and Hunt both on the scoresheet in a 2-1 win for the German side after extra time. Dortmund's performance was praised across the English press, with Liverpool's reliance on Hunt in attack identified as a key shortcoming.

West Germany in white shirts, black shorts and white socks kicked off the World Cup Final against England in red shirts, white shorts and red socks at 3pm on Saturday, 30 July 1966. Six minutes in, Stiles dispossessed Beckenbauer for the first time, and shortly afterwards he crossed for Hunt in the penalty area. Tilkowski's clearing punch found only Bobby Charlton, and Hurst and Tilkowski then fought squarely for the ball from Charlton's return cross. The goalkeeper, who was a doubt ahead of the match after sustaining a shoulder injury in the semi-final, came off worse. Wolstenholme quipped, 'He's probably saying to himself, "I heard Muhammad Ali was here but I didn't think he was on the field."' Peters shot from distance moments later. 'Blood was dripping from my mouth,' remembered Tilkowski. 'After a short break for treatment, I was still a bit dazed when Peters let fly. With some difficulty I diverted the shot for a corner.'

On ten minutes, one of the more robust challenges of the afternoon saw Wilson slide into the back of Seeler on the halfway line. From the resulting free kick, West Germany switched the play to the left side, where they directed much of their play in the opening exchanges. Held dispatched a hopeful high ball into the penalty area – a tactic he would employ on numerous occasions – and Wilson's poor defensive header landed at the feet of Haller, who shot on the turn and beat Banks to open the scoring in the 12th minute. Wolstenholme immediately reminded his audience that in the previous three World Cup finals, the team that scored first ended up on the losing side.

Fifteen minutes into the match, a late tackle from Overath on Ball resulted in a word of warning for the Köln midfielder from the Swiss referee Gottfried Dienst. A minute later, there was no hesitation from the referee in awarding another free kick when Overath tripped the advancing Moore inside the West German half. The England captain grabbed the ball, set himself quickly, and launched a floating pass into the penalty area, where the opposing defence was unprepared. Hurst was completely unmarked and rose to meet Moore's gift about seven yards out. As with his precious goal against Argentina, Hurst's accurate header sent the ball past the goalkeeper, and the score was 1-1 after 18 minutes. 'England were beginning to look a wee bit down,' said Wolstenholme. 'Now, they're all looking ten feet tall.'

The equaliser is the least famous goal Hurst scored that day, but he considers it his best. He has answered the same questions countless times, and I quote just one example in which he emphasises the importance of his collaboration with his club-mate Moore for his first goal:

'At West Ham … we always felt that from throw-ins, corners, and free kicks, if something was on, use your brain and take it … We understood that you leave the space in the middle of the box, that's where the ball's got to get to, and both the ball and the man arrive at the same time. And amazingly enough for great German players, who when they mark you, for 90 minutes they're inside your shirt – if you look at the picture of the goal, my German marker Höttges was probably about ten yards away from me, and that was because of that amazingly quick free kick and that understanding.'

A few minutes later, Dienst booked Peters for pulling back Overath, who was seemingly involved in every midfield incident. Shortly thereafter on England's right flank, two of the great names of world football were face to face for the first time that afternoon. Bobby Charlton received the ball back from Cohen after his own throw-in and then took it past Beckenbauer with a drop of the shoulder and a dart infield. The young German star could only hope to catch Charlton next time. Unfortunately for England, nothing came of the opening because Cohen on his weak foot shot wildly off target.

Just after the half-hour mark, Hurst had another opportunity with his head when Cohen played in a long ball of the type that Held and Emmerich had been playing towards Seeler at the other end. Tilkowski made a low save but spilled it at the feet of Ball, who was unable to make anything of the opportunity. England's normally unflappable defence was then momentarily unsettled when Cohen's indecision in possession led to a corner, taken by Held. The ball fell to Overath on the edge of the penalty area, and the midfielder met it with a left-footed shot that Banks could only parry. Emmerich's follow-up effort, dispatched under pressure from Cohen and Peters, was saved by Banks.

Five minutes before half-time, Moore showed his composure with a precise saving tackle on Emmerich, who had ridden a challenge by Jack Charlton and was advancing on England's goal. A minute later, a misjudged header in the West German defence caused the ball to drop in front of Hunt inside the penalty area but the Liverpool forward struck his shot from a narrow angle straight at Tilkowski. The half ended soon after Seeler struck a fierce shot from distance which Banks had to tip past his post, but not before Bobby Charlton had skipped over another attempted tackle from his close marker Beckenbauer, this time on the left. It had been a well-contested first half, with some robust challenges, although nothing which recalled the cynicism of the quarter-finals, and Tilkowski had been somewhat more involved in the action than his opposite number Banks.

The second half began with an incident which in the modern day would prompt clamorous appeals for a penalty, but to which Dienst simply waved play on. Nor did Bobby Charlton, apparently fouled by Schulz in the penalty area, make much of the moment or remonstrate in any way.

The splendid sunshine of the first half was now replaced with rain showers, on a Wembley afternoon that had it all, including what Glanville called 'a protracted period of stalemate' in the second half. Overath's commitment in midfield did not diminish, and he was penalised for a tussle with Hunt on England's left. This gave Moore another chance to play a quick free kick into the danger area, but Jack Charlton's far-post header went just wide. A reckless challenge from Stiles on Haller then earned the Manchester United midfielder a warning from Dienst as Haller rolled up his shorts and endeavoured to show the marks that Stiles had left on him. Another England chance that might have resulted in a penalty came when Moore made an overlapping run outside Ball and then crossed, again looking for Hurst. The knock-down fell for Bobby Charlton, but he was impeded by the ever-attendant Beckenbauer. The chance ended in a painful collision between Beckenbauer and his own goalkeeper.

With a little over ten minutes of normal time remaining, England took the lead. A West German attack had been snuffed out to great applause when Ball dispossessed Emmerich, and the subsequent England move ended with Ball also winning a corner when his shot was saved low down by Tilkowski. Ball took the corner himself, and a header from Schulz only reached Hurst on the edge of the penalty area. Hurst's shot, threaded between the oncoming Schulz and Seeler, hit the despairing Höttges and looped into the path of Peters, who made no mistake from six yards. England were leading 2-1 after 78 minutes of the World Cup Final, and Wembley now turned into what Tilkowski described as 'a total madhouse'.

Shortly after England's second goal, a tired Höttges committed his second serious foul on Ball, much to the irritation of the vociferous crowd. In response to a pass back to Banks with just under ten minutes remaining, the crowd jeered and began chanting, 'We want three!' Wolstenholme described the tension at this point as being 'unbearable'. With five minutes to play, Moore was penalised for dangerous play – a high foot – and West Germany won a corner after the resultant free kick. After Moore expertly marshalled the ball out of danger from this corner, a brilliant reverse pass from Ball released Hunt on a breakaway that was met with a thunderous roar from the goal-hungry crowd. Yet when Hunt squared to Bobby Charlton, Overath was there to put him off his stride and prevent that famously unerring shot from troubling Tilkowski. Glanville was less charitable towards the England attack concerning this chance to put the game to bed, calling it 'a three to one situation, in which simple accuracy must have brought a goal. But Hunt's pass was too shallow and square, Charlton's shot a hastily hit fiasco.'

At the very end of normal time, the outstanding Overath then took the ball past Peters and shot wide from 25 yards out. While Banks gathered the ball for his goal kick, Wolstenholme began what sounded like closing statements, invoking England's famous defeat to Hungary in 1953 and the fashioning of a new team in the intervening years. Just at that moment, Dienst awarded a free kick 'of doubtful origin' to West Germany for a foul by Jack Charlton. A minute remained as the referee performatively paced out his ten steps from the spot of the infringement. Without delay, the left-footed Emmerich hit a fierce shot into the crowd. The ball fell to Held on the left edge of the six-yard box, and he dispatched another shot into a mass of bodies, where it hit Schnellinger. Too many red shirts had been employed in the five-man wall to defend the original free kick, and now only Wilson and Banks were anywhere near the loose ball in front of goal. The Köln defender Weber took full advantage and became an unlikely goalscorer by stabbing the ball home from three yards at the far post.

'Suddenly, between hundreds of legs – I only saw legs – the ball was lying in front of me,' remembers Weber. 'I thought, "I have to put it in the net quickly, before the referee blows the final whistle.'" Glanville was among those to assert – with unreasonable certainty, given his misidentification of Schnellinger – that 'Haller, in the goalmouth, played the ball down blatantly and undeniably with his hand.' In the dying seconds, the redoubtable England defence had lost its composure for a mere instant, and the World Cup Final was now heading for an additional half an hour. 'Only the two sets of actors down on that green stage could have truly felt the bitter disappointment or the elation of that moment,' mused Green.

Early in the first period of extra time, Ball drew a fine save from Tilkowski with a shot from distance. After another collision between Hurst and the West German goalkeeper, a rare opportunity presented itself for Bobby Charlton to strike at goal. The shot hit Tilkowski's left upright and then hit him in the face. 'The goalkeeper's taken another one in the mouth,' said Wolstenholme. As England began to settle after a fast start to extra time, Held ran fully 60 yards on the left flank and eluded Ball and Jack Charlton before crossing from the bye-line, but there was no one there to meet it.

The summer sunshine now lit up Wembley's sodden turf again after the second-half spells of rain. Stiles released the irrepressible Ball down the right flank with a weighted pass, and the flame-haired midfielder hit a first-time cross into the penalty area. The ball was behind Hurst as it came to him near the penalty spot but he knocked it down with his right foot, shielding it from Schulz while at the same time gaining space. He took a few more steps and, while on the turn but also falling backwards, hit the ball directly above Tilkowski from about eight yards out. It struck the crossbar, ricocheted directly downwards, and bounced back out before the onrushing Weber headed it clear over the bar. Seemingly everywhere, confusion now reigned.

Many volumes have been written and interviews conducted in efforts to disentangle what occurred in these few moments, but the discernible facts are merely that the referee Dienst consulted with his linesman, Tofiq Bahramov, and then awarded a goal to England based on what he was told. There is also ample footage which proves that the ball bounced down on to the goal line, and thus that it did not cross the whole of the line in its entirety as necessitated by the laws of the game for a goal to be given. This was conclusively proved in a study by Oxford University researchers Ian Reid and Andrew Zisserman in 1995. It ought to be an uncontroversial historical imperative to state that the ball did not cross the line, but, of course, this does not change the facts of either the decision in isolation or the result of the 1966 World Cup Final. What remains unclear is whether Wolstenholme was aware of the delicious irony of his remark a few minutes later, when Tilkowski threw the ball out to Haller after a wayward pass from Bobby Charlton appeared to have gone out of play, 'That seemed to have been over the line for a goal kick. Still, nobody worried about such niceties.'

In the second period of extra time, the two tiring prizefighters barely exchanged blows, struggling just to remain standing as they went the distance. Weber's 90th-minute equaliser surely played a big part in the psychology of both teams, with England so close to glory again and the Germans clinging to a belief that they could yet force a replay on the following Tuesday. Wolstenholme now announced the passing of every minute as West Germany wearily probed for openings wherever possible. A chance came with one minute remaining, when Schulz put another hopeful ball into the penalty area and Haller beat Jack Charlton to the header, but the knockdown just eluded Seeler as it flashed across the six-yard box.

Another cross from Schulz was then cleared by Cohen for a corner in the last seconds of this extraordinary final. Haller's corner was punched well clear by Banks but one more ball was played into England's penalty area as Dienst studied his watch. Moore calmly swept up in defence, looked up into the far distance as Dienst motioned him to keep playing, and almost nonchalantly directed a long pass to Hurst. At the far end of the pitch, fans were running on to the field of play, convinced that Dienst had blown the final whistle after that last West German attack. Unperturbed, Hurst advanced on goal with only the seemingly tireless Overath in pursuit. Driving into the penalty area, Hurst unleashed a left-footed shot that flew into the top corner of Tilkowski's net and sealed a glorious win for England. Hurst, who remains the only player to score a hat-trick in a World Cup Final, did not know at first if this goal had counted, and he also maintains that he was merely trying to waste time by hitting the ball as hard as he could into the Wembley crowd. Wolstenholme's famous commentary encapsulated the surreal and exhilarating finish, 'Some people are on the pitch – they think it's all over; it is now!'

* * *

Alf Ramsey's three years of hard-headed scheming were vindicated by England's win. In *The Times* of 1 August, Green's match report is headed by the words 'Ramsey Proved Right in World Cup', and in a separate article Green candidly forswore his criticism of Ramsey's three-year-old promise that England would win the tournament, 'Certainly there were some of us who felt he was living under a sword of Damocles of his own making. But he has triumphed and I, for one, salute him, having doubted him. The sword has been swept away and replaced by a laurel wreath.' David Miller in the *Sunday Telegraph* credited the victory to 'the most patient, logical, painstaking, almost scientific, assault on the trophy there has ever been – and primarily the work and imagination of one man'.

If there remained a caveat within these writers' now fulsome praise for Ramsey, it came in descriptions of the team's style as 'methodical rather than brilliant', and variations of the view that while this was 'not the best England team there has been', it was 'incomparably the best organised'. Perhaps Ramsey's last acts in his preparation and management of the final were his most important of all. Bobby Charlton recalled how, on the eve of the game, Ramsey explained the role he wanted him to assume:

'I want you to stick on Beckenbauer for every minute, every second of the match. This boy is the only German player who can beat us … I want you to stay with him throughout the whole game, don't go anywhere else. He is your responsibility … If you do your job he will not do any damage and I'm sure we will win the World Cup.'

As it happened, Schön gave a similar assignment to Beckenbauer regarding Charlton as both managers looked to nullify their opposition's outstanding player, and from the German perspective, 'Charlton was more often forced to follow Beckenbauer than the other way around!' The principal objective of preventing goals from two star players who had scored seven between them during the tournament was achieved by both managers. In terms of Ramsey's management on the day, there is a consensus among the players that his words to them at the beginning of extra time, just after they had suffered the sucker punch of Weber's equaliser, made a telling difference. As Green noted, 'Psychologically Germany should have had the edge in that extra time,' but Ramsey told his players to stand tall and not allow the opposition to see signs of exhaustion. Quotations of what he told the players range from the succinct 'You let it slip. Now start again!' to the more rousing 'We've won the World Cup once, now go out and do it again.' The underlying sentiment is common to all accounts, however, as exemplified by Bobby Charlton:

'Bobby Moore was not a man easily impressed by words intended to be inspirational but he would always insist that this was among Alf's finest moments. He touched all the players. He reminded us of all that had been achieved, how far we had come and, most of all, how it would be absolutely intolerable if the prize was allowed to slip away.'

On the West German side, there was ample praise for the effort, commitment and sportsmanship of the *Nationalmannschaft* in a match that was much admired by all. Indeed, in reference to England's controversial third goal, the headline in *Kicker* magazine of 1 August exclaimed, 'This game did not deserve that – the ugly stain on a great final.' Editor Robert Becker concluded, 'Germany has every reason to congratulate our team. Nobody should be ashamed of this defeat, which came about in such unfortunate and mysterious circumstances. That should not prevent us from also giving our opponents the respect they have earned.' Writing in the present tense to convey his feelings at the time, the goalkeeper Tilkowski recalled the pride and magnanimity that accompanied the West German team's obvious sadness at the final whistle, 'We are disappointed. Not because we have lost, but because of the way in which the result has come about. We can be proud of our performance. And we congratulate the winners. We don't begrudge the English this triumph. The motherland of football has had to wait long enough for this.'

Uwe Seeler, meanwhile, has reiterated time and again his appreciation of the reception he and his team were given by the

English public after the match. Ahead of the 50th anniversary in 2016, he recalled how Schön in the dressing room told his players that it was better to be a good loser than a bad winner, and that they had done Germany proud. Seeler continued:

'As soon as we left the stadium we realised that it wasn't just our manager who thought this way. Everywhere we went, we were cheered. I had never experienced anything like that abroad before. After the FIFA banquet, about nine or ten of us went into central London for a few beers. In one huge disco, our joker of the pack [Werder Bremen midfielder] Max Lorenz went up on stage to conduct the band. I just thought, "Oh God, this isn't going to go well, he's about to get a smack in the mouth." … The English understood everything, joined in, and jumped up. Standing ovations for us – sensational!'

Seeler, West Germany's captain and leader that day, was too young to have been involved in the 1954 World Cup under Sepp Herberger, and he finished his international career before Schön's successes in the early 1970s. Along with Michael Ballack at the start of this century, he is perhaps the greatest German player never to win an international title. It was not easy for him at the time to process what he called 'this extremely unlucky, indeed unfair defeat at Wembley'. Yet after all that time had passed, he was able to reflect on more positive developments, 'Today, after 50 years, I can say that I, and happily all my team-mates too, have long made our peace with this game. Its special circumstances haven't pulled us and our opponents from that day apart. On the contrary: rivals have become true friends.' Remembering Wolfgang Weber's pained words to him in the dressing room after the match – 'Uwe, these tears will never dry!' – Seeler concluded, 'The tears dried up after all, the aching wounds healed well. I can laugh about a lot of things nowadays, and I think that's the way it should be in sport.'

Das Wembley-Tor

Even though the *Nationalmannschaft* has gone on to make many happier memories at Wembley as we shall see, the controversial third goal of the 1966 World Cup Final will always be known in Germany as *das Wembley-Tor*, or the Wembley goal. As indicated by Seeler's sentiments, time – and success – have proved great healers, and many Germans today will discuss the subject with a wry smile and a variation of the remark, 'When you've won four World Cups, you can afford to let one go.' It is nonetheless important to note the intense feelings of anger and injustice that the decision generated in the moment. I asked leading *Kicker* journalist Manfred Münchrath to explain how Germans felt at the time, and in response he used the adjective *stinksauer*, for which any translation is surely redundant. 'I think the people were simply very disappointed and upset by the decision,' he continued.

'Of course we have much better technical capabilities these days; back then there weren't many pictures of the situation, and it simply wasn't clear, with the available images, what had happened. But it did *seem* to most Germans that the ball was not in, and that was something where people said, "That's not OK, something's been taken from us here" – but not so much by the English; rather by the referee and the linesman, they were the ones who made the wrong decision. It was obvious that the players would think that it had crossed the line, but it wasn't an Englishman who took the decision, it was a Swiss and a Russian who decided it was a goal. It was definitely something where you said, "We need to get revenge somehow."'

I asked Münchrath if he thought that *das Wembley-Tor* led directly to the West German team's subsequent successes in the 1970s. He replied:

'No. It's a coincidence. It was a brilliant generation of players – most people to this day say that a German team has never played better than in 1972 – because they were very atypical, elegant German players; Germans had long been known for physical attributes as opposed to skill, but there we had people like Beckenbauer, Overath, Netzer, people who really knew what to do with the ball, and that was an unbelievable coincidence, a happy coincidence.'

The first half of Robert Becker's *Kicker* match report, which appeared two days after the final, focussed almost exclusively on refereeing; not just the actions of Dienst and Bahramov, but also FIFA's decision to allow the German referee Kreitlein to officiate England's quarter-final against Argentina, given what had transpired between West Germany and Argentina in the group phase. On Bahramov's appointment for the final, Becker then wrote:

'It had to be a Russian! After we had just eliminated the USSR in the semi-final, in which they lost a player to a sending off. I do not know what Bahramov was thinking of, when in the 12th minute of extra time he explained to Dienst that he had seen a "goal". He could not have seen it. Nobody apart from him saw it. He had not even signalled for it.' As is now well known, Bahramov was born in Azerbaijan and held Soviet citizenship at this time. The former Azeri national football stadium in Baku is named in his honour, Tofiq Bahramov Republican Stadium.

Among the most popular exhibits at the German National Football Museum today is the *Wembley-Tor* 'crime scene investigation', which meticulously catalogues the location, the incident, the witnesses, the available evidence, and the subsequent analysis and evaluation of the most infamous goal in the history of German football. The key witnesses are of course those closest to the action, the scorer and the goalkeeper. Geoff Hurst has always maintained that given the circumstances, he wanted more than anything to believe that the ball had crossed the line, but in his 2002 autobiography entitled *1966 and All That*, he wrote, 'Having listened to all the arguments over the decades and watched the replay hundreds of times on TV, I have to admit that it looks as though the ball didn't cross the line.' Tilkowski described his experience, 'I can still change the trajectory of Hurst's shot slightly, and I turn my head in the direction of my goal as I fall. Press photographs prove this. Over my shoulder I can see the ball coming off the crossbar and clearly not landing over the line.' Several other significant *Wembley-Tor* quotations are collated below:

> Wolfgang Weber: 'It wasn't a goal. I should know, after all.'

> Roger Hunt: 'Normally in that situation I would have gone in and, looking back, I still don't know why I didn't. I don't think, in fact, I'd have got to the ball. It bounced down and high up to my left and Weber

headed it away. I have thought many times since, "Why didn't I go in?"'

Gottfried Dienst: 'I was uncertain, there's no reason not to admit that. I looked at my Russian colleague Bahramov, who was holding his flag at eye level. I didn't know exactly what he meant by that, so I went to him and asked him if the ball had crossed the line, to which he said yes and demonstratively walked towards the halfway line.'

Tofiq Bahramov, 'I did not see that the ball had crossed the line. But I saw how the Englishman Hunt threw up his arms after the shot from Hurst. I also saw the German goalkeeper looking disconsolate. So it must have been a goal.'

Bobby Charlton: 'Down the years and after close inspection of film evidence, I have come to accept [the goal] was maybe not legitimate. I was convinced it was over the line and whether or not I willed it to be so was a question that only gathered strength down the years.'

Franz Beckenbauer: 'At the time of England's third goal I was in the penalty area with quite a good view. I was convinced the ball touched the goal line – but was not completely over – when Geoff Hurst's shot bounced down from the crossbar and therefore it was not a goal. What language did the Swiss referee and the Azerbaijani linesman use when they discussed the incident? Who said what? We'll never know.'

7

The Nimbus of Invincibility
1968–1970

The year 1968 was one of protest, revolution and change on a global scale. At the end of January, the Tet Offensive launched by Vietcong and North Vietnamese Army troops brought conflict to Vietnam's city streets. It was a major escalation which indicated to the American public for the first time that the war would be unwinnable, and anti-war demonstrations and riots were widespread by the summer. The assassination of Martin Luther King Jr. on 4 April also triggered violent protests across the United States, the final impetus for the passing of the Civil Rights Act of 1968 on 11 April.

The protest movement in Europe was dominated by students fighting for civil liberties, most notably in France, where the economy ground to a halt during May and June. Civil rights marches also began in Northern Ireland, where students and activists protested against the brutality of the Royal Ulster Constabulary.

In West Germany, meanwhile, the protests of 1968 were of an idiosyncratic nature linked to the country's problematic past. As discussed in chapter four, the postwar process of denazification overseen by the Allies was more or less abandoned amid emerging Cold War tensions and, by the late 1950s, former Nazis occupied positions of power and influence in the new republic. Events such as the publication of the diary of Anne Frank in 1955 and the trial of Adolf Eichmann in Jerusalem in 1961 brought the horrors of the Third Reich back into the forefront of the national consciousness, and to the attention of a new generation of Germans, born during or just after the Second World War.

The formation, after the 1965 federal election, of a grand coalition government under Chancellor Kurt Georg Kiesinger gave rise to the West German student movement, which expressed unease at the lack of opposition in parliament. The movement, which peaked in 1968 after the attempted assassination of a leading student activist, focussed on the young republic's relationship with its past, targeting officials with links to national socialism. As historian Harold Marcuse explains, the Adenauer government in its last years had become 'increasingly sensitive to charges of continuity with the past', and now Kiesinger's former affiliations with the Nazi party prompted outrage. At the Christian Democratic Union (CDU) party convention in November, the journalist and campaigner Beate Klarsfeld slapped Kiesinger in the face and called him a 'Nazi'. Overall, 1968 'marked a watershed in the broader public awareness of Nazi criminality' and heralded generational change in West German society.

In the story of the England v Germany football rivalry, it was likewise a pivotal year. After a first win over the English in June 1968, West German football would ascend to the summit of both the international and the club game, while England slid from the position of world champions into the international wilderness. Alf Ramsey had responded to questions about his future after the 1966 World Cup Final in characteristically pragmatic fashion, 'Everyone seems concerned about what I'm going to do. But there is another World Cup in Mexico in four years. It's good to have won at home; it would be good to win there.' There was, of course, every reason to be optimistic. England were world champions at last, and four years hence the senior men Bobby Charlton and Gordon Banks would still be 32; the likes of Bobby Moore, Geoff Hurst, Nobby Stiles, Martin Peters, and Alan Ball all in their mid-to-late 20s. Even Jimmy Greaves, born in 1940, could be a major asset if he found his way back into form in an England shirt.

A dismal record in the Americas, discussed in chapters four and five, would have to be reversed, however, if England were to become the first European nation to prevail in a World Cup outside its home continent. To this end, England would travel again to Mexico City, Montevideo and Rio de Janeiro for a preparatory tour in the summer of 1969.

The first task after the heady days of July 1966, however, was the bread and butter of the annual Home Championship, the next two editions of which would also constitute a qualification group for the 1968 UEFA European Championship in Italy. On 15 April 1967, England welcomed Scotland to Wembley. Ramsey's team were defending an impeccable record of 19 international matches without defeat, but this was to be one of Scottish football's finest hours. Scotland's 'Wembley Wizards' featured four players from the Celtic side which six weeks later became the first British team to win the European Cup, against Internazionale in Lisbon. For the home side, the only change from the XI that had played in the World Cup Final was the return of Greaves in place of Hunt in attack.

The 3-2 win over England prompted Scotland fans to name their team unofficial world champions, and it remains a part of Scottish football lore to this day. From an English perspective, the injuries during the course of the match to Jack Charlton, Ray Wilson and Greaves were cited in mitigation. Nonetheless, the result was greeted with maudlin sentiment in the press, 'It is a long, long time from the mid-summer glory of July to April's first intimations of another spring,' wrote Donald Saunders in the *Daily Telegraph*, 'time enough, indeed, for a great football team to wither away and die as, inevitably, all champions must.' The article's headline called for Ramsey to 'begin rebuilding now'.

By the time of the next meeting between the auld enemies on 24 February 1968, there were four new faces in the England team: Blackburn Rovers full-back Keith Newton, Tottenham Hotspur midfielder Alan Mullery, and Everton centre-half Brian Labone had all made a handful of appearances, while Manchester City forward Mike Summerbee made his international debut in this match. Of the world champions, only George Cohen had played his last match for England by this time, but several others were unavailable to Ramsey. The 1-1 draw, reportedly played in front of a crowd in excess of 130,000 at Hampden Park, determined England as the winners of the 1967/68 Home Championship but also as qualifiers for the quarter-final stage of the upcoming

European Championship, to be played over two legs in April and May 1968.

West Germany were already out of the running by this point, after failing to progress from a three-team group with Albania and Yugoslavia. The final match of the group, a scoreless draw in Albania, is referred to as *die Schmach von Tirana*. This phrase denotes the ignominy of the only failure to qualify for a major tournament in the history of the German and West German national team. Manager Helmut Schön was the focus of severe criticism after the setback, which was dubbed 'a black day for German football' in the press. England, meanwhile, faced Spain at Wembley on 3 April 1968, looking to progress to the final four of the European Championship for the first time. Coincidentally, the two-legged tie was played out around the same time as Manchester United's European Cup semi-final against Real Madrid. Bobby Charlton played in all four of these crucial games, as did three of the Real Madrid stars.

Charlton gave England a 1-0 first-leg lead with his late goal at Wembley, and then on 8 May a 2-1 win at the Santiago Bernabéu Stadium followed. Ramsey lost Hurst to a toe infection ahead of the game and was forced to bring Norman Hunter into the attack, and it was the Leeds United player who scored the winning goal with just a few minutes remaining, one of only two international goals in his career. 'Tonight England played one of their finest matches,' wrote Albert Barham in *The Guardian*. 'They knew they had to contain a Spanish side which included six Real Madrid players, all the forwards famed throughout the land for their ability, skill, and speed.' A week later, Manchester United booked their passage to the European Cup Final with a thrilling 3-3 draw in the same stadium.

1 June 1968
West Germany 1-0 England
Niedersachsenstadion, Hanover

Three days before West Germany welcomed England to Hanover for a friendly international that, for Ramsey, served as preparation for the European Championship in Italy, Manchester United beat Eusébio's Benfica to become the first English winners of the European Cup. This was the second time the showpiece final had been hosted at Wembley, and it was also another famous night on the hallowed turf for World Cup winner Bobby Charlton, who scored twice in United's extra-time win. In the Cup Winners' Cup, meanwhile, FC Bayern München and Hamburger SV both reached the semi-finals, and Hamburg progressed to the Rotterdam final against Bayern's conquerors, AC Milan. Uwe Seeler's side were beaten 2-0 by the great Milan team which featured Gianni Rivera, Kurt Hamrin, Giovanni Trapattoni, and, notably, Karl-Heinz Schnellinger.

The contexts of European club competition finals and the upcoming championship in Italy form the background for an underwhelming match in Hanover which nonetheless represents a landmark in the development of the England v Germany football rivalry. Ramsey fielded Banks, Moore, Ball and Hurst, but had to do without Peters and Bobby Charlton. A young Colin Bell joined his club-mate Summerbee in attack, and Tottenham Hotspur left-back Cyril Knowles made his last of only four England appearances. Schön, meanwhile, called on three World Cup finalists in Franz Beckenbauer, Wolfgang Weber and Wolfgang Overath. Apart from these three players, only Weber's and Overath's fellow Köln player Hannes Löhr had more than ten caps, with 11.

The match was a hard-fought physical battle, in particular because of the presence of Hunter, who at the age of 24 was already earning a reputation as one of English football's fiercest competitors. In March 1968, Hunter had played in Leeds' stormy League Cup Final against Arsenal, winning the first of six major honours under manager Don Revie. By some accounts, it was at that match that a Leeds supporter's banner with the words 'Norman Bites Yer Legs' first appeared, giving rise to Hunter's famous nickname. In Hanover, members of the English press were forced to concede that some of the so-called excesses were 'wholly reprehensible', and that Hunter was 'of value only as a hatchet man'. Hugh McIlvanney in *The Observer* called England's more extreme tackles merely 'regrettable', noting, 'The opposition's tendency to dramatise their injuries exaggerated the roughness.' On the German side, Robert Becker simply stated, 'Hunter, who gave Weber and Overath a brutal kicking, should have been off the pitch.'

Indeed, on few occasions in the history of this rivalry have press reactions to a match varied so greatly. As a highly anticipated spectacle to follow the drama of the World Cup Final two years earlier, it was undeniably a disappointment to the crowd of around 80,000 which again included many British servicemen. Yet the result appears to have made all the difference to subsequent analysis. The match was won eight minutes from time when Beckenbauer's left-footed shot deflected off Labone to beat Banks, and while English football writers were all too keen to dismiss the significance of the defeat, the German press hailed a first win over the old football masters and current world champions. The report with perhaps the most bitterness coursing through its lines the following day is that of Brian Glanville in the *Sunday Times*:

'You could, if you wished, try to breathe life into [this match] in terms of spurious significance; a revenge for 1966 (but the team England picked surely obviated this except for the most fervent German extremist), the latest of a series of games in which England had remained unbeaten for 67 years. There was even a huge, noisy crowd to encourage such delusions; though more symbolically apt were the two huge floodlight pylons, looking with their myriad blind lights, like giant futuristic flowers, craning over the proceedings with apparent incredulity.'

McIlvanney, meanwhile, remarked, 'Comparing this miserable hour and a half ... with the last great meeting between the countries is entirely fatuous,' and David Miller in the *Sunday Telegraph* churlishly suggested that this repeat of the World Cup Final 'would, like comebacks by boxers and actresses, have been better not attempted'. No doubt aware of such reaction from his English counterparts, *Kicker* editor Becker pointedly reminded his readership of England's win against Sepp Herberger's world champions at Wembley in 1954:

'It is not our concern to look for excuses for England, any more than the English did for us when in 1954 at Wembley they beat a Germany side that were world champions, but which had travelled to London with the bare bones of the team that had claimed the title in Bern half a year earlier.'

Becker cited the heat in Hanover and the long, hard season that both sets of players had behind them as mitigating factors for the poor quality of the match. Above all, he praised the commitment of the West German defenders in securing the famous result, noting the 'tenacity' of Berti Vogts, the tackling of Ludwig Müller, the 'clever, attentive positional play' of Klaus Fichtel, and the 'iron grip' with which Weber kept Hurst at bay.

Schön was accompanied on the bench in Hanover by a smartly suited Uwe Seeler, who had announced his international retirement just the previous day. The manager would ultimately convince him to return, however, and Seeler thus played at the 1970 World Cup at the age of 33. Schön's words also played an important part in the *Nationalmannschaft* finally ending that long wait for a win against the football pioneers, 'You always think you don't have a say against England. Go out on that pitch with your heads held high! Look them in the eye with confidence! You've got to think: we're somebody too!' The victory represented the end of a variously defined historical period: 38 years since the first official match recognised by both associations; 60 years since the first match against England recognised by the DFB; 67 years since a German team's first visit to England; even 69 years since that first FA tour of Germany in 1899 – viewed whichever way, there could be no ambiguity and 1 June 1968 marked the first win by a German national team over its English counterpart.

In Becker's words, it was a result which cost the visitors 'the nimbus of invincibility'. Besides this, England also lost an unbeaten record on the European continent that stretched back to that 5-2 reverse in Paris at the very start of Ramsey's tenure, over five years before. Nonetheless, manager and press alike remained in confident mood because of the prospect of redemption and renewed success that awaited in Italy. 'He is well aware that he can make a more than adequate riposte by winning the European Nations Cup next week,' wrote McIlvanney of Ramsey. Geoffrey Green also tempted fate the following day, when he remarked that defeat was 'better on this occasion at Hanover yesterday with nothing at stake beyond a reputation, than this coming Wednesday, when England meet tough and technical Yugoslavia'.

In the event, England lost both matches. To make matters worse, Alan Mullery became the first England player in history to be sent off, after he lashed out in retaliation at the end of a fractious 1-0 win for Yugoslavia. England won the competition's third-place play-off against the Soviet Union in Rome, with goals from Bobby Charlton and Hurst, but the trip to Italy had been a failure. The hosts won the third edition of the continental championship, Italy's first postwar title, after a replay against Yugoslavia.

* * *

One matter on which English and German football writers could find agreement in Hanover, besides the poor entertainment value of the contest, was the ability of Beckenbauer, still aged 22 at the time. Glanville called him 'by far the most attractive and creative player on the field', and Green described him as a 'talented midfield manipulator'. Becker relayed the opinion of former manager Herberger, who was at the game, that Beckenbauer ought to be employed alongside a midfield partner (he used the word *Wand*, meaning 'wall') who could play slightly further forward and exchange passes with him. Herberger nominated Overath, who captained the side in Hanover, as the ideal player for this task.

These emerging ideas of building a team around Beckenbauer point to a crucial development in club football at the end of the 1960s that must be considered in any discussion of the West German national team's success in subsequent years, namely the rise of FC Bayern München. From a 21st-century perspective, it is important to note that, at the end of the 1967/68 season, the club possessed a relatively modest trophy cabinet with one national title (1932) and three German Cups (1956/57, 1965/66, 1966/67). Added to these domestic successes, Bayern won the 1966/67 UEFA Cup Winners' Cup under the Yugoslav manager Zlatko 'Tschik' Čajkovski, who had played against Herberger's West Germany at the 1954 World Cup. The club won its first continental title, in extra time against Rangers in Nuremberg, with a young team that included Sepp Maier in goal (then aged 23), winning goalscorer Franz Roth (21), Gerd Müller (21) and Beckenbauer (21).

The 1968/69 season brought a first Bundesliga title, and indeed a league and cup double, under new manager Branko

Zebec, another former Yugoslav international with a history of World Cup appearances against West Germany. It was under Zebec that Beckenbauer moved back into the *libero*, or sweeper, role which he would mould in his own image in the ensuing years. Müller finished as top scorer in the Bundesliga for the first time that season with 30 goals, and he also scored both of Bayern's goals in the 2-1 win over Schalke 04 in the DFB-Pokal Final. The stocky striker from the small Bavarian town of Nördlingen had made his international debut shortly after the World Cup in England, but he played regularly for West Germany from the 1968/69 season onwards. The famous 'golden axis' of Maier, Beckenbauer and Müller was by now firmly established at FC Bayern, and as Maier gradually displaced Eintracht Braunschweig's Horst Wolter it also became a fixture of Schön's *Nationalmannschaft*.

The historic victory over England in Hanover was followed two weeks later in Stuttgart by a first win – at the third time of asking – against Brazil. Schön made just two changes from the England game, recalling the Dortmund players Sigfried Held and Willi Neuberger, who had been on a post-season tour with their club. Held scored the early opening goal, and Hamburger SV forward Gert Dörfel added a second before the double world champions hit back immediately with a goal from the great Tostão. Six months later, in December 1968, West Germany undertook a mid-season tour of the Americas, with games in Rio de Janeiro, Santiago and Mexico City. Schön's team put in another impressive performance against the illustrious Brazilians, drawing 2-2 in the Maracanã. 'Even optimists would not have predicted such a brilliant start from the German national team to its tour of Latin America,' proclaimed *Kicker* in delight.

In both matches against Brazil, Schön employed Beckenbauer as a *libero* behind the defensive line, and in Rio de Janeiro he gave him a specific assignment – Pelé. According to German journalist Walter Setzepfandt, Beckenbauer throughout the match was instinctively in the right place at the right time to anticipate Pelé's play. Moreover, 'a murmur passed through the crowd' when Beckenbauer later gave up the sweeper role to join the attack. Setzepfandt impressed on his readers that the second half, in which West Germany came back from 2-0 down to equalise through goals from Held and the Braunschweig forward Klaus Gerwien, would not be forgotten by the few Germans who were present, and neither by the Brazilians. 'A great day for German football,' he concluded.

The important matter of World Cup qualification was yet to be settled, however, with three games to come in 1969, all at home. Wins over Austria and Cyprus in May meant that the match against Scotland in Hamburg in October would be decisive. Back in Hanover 15 months earlier, *The Times* football correspondent Geoffrey Green had taken a swipe at Scotland manager Bobby Brown, who was reportedly 'cock-a-hoop with protestations of coming victory' against West Germany in World Cup qualification having seen them labour against England, 'It is worth Mr Brown considering that the Germans are great competitors at top level and that the side he saw yesterday will, in due course, be reinforced by talented experienced men ... But that is his business.'

Having earned a 1-1 draw at Hampden Park in April 1969, the *Nationalmannschaft* now achieved a historic first win over Scotland at Hamburg's Volksparkstadion. Schön's line-up anticipated his team at the World Cup in Mexico to a large extent, with Seeler now back in the team alongside Müller, and the Schalke 04 winger Reinhard Libuda on the right flank. His club-mate Fichtel played alongside Overath and Haller in a midfield three, and with Libuda and Fichtel both on the scoresheet in a hard-fought 3-2 win, there was cause to exclaim, 'Schalke fired us to Mexico!'

As holders of the Jules Rimet Trophy, England meanwhile extended their period of exemption from World Cup qualification to eight years, and again the Home Championship was the immediate priority for Ramsey, as well as the tour of Latin America at the end of the 1968/69 season. The 0-0 draw at the Azteca Stadium in Mexico City on 1 June proved a worthwhile reconnaissance exercise, as it demonstrated the effects of playing at altitude and in searing heat. After so many lessons appeared to go unheeded in the era of Walter Winterbottom, physical preparation was now finally a priority for England when it came to a World Cup challenge on the other side of the Atlantic. For the tournament in Mexico 12 months hence, there was simply no other way. Green explained how during the second half of this game, which kicked off at noon, 'The altitude beat the air out of English lungs and destroyed their rhythm. We saw this over the last half hour when England were virtually on their knees.'

Donald Saunders used the example of England's most energetic World Cup winner to convey the effect of the conditions to his readers, 'When I report that Alan Ball, who might be among the fittest and most enthusiastic footballers in the world, once failed to chase a pass that was only a yard ahead of him, I need scarcely add that England were a very, very tired team during the closing stages.'

The Mexican conditions also prompted Green to consider Bobby Charlton's role in the team:

'I wonder if too much is to be asked of Bobby Charlton here next summer as the attacking hub of the England wheel at the age of 31 [by then 32] in this heat and at this altitude. He could be burnt out by the effort. Better, perhaps, to transfer this midfield weight to the younger shoulders of someone like [Colin] Bell ... thus leaving Charlton up front as one of the striking bombardiers. It is his explosive shooting that England will need.'

Before moving on to South America, England played another tour match against a Mexican XI to give the rest of the travelling party an experience of the conditions, although Moore, Ball and Peters notably played in both fixtures, just 48 hours apart. This game, at the Estadio Jalisco in Guadalajara, is also notable for the appearance in goal of a young Peter Shilton, who would play in a World Cup semi-final against West Germany all of 21 years later. Less auspicious were Ramsey's derogatory comments about the Mexican public, reported in the local press. His complaints about being kept awake at night and jeered in the stadium compounded the insult of his 'animals' slur on Latin American players in 1966. The wounds would fester for another year until England returned for the World Cup.

After a 2-1 win over Uruguay in Montevideo, England's tour finished in front of an enormous and excitable crowd at the Maracanã in Rio de Janeiro on 12 June. Leading 1-0 after an early goal by Bell from a Peters cross and a first-half penalty save from Banks, England were just over ten minutes away from becoming the first European nation ever to win in Brazil. Two quick-fire goals from Tostão and Jairzinho ended this dream, and even on the dark, grainy footage which survives, the explosion of noise and emotion that greets the home side's comeback is clearly evident. Despite ending in defeat, the tour was still judged a success. Saunders wrote in the *Daily Telegraph*, 'I, like most who have watched [England] closely in Latin America, am satisfied they are an even better side now than in 1966 and must have a chance of clinging to the title.'

1970 FIFA World Cup
Mexico

A year on from the exploratory tour, England finalised preparations for the 1970 World Cup in Mexico in extraordinary circumstances. Four matches, including two full internationals, were scheduled in Bogotá and Quito at the end of May, after the squad had already spent two weeks in Mexico City acclimatising to the difficult conditions. Ramsey was keen for his players to face a competitive challenge in the run-up to the tournament, and the venues for these games lay at even higher altitudes than Guadalajara, where England would play their three World Cup group matches. England beat Colombia 4-0 on 20 May with goals from Bobby Charlton, Ball, and a brace from Peters, now of Tottenham Hotspur. A 2-0 win over Ecuador, with goals from Franny Lee and substitute Brian Kidd, followed four days later.

The intrigue developed far from the pitch, however. England flew back from Quito to Mexico City via a stopover in Bogotá, where they checked in to the Hotel Tequendema, which they had used for their stay in the city a few days earlier. While the squad watched a film to pass the time, two plain-clothed policemen quietly arrested England captain Bobby Moore, who was alleged to have stolen a bracelet from the hotel's gift shop on the day of England's first arrival in Colombia a week earlier. On that occasion, the commotion caused by the accusation had been resolved by Ramsey and the FA, and details of the embarrassing scene were kept out of the press by mutual agreement. Ignoring the misgivings of accompanying journalists, however, England made the mistake of returning to the scene of the alleged crime. A second witness had come forward in the intervening days and identified Moore, who was now placed under house arrest at the home of Alfonso Senior, the president of the Colombian FA and founder of the Bogotá club Millonarios. Moore could continue training here and was spared time in a prison cell, but his fate remained uncertain.

Ramsey and his squad flew on to Mexico without Moore, and news of his arrest was only revealed to players and journalists on the flight. To make matters worse, the plane was forced to land in Panama because of a storm, and the West Bromwich Albion striker and nervous flyer Jeff Astle began drinking to calm his nerves. On arrival in Mexico City, it was impossible to hide Astle's drunkenness, and the local sports paper *Esto* combined the scene with the sensation of Moore's arrest to call England a team of 'drunks and thieves' ('*borrachos y ladrones*'). With a UK general election just three weeks away, the *Daily Telegraph* reported on its front page of 27 May that Prime Minister Harold Wilson had intervened in the matter, and that this in turn prompted a Conservative MP to opine, 'It sounds like another election gimmick to enable Mr Wilson to get into the news.'

Moore was released the following day and duly flew to Mexico to join up with the rest of the players. A relieved Ramsey looked to draw a line under the whole affair and told the gathered press that his squad had the qualities to retain the World Cup in Mexico. David Miller in the *Sunday Telegraph* at the end of this strangest of weeks praised Moore's 'equanimity' throughout the saga and added that Ramsey possessed the same quality. Miller quoted a German correspondent who told him, 'Give us your manager, and we can win the World Cup.'

West Germany arrived in Mexico somewhat later than England, opting to play warm-up matches against Ireland and Yugoslavia at home in mid-May, before departing from Frankfurt on 19 May. *Kicker* magazine's new editor-in-chief Karl-Heinz Heimann flew with the squad and reported a few days later from the team base, the Balneario Comanjilla hotel outside León in central Mexico. At the ping-pong table he mostly found Gerd Müller, top scorer in the Bundesliga that season with 38 goals in 33 games. *Der Bomber* was ready to take the World Cup by storm. Fearing injuries and prioritising acclimatisation, Schön rejected invitations for warm-up matches from local club sides, and Heimann at this point saw the front line of Seeler, Müller and Köln forward Hannes Löhr as more or less fixed; likewise, the midfield trio of Beckenbauer, Overath and Haller. A question remained in defence, where the Italy-based Schnellinger had excelled in the *libero* role in the final warm-up match against Yugoslavia. As such, Schnellinger, Schulz and Weber were still competing for two positions alongside the full-backs Höttges and Vogts.

West Germany's group stage in Mexico belonged to Müller, as the FC Bayern striker scored the winning goal in the first game against Morocco, two goals against Bulgaria, and then a first-half hat-trick against Peru. His economy of movement and deadly accuracy inside the penalty area made him the ideal player for the conditions. By the end of the three matches in the small venue of León, many local people had taken Müller, and the West Germany team as a whole, to their hearts.

England's group, meanwhile, had been all about just one match since the draw was made in January. The meeting between Brazil and England in Guadalajara on 7 June pitted the winners of the previous three World Cups against each other in perhaps the most famous group-stage match in the competition's history. This was the game of Pelé's downward header and Banks's stunning save, of Moore's tackle on Jairzinho, of Jairzinho's emphatic finish and leaping celebration, and of Moore and Pelé swapping shirts and sharing an embrace of sheer sportsmanship and mutual respect. Many people, not least the Brazilian players themselves, considered this match to be a mere preview of a probable World Cup Final in Mexico. Indeed, Green thought a repeat was 'the climax most people in their secret hearts desire'.

The defensively minded Mullery had been given the daunting responsibility of marshalling Pelé in Rio de Janeiro a year earlier, and he had some success, but Brazil's thrilling 4-1 win over the Czechs in their first group match showed that, at the World Cup, Pelé was a different proposition altogether. Green summarised the contest, which was settled by a single goal in Brazil's favour, as 'a match between a better team, England, and better creative artists, Brazil'. The veteran football writer of *The Times* retained hope that England could yet emulate the feat of West Germany in 1954, who lost to Hungary in the group stage only to beat them in the final. The final group game dampened expectations somewhat, however, as England, with the reserve forward line of Astle and Leeds United's Allan Clarke, stuttered to a 1-0 win over Czechoslovakia by means of a controversial penalty.

14 June 1970
FIFA World Cup quarter-final
West Germany 3-2 England (after extra time)
Estadio Nou Camp, León

England's defeat to Brazil ultimately meant a second-placed finish in the group and the obligation to leave the comfort of the Guadalajara Hilton behind for the quarter-finals. Ramsey's men were bound for León, by now West Germany's home away from home. On Sunday, 14 June at high noon and in punishing heat, all four quarter-finals of the 1970 World Cup would kick off simultaneously, including the repeat of the Wembley final.

With the Bogotá bracelet affair behind them, England were beset by new problems in the build-up to this crucial match. First, the Mexican authorities denied them the chance to fly from Guadalajara to León, which meant that the team had to travel by coach for several hours on the day before the game. Upon arrival, they found that the accommodation that had been earmarked by the FA was now unavailable, and the party ended up in a sub-standard motel. As Jeff Dawson put it in his book on England at the 1970 World Cup, 'Given that the Germans have, in customary fashion, pre-booked their hotels all the way through to the final, it seems remarkably shortsighted that, for all the effort that went into England's pre-tournament planning, such a likely eventuality as finishing runner-up in their group has not been budgeted for.' A bigger problem was the condition of goalkeeper Banks, who felt unwell with presumed food poisoning on the evening of 12 June but had seemingly recovered and joined the rest of the squad for the coach trip to León. Banks spent Saturday afternoon in bed while the rest of the team trained on the Nou Camp pitch, and when Ramsey named his team the following morning it still included the England number one. Yet just before the short trip to the stadium, reserve goalkeeper Alex Stepney found Banks suffering a relapse in his room. Ramsey's hand was forced, and he told Chelsea's Peter Bonetti, long-time deputy for Banks, that he would play in goal against West Germany. McIlvanney did not even know what had befallen Banks when he gravely reported for the matchday edition of *The Observer*:

'If the alarming inadequacies of England's qualifying performance against Czechoslovakia are compounded by the effects of travelling 150 miles to a city that is about a thousand feet higher and noticeably hotter than Guadalajara, there should be little chance of interrupting West Germany's confident progress towards the semi-finals of the World Cup.'

The England line-up was otherwise the same as had played against Romania in the opening game, with Newton and Leeds United's Terry Cooper at full-back and Labone alongside Moore in central defence. Ball and Peters joined Mullery and Bobby Charlton in midfield, with Hurst and Lee up front. On the West German side, Schnellinger played himself into the sweeper's role in the matches against Bulgaria and Peru, displacing Schulz. Beckenbauer, with Overath in support, would again play in midfield and dedicate himself to containing Bobby Charlton. Seeler and Müller played every minute of the group stage up front together, confounding those members of the German press who had told Green of their fears that the two strikers would 'mix like oil and water'. Outside them, two orthodox wingers, Libuda and Löhr, would face Ramsey's 'wingless wonders'. The irony was sharpened by Libuda's nickname, Stan, which he had earned for his tricks on the right flank that reminded football fans of the great Stanley Matthews.

Schön picked Libuda and Löhr in place of the 1966 veterans Held and Haller after an underwhelming first display against Morocco, and he also used the Eintracht Frankfurt winger Jürgen Grabowski as a substitute in each of the three group matches. The tactical switch had been such a success in the games against Bulgaria and Peru that McIlvanney, who observed that England had 'found scoring about as easy as skiing on marmalade' in a formation that 'seldom becomes more adventurous than 4-4-2', was moved to sound a warning on the eve of the match:

'It will be hard to accept that [England] are no longer the strongest team in Europe, let alone the world, and all the harder for Sir Alf Ramsey because any success the Germans enjoy tomorrow will be inseparable from their use of the conventional wingers he has scorned for so long.'

Half an hour into the contest, however, England served up what ITV commentator Hugh Johns described as 'the most heartening sight we've seen in this whole competition'. Mullery started a move deep inside his own half and then swept a long pass to the right flank to find Newton in space. The camera zoomed in on Newton but, out of shot, Mullery only kept running, straining every sinew to break into the penalty area and receive Newton's return ball. 'Mullery! Alan Mullery!' screamed Johns, almost incredulous that it was the Spurs midfielder who diverted the ball into Maier's net with a right-footed finish under pressure. Just four minutes into the second half, England doubled their lead through Peters, who eluded Schnellinger at the far post to steer home another good cross from Newton. Ball then indulged in an infamous moment of gloating, as he himself admitted, 'When our second one went in, I ran around the field shouting to all the Germans, "Good night, God bless, see you in Munich."'

Schön had been forced to rearrange his defence at half-time because Höttges suffered an injury in a collision with Bobby Charlton on the half-hour mark. Höttges was replaced by Schulz, who played in the centre of defence, and Fichtel was asked to cover at left full-back. When England scored their second goal, the West German defence was evidently still adjusting to the change, as the area of the pitch formerly occupied by Höttges was conspicuously vacant and Newton took full advantage to cross for Peters.

On 56 minutes, Schön resolved to make use of the tactical substitution that was now permitted at the World Cup. The move was expected as he had already substituted wide players in the punishing Mexican conditions in each of West Germany's three group games. On this occasion he introduced Grabowski for the ineffectual Libuda, who was well covered by Cooper and failed in the first half to live up to his English nickname. In the heat of León, the introduction of a pacy winger with fresh legs had an immediate impact. Grabowski took a short corner as his first act and then unleashed a powerful right-footed shot that was blocked by Cooper. Moments later, Bonetti picked a high ball from Löhr out of the air with Müller ready to pounce. 'The first time that Peter Bonetti's been put under pressure,' remarked Johns. On the hour mark, Schnellinger played another teasing high ball into the box and Seeler beat Moore to the header, displaying his remarkable ability to rise above taller defenders. 'Incredible how this little man climbs in the sky,' noted Johns.

Then came the key moment in the match. With 68 minutes played and England settled in their own half with nine men behind the ball, Lee – misidentified by Johns as Moore – was floored by an attempted pass from Fichtel that hit him 'in the you-know-what', according to the player himself. The ball found its way to Beckenbauer, who dropped a shoulder to get past Mullery while Bobby Charlton could only watch on, hands on hips. Beckenbauer hit a right-footed shot across goal from the edge of the penalty area to score in the manner so often seen before. *Kicker* called it a 'magnificent' goal and, less justifiably, described it as 'unsaveable'.

Even in the English match reports of the following day, criticism for Bonetti's part in the goal is conspicuous by its absence. Green wrote that Beckenbauer's shot 'beat Bonetti's dive to the far corner'; Barham observed how the midfielder 'fired the ball into the corner of the net'; the *Daily Mirror's* Ken Jones described how he 'struck a firm shot beyond the diving Peter Bonetti'. Only Saunders in the *Daily Telegraph* perhaps implicitly blamed the goalkeeper in repeating his surname, unless this was a misprint, 'Beckenbauer picked up a loose ball, moved smoothly past Mullery and hammered Germany's first goal past Bonetti. Bonetti.' One man who certainly did not spare Bonetti's feelings was 'Worldcup-Willi' Schulz, who was quoted a few days later as saying, 'We shouldn't forget: Bonetti was a *Fliegenfänger*. That would never have happened to England with Banks.' The pejorative term literally translates to 'flycatcher', but, in the context of goalkeeping, its English equivalent is 'butterfingers'. Certainly in the years that followed, the idea that Banks would have saved the shot comfortably, and by extension that England would have held on to their lead if he had played, became a commonplace.

Ramsey's next act was to remove Bobby Charlton and replace him with Colin Bell. He had also taken his star player off after just over an hour against Brazil and Czechoslovakia, so this was not an unexpected change, but much like Bonetti's error it has since become mythologised in English football lore. It is thus important to state the fact that Ramsey did not take off Charlton and Peters while his team held a comfortable two-goal lead, as is so often thought. The game arguably began to turn on the introduction of Grabowski, and with Beckenbauer's goal the West German players then received the impetus they needed. Again, it is worth noting the view of the half-time substitute Schulz, 'I never really doubted that we could win. After the 0-2 I hadn't given up hope yet. As a substitute I noticed how tired the English players were at the beginning of the second half.'

The perception that England were 'out of sight' derives in part from the players' own embellishment in interviews of their performance in the first hour – Mullery has said, 'We were easily the better side and dominated the game,' for example. Yet it is also sustained by the highly partisan commentary from Johns which features on the most readily available video footage of the match today. Apart from his characterisation of the West German players as 'tragedy actors from a touring Shakespeare show' and his insistent reminders of referee Angel Coerezza's Argentinian nationality as if to impugn him, Johns was also happy to describe a tiring England team after 65 minutes as 'quite prepared to play at walking pace' before noting that West Germany looked 'far more tired than England' when slowing play in extra time. Moreover, when Lee was brought down in the penalty area by Schnellinger shortly before half-time, the incident was met with an excited shout of, 'That must be a penalty!' When Vogts was robustly challenged by Cooper in the same area of the field in extra time, Johns merely said, 'The Germans claiming a penalty, Cooper saying "get up!"' Without the benefit of various camera angles and slow-motion replays, it is impossible now to assess the relative validity of each penalty claim, but the commentary has nonetheless shaped many write-ups of the match over the years.

An indication that the players' behaviour was under scrutiny on both sides comes from the German journalist Werner Schilling, who gave his reaction to the match a few days later:

'It was not in the noble English tradition, the way Lee gave Sepp Maier an uppercut ripe for the boxing ring. Mullery, whom Uwe had to thank for a bruise on his thigh, and Labone, who elbowed Gerd Müller in the ribs, whereupon *der Bomber* retaliated with a slap to the face. All this was just evidence of unchecked passion.'

The most glaring misconception of all is the notion that Seeler's equaliser was a stroke of luck. At 168cm, or 5ft 6in, the Hamburg striker always looked an unlikely candidate for aerial prowess, but his spring and anticipation allowed him to score with his head time and again. For anyone who watched Seeler's career, there is no doubt that this exceptional finish, a craning header while falling with his back to goal, was also intentional. Before he hit the ground, he had spun his head round and knew precisely where to look – beyond Bonetti and in the back of the net.

Heimann wrote that the equaliser 'reawakened a fighting spirit in the German team that had seemed to burn out in the heat of the León stadium'. When the final whistle went, signalling that 30 minutes of extra time would be played, there was no possibility of standing tall and sending a signal to the opposition that belied exhaustion, as England had done four years before. In these conditions, the priority was to seek shade and water for even a moment's respite. At the beginning of the first period of extra time, West Germany won five successive corners and Beckenbauer had another fierce shot tipped over the bar by Bonetti. England's best chance fell to the wrong man after a corner, when Bell played a low cross that found Labone unmarked near the penalty spot, and the defender could only skew his finish high into the stand.

The decisive moment came just a couple of minutes after the change of ends in extra time, and it came from that most decisive of players, Müller. McIlvanney's warning about the threat of West Germany's wing play now became a prophecy, as Grabowski once more took on an exhausted Cooper on the right flank and hit a teasing high cross that his fellow winger

Löhr headed back across the six-yard box, beating Newton in the air. Labone, marking Müller, had followed the path of the original cross from Grabowski, thereby affording the FC Bayern marksman the split second he needed to anticipate what would ensue and find his pocket of space. He scored with an acrobatic, high-footed finish from two yards out before Bonetti or Moore could reach him. There could hardly be a better archetype for a Gerd Müller goal.

In the case of England's final penalty claim, just five minutes from the end of extra time, no alternate angles or high-definition replays are needed to verify that Bell was fouled by Beckenbauer and that a penalty should indeed have been given. Coerezza waved play on, however, and Beckenbauer escaped to victory. We may surmise that the referee was unwilling to make a decision that would in all probability have led to a coin toss to determine the winner, but this is mere conjecture.

In *The Times* of the following day, Green praised the West German team and in particular its midfield pairing, which grew into the game after a listless first half:

'The better side won in the end. And they won because, once Beckenbauer had put the Germans back into the match when it was three-quarters gone, England wrongly proceeded to pull in their horns, pack the perimeter of their penalty area and concede the central areas to the twin German generals, Beckenbauer and Overath, supported by that wise old owl, Seeler. That was the heart and core of this extraordinary upheaval when all seemed done.'

Saunders in the *Daily Telegraph* was more damning of England, asserting, 'They allowed a match that appeared to be firmly in their grasp to slip through their fingers.' Schilling, meanwhile, reported a fascinating exchange of views between Karl-Heinz Heddergott of the DFB and his FA counterpart Ron Greenwood, the future England manager. According to Schilling, Heddergott and Greenwood agreed that Bobby Charlton had allowed England's early supremacy to tempt him into setting an unsustainable tempo, to which first he and then the whole team fell victim. Meanwhile, 1966 veteran Höttges was adamant that West Germany had better accounted for the conditions than England, who played well for only an hour. 'I am absolutely convinced that no other team in the world could still have recovered from this 0-2 deficit,' said Höttges proudly. After all was said and done, it was Jones in the *Daily Mirror* who best encapsulated the drama and historical significance of this latest 120-minute contest between the two nations, 'The World Cup was torn from England here today in a dramatic, tragic reversal of the 1966 final against West Germany.'

* * *

One of the wry, sardonic opinions that is commonly offered in Germany when the Anglo-German football rivalry is discussed centres on the fact that many important meetings between the two nations have been directly followed and overshadowed by an even more significant match – for Germany. The first time that this was the case was at the 1970 World Cup in Mexico, since a mere three days after beating England in León, the *Nationalmannschaft* went the distance once more in the enormous Estadio Azteca in Mexico City.

The semi-final against Italy, which featured five goals in an extraordinary half an hour of extra time, became a new 'Match of the Century' to rival England v Hungary in 1953. Again, the majority of the Mexican crowd supported West Germany, this time against the team that had eliminated the host nation in the quarter-finals. An early goal from Internazionale forward Roberto Boninsegna was the worst thing that could have happened to Schön's side as it allowed the Italians obstinately to defend their advantage, by fair means or foul. West Germany's relentless second-half pressure, amid growing frustration at Mexican referee Arturo Yamasaki's indulgence of the Italians, finally found its release deep into injury time. Again it was the irrepressible Grabowski who provided the all-important cross, this time from the left, and Schnellinger was unmarked on the edge of the six-yard box to divert the ball past Enrico Albertosi, triggering the most famous period of extra time in World Cup history.

Much like Weber's goal at Wembley in 1966, this moment helped to consolidate West Germany's reputation, first forged in Bern in 1954, for refusing to give in until the final whistle. The match is also famous for the image of Beckenbauer playing with his arm in a sling during the second half and extra time, after he was brought down by the Cagliari defender Pierluigi Cera and suffered a dislocated shoulder. Müller scored twice in extra time, bringing his total for the tournament to ten, but Italy scored three times, including a beautifully taken goal from Cera's club-mate Gigi Riva. Italy's fourth goal, from the great Gianni Rivera just a minute after Müller's second, put the *Azzurri* 4-3 ahead and was at last too much for West Germany to answer. As Uli Hesse writes, the heroic performance, coupled with Yamasaki's questionable refereeing, 'explains why the team were regarded at home – for the second time in four years – as unlucky losers, even the moral victors. Sixty thousand people gathered to welcome the squad on their return.'

8

From the Depths of Space
1972–1978

On 18 June 1970, just four days after León, voters in the United Kingdom went to the polls and elected the Conservative leader Edward Heath as prime minister. The surprising result ended nearly six years of Labour rule under Harold Wilson, who remained leader of the party in opposition. For all his faults, Heath possessed the vision to bring Britain into the European Economic Community, persuading French president Georges Pompidou to revoke his predecessor Charles de Gaulle's veto on British entry. Heath signed the Treaty of Accession in Brussels on 22 January 1972, and Britain's membership took effect on 1 January 1973.

This was a transformative development in British history that played out amid a variety of domestic crises. Heath's Industrial Relations Bill of 1971, although supported by the general public, created widespread resentment in the trade union movement and led to damaging protests, including a national miners' strike at the beginning of 1972. At the same time, violence in Northern Ireland reached its peak, in part because of the new Conservative government's handling of the problem. In August 1971 it had used a policy of mass internment as a proposed solution to the security threat. It was against this measure of imprisonment without trial that a group of Catholic demonstrators were marching on 30 January 1972, now remembered as Bloody Sunday, when British soldiers opened fire on the streets of Londonderry and killed 13 civilians. In the aftermath, Heath's government passed emergency legislation to impose direct rule on Northern Ireland from Westminster.

The year 1972 also notably marks the first peak of violence perpetrated by the Rote Armee Fraktion, the West German far-left militant organisation also known as the Baader-Meinhof Group. Indeed, in the two days before England's visit to West Berlin for the European Championship quarter-final second leg, the group carried out bombings in Frankfurt, Augsburg and Munich. In mainstream German politics, however, the student movement of 1968 had brought about real change, as the grand coalition was replaced in 1969 by a new Social Democrat Party (SDP) government under Chancellor Willy Brandt, who had been a political exile from the Third Reich. The principle of *Vergangenheitsbewältigung*, the struggle to come to terms with the past, was now embodied at the highest level of politics. On 7 December 1970, as part of his *Ostpolitik* doctrine of normalising relations with eastern Europe, Brandt signed the Treaty of Warsaw with Polish Prime Minister Jósef Cyrankiewicz. The agreement ratified the existing border between Polish and German territory that had been imposed by the Allies in 1945. That same day, in a gesture now remembered as *der Kniefall von Warschau*, Brandt knelt respectfully before a memorial to the Jews killed in the 1943 Warsaw ghetto uprising. As German historian Ulrich Herbert puts it, 'This was a silent gesture of humility which was perceived all over the world like no other as an admission of German guilt and a plea for forgiveness.'

In German football, meanwhile, the first decade of the Bundesliga culminated in its greatest scandal in 1971. After the DFB neglected to adopt full professionalism when agreeing to implement the national league in 1962, illegal payments to players became pervasive. As Uli Hesse so memorably puts it, 'In the 1960s Bundesliga, there were probably more hidden accounts and suitcases stuffed with cash than in all the world's dubious offshore tax havens put together.'

Hertha Berlin had been the first club to fall foul of the authorities, in the earlier scandal of 1965, after encountering difficulties in attracting players to the politically isolated city. After Hertha were relegated, the DFB's insistence on Berlin representation in the Bundesliga led circuitously to the 11th-hour promotion of seriously underprepared local club Tasmania Berlin to the 1965/66 Bundesliga, as well as the expansion of

battle for supremacy in German football, 'Politics, philosophy, art and sometimes even sport – whatever there was that needed classification, you could bet somebody was there who would argue it all boiled down to Gladbach v Bayern, Netzer v Beckenbauer, Good v Evil.' After Bayern's first Bundesliga title in 1969, the two clubs won the next eight championships; three in a row for Bayern between 1972 and 1974, and the other five for Gladbach.

One of the reasons for Bayern's perceived good fortune in comparison to their rivals loomed large in 1972. While West Germany would once again welcome England to Berlin for the second leg of the quarter-final tie, the next international after that, against the Soviet Union on 26 May, served to inaugurate the Olympiastadion in Munich that was built for the Olympic Games later that summer. Bayern had shared the Grünwalder Stadion to the south of the city with rivals TSV 1860 München since 1925, but the club would now play at the new venue with an initial capacity of 80,000, resulting in significantly higher matchday incomes.

Netzer would leave the great debate behind him by signing for Real Madrid in 1973, which upset Schön's traditional sensibilities. At the 1974 World Cup, Netzer would lose out in terms of selection to Beckenbauer's trusted midfield sentinel Overath, but here at Wembley the long-haired maestro, nicknamed 'Karajan' after the famous conductor, made perhaps his greatest impact on the *Nationalmannschaft*. He had already impressed against England at Wembley at the age of 21, in the friendly international at the start of 1966. At 27, Netzer was now in the prime of his career, winning the first of two consecutive German Footballer of the Year awards in the 1971/72 season.

The English press pack were duly wary of Netzer, with Geoffrey Green, Donald Saunders and Albert Barham all identifying him before the match as a threat. As such, all three writers agreed that Alan Mullery was needed for defensive solidity in the England midfield. While Green took Mullery's selection for granted, Saunders in the *Daily Telegraph* was keen to state the case for the Tottenham midfielder's inclusion, 'This season England have rarely looked convincing in that all-important part of the pitch. Tonight they must try to take command away from Netzer, the powerful, skilful German general. Mullery, a player of vast experience and commendable tenacity, would be my choice for that job.'

Notwithstanding their due respect for the talents of Netzer, Beckenbauer – 'a great player of world quality whose creative talents surely are wasted as a defensive sweeper' – and Müller, the English writers were also in agreement that England would win, and that a two-goal margin to take to Berlin was the priority. Indeed, Green quoted Moore's response when asked if the team would win well in the first leg at Wembley, 'Don't be silly ... We'll win both.'

There was precious little expectation of success on the West German side, meanwhile. The unavailability of the Schalke players embroiled in scandal caused problems for Schön, and injuries excluded Overath, Vogts and Schnellinger, who had expressed delight at a recall to the national side but then suffered a thigh injury in AC Milan's semi-final second leg against Tottenham Hotspur in the UEFA Cup, the new continental competition inaugurated that season. Even the team's strong FC Bayern contingent was thought to be suffering from low morale following a chastening 2-0 defeat away to Rangers in the second leg of the Cup Winners' Cup semi-final ten days before. Heimann was moved to appeal for calm in his preview of the match, 'No matter how bad the omens may be, there is no reason to retreat in fear at Wembley.' The headline exhorted, 'Leave the fear at home!'

What transpired was one of West Germany's greatest victories, the first win for any German national team on English soil, and the latest abrupt wake-up call for Ramsey's England. West Germany won 3-1, with two late goals bringing victory, but it is the style of football on show that is fondly remembered today, immortalised by *Bild*'s 'Ramba-Zamba-Fußball' headline and the French sports newspaper *L'Équipe*'s description of 'football from the year 2000'. If the English journalists had been rather grudging in the wake of West Germany's landmark win in Hanover, now there was unambiguous acclaim. McIlvanney began his report with an epochal assertion, 'No Englishman can ever again warm himself with the old assumption that, on the football field if nowhere else, the Germans are an inferior race.'

Miller in the *Sunday Telegraph* asked exasperatedly, 'Where ... is our Netzer? This long-striding Germanic Bobby Charlton was more dangerous than England's midfield trio put together.' The *Sunday Mirror*'s Frank McGhee saw no way back from the shock defeat, 'There will be a funeral in Berlin in a fortnight's time. England's hopes of success in the European Nations Cup will then be finally and completely buried.'

All this, despite the fact that with just six minutes to play, the score was 1-1 and, by some accounts, England were superior during the second half. Hoeneß had opened the scoring with a shot from the edge of the penalty area midway through the first half, a cruel deflection taking it past Banks. The chance had materialised when Moore uncharacteristically lost possession in the penalty area. As football historian Tim Vickery astutely points out, the goal was ultimately caused by problems with England's personnel, specifically the pairing of Hunter and Moore in central defence:

'The problem here is not only that these are two players who carry out the same function, it's also that Hunter is left-footed, which means that Moore has to switch to the right, which is not his natural side to play on. And that's the first goal – because he does a movement then, when he turns to the right, usually that would be taking him away from the goal – this time, it takes the ball right into the goalmouth and leads to the goal for Hoeneß.'

With 12 minutes of the match remaining, England equalised through Lee, who took full advantage when Maier was unable to hold a shot from Bell. 'I wanted to push the ball to the side, because it was too slippery to catch,' said Maier, 'but it hit my hands with too much pace, so it lost momentum and fell right at Lee's feet, who just had to poke it in.' A few minutes later, Moore brought down Held on the very edge of the penalty area. He certainly began his sliding challenge well outside, but then made contact with the Offenbach forward when Held was already inside the box, for what Brian Glanville saw as an 'indisputable penalty'. McIlvanney dryly remarked, 'English complaints about the award of a penalty were no more sustained than they had a right to be.'

A first victory on English soil was now palpably close, just 12 yards away in fact. Remarkably, Netzer later revealed that customary penalty-taker Müller shied away from the spot kick, and that Beckenbauer once remarked, 'You'd have to be crazy to take a penalty in that situation.' The man for the moment, Netzer remembered the great fortune he had when Banks tipped his shot on to the post but the ball ricocheted into the net.

West Germany's third goal came with just two minutes remaining, compounding a miserable evening for Ramsey. After Held dispossessed Hughes, Hoeneß received the ball and broke into the penalty area, skipping past attempted tackles from Hunter and Peters, and then drawing Moore towards him and away from the ever-alert Müller. Hoeneß with a neat reverse pass found his Bayern colleague, who trapped the ball, turned, and shot, all before Hunter and Peters could reach him.

Müller's strike beat Banks low to his right and hit the inside of the post on its way into the net. In terms of England's tactics, the most obvious failure had been the cession of expansive areas of midfield space on the Wembley pitch. Glanville was among those who did not hide their irritation that Ramsey had neglected to select Mullery in favour of the same midfield trio that underwhelmed in a qualifying match against Greece the previous year:

'His mistakes were, both in prospect and in retrospect, so obvious and salient, their consequences so inevitable, that it is still hard to credit them. When one heard that England, just as in Athens when they last played, would take the field with a middle trio of Peters, Ball and Bell rather than with Mullery, with three men essentially dedicated to creation rather than destruction, to using rather than winning the ball, one was astounded.'

It is what Schön's team did with the available space that is now remembered in German football lore and, to an extent, in wider German culture. The two great rivals of the club game, Beckenbauer and Netzer, complemented each other perfectly on this occasion. Beckenbauer was the nominal *libero* while Netzer played in midfield alongside his club stalwart Wimmer, who 'diligently carried water so that Netzer could walk on it', to borrow Rob Smyth's artful phrase. The key tactic behind the performance at Wembley originated at Gladbach. In an interview with *Bild* to mark the game's 50th anniversary in 2022, Netzer was asked how the idea of the two star players intermittently switching positions, allowing each other the freedom to maraud into attacking spaces, was conceived:

'In the Bundesliga I was only getting kicked in midfield. In every game there would be a player whose sole assignment was to kill me. I was in great danger. At some point I said, I'm not tired of life. That's why we invented this interplay at Gladbach with our *libero* Hans-Jürgen Wittkamp. And then I said: If it works so well with Wittkamp, then surely it will work even better with Beckenbauer. So we did it.'

It was this so-called *Wechselspiel*, or interplay, which allowed Netzer to emerge from a defensive position and run with the ball into vacant space, particularly in the early stages of the match before England could respond. With his flowing blond locks and green number ten shirt, it became an enduring image, consolidated in the cultural memory by one observer's turn of phrase. The German historian Wolfram Pyta explains the morphology of the phrase *'Aus der Tiefe des Raumes'*, meaning 'from the depths of space', which has long since broken loose from its original context. It was first used by the scholar and essayist Karl Heinz Bohrer, once a London correspondent for the *Frankfurter Allgemeine Zeitung*. In an article foregrounding his appreciation of the unique atmosphere at Wembley during England's World Cup qualifier against Poland in October 1973, Bohrer fleetingly recalled West Germany's victory on the hallowed turf in 1972. In reference to Netzer's inimitable playing style, he used the words *'Der aus der Tiefe des Raumes plötzlich vorstoßene Netzer hatte* "thrill"' to articulate how the player would suddenly appear from the depths of space, exuding a 'thrill' for which there was evidently no equivalent in the German language.

After the match, a delighted Schön was prepared to proclaim that he had just overseen the most significant victory of his tenure, 'Above all, we have to remember that we played at Wembley, on English soil, on the hallowed turf, and if we win here in a game in which something is at stake, then of course it's a big occasion, and that's why I would put this game at the very top.'

13 May 1972
UEFA European Championship quarter-final second leg
West Germany 0-0 England
Olympiastadion, Berlin

Two England players in the side for the second leg in Berlin are emblematic of the difficulties Ramsey had in adapting to the vicissitudes of football in the 1970s. Norman Hunter had only played at Wembley because Derby County's Roy McFarland, a tough-tackling central defender who had established himself in the national team during 1971, was withdrawn from the squad by his club manager Clough, apparently due to an injury. McFarland played for Derby in their crucial last-day win over Liverpool just 48 hours later, causing Ramsey to say of Clough, 'This man calls himself a patriot but he has never done anything to help England. All he does is criticise us in the newspapers and television.' The Queens Park Rangers forward Rodney Marsh, meanwhile, was one of football's so-called mavericks in the early 1970s. They followed the trail blazed by Belfast-born Manchester United star George Best, who burst on the scene at the age of 19 with two goals against Benfica in Lisbon, in the 1965/66 European Cup quarter-final second leg. His dazzling displays and long-haired insouciance earned him celebrity status and the 'fifth Beatle' nickname.

English mavericks included the 'working man's George Best' Frank Worthington, Chelsea's Peter Osgood and Alan Hudson, and Marsh, who in the defeat to West Germany had made only his second appearance under Ramsey at the age of 27. Marsh came on for Hurst after an hour, the calls for 'Rodney' from the Wembley crowd having grown louder and louder since the first half. These players' careers had all begun after the abolishment of the maximum wage in English football in 1961, and their professional environment was now a world away from the postwar Football League in which Ramsey had played. The biographer Leo McKinstry astutely explained why Ramsey found it difficult to adapt and compromise on his loyalty to the 'old guard' after Mexico 1970:

'It is fair to say that Alf felt far less connection to the colourful stars of the 1970s than he had to the more solid, mature figures of the mid-1960s. There was an affinity of outlook between Alf and men like George Cohen, Ray Wilson and Bobby Charlton. They had all done military service for their country and experienced the maximum wage. Modest and dignified, they had a sense of privilege about earning their living as a professional footballer. They belonged to an era when extravagant emotions were frowned on. But Alf was a man out of time by the early 1970s.'

After the shock of defeat at Wembley, Ramsey selected Marsh in place of Hurst in Berlin, and McFarland was available once more. In essence, however, the beleaguered England manager overcompensated for his errors in the first leg, bringing in Arsenal's famously combative Peter Storey to play alongside Hunter in a midfield bent on destruction as opposed to creation. An ugly game on a sodden, grey day in Berlin ended scoreless, leaving Ramsey's reputation almost as bruised as Netzer's legs. Under an indignant headline 'Hunted and kicked like an animal', *Kicker* journalist Hildebrand Kelber quoted the walking wounded after the match.

'This time the English players set a new record and got me in three different places,' said the Gladbach midfield dynamo, who was designated fair game by his opponents and continuously suffered bad fouls to prevent him from directing Germany's play in the usual way. 'Honestly,' declared the embittered Netzer, 'I've never experienced so much foul play.'

Accordingly, the German press were damning of the visitors, asserting that 'of England's glory only ashes remain'. If Hanover 1968 had removed the weight of history from West German shoulders, this European Championship tie in 1972 dispelled not only all remaining preoccupations with inferiority, but also the last vestiges of admiration for English 'fair play' ideals.

* * *

The career of England's greatest goalkeeper, Gordon Banks, came to a sad and abrupt end in October 1972. Banks was injured in a car accident near his home, with fragments of the broken windscreen of his car lodged in his right eye. He regained partial sight after an operation to remove the glass, and he retained hopes of resuming football, but was eventually forced to retire when he lost all sight in the eye. His international career ended with 73 caps and the unforgettable image of his 'Save of the Century' from Pelé's header at the 1970 World Cup.

Famously absent for the quarter-final in León, Banks played six times against West Germany between 1965 and 1972. On winning the World Cup with England in 1966, he wrote, 'I felt as Christopher Columbus must have when realising he hadn't sailed off the edge of the world.' Gordon Banks passed away on 12 February 2019 at the age of 81.

1972 UEFA European Championship
Belgium

The national team's triumph at the 1972 European Championship in Belgium, in which West Germany defeated the hosts in the semi-final with a brace from Müller before convincingly beating the Soviet Union with another stylish and commanding display in the final, was emblematic of the climax of the country's progressive period of social liberalism under Brandt between 1969 and 1974. On 27 April 1972, an unsuccessful vote of no confidence against the chancellor gave rise to concerns that Brandt's 1970 treaties with Poland and the Soviet Union might yet be obstructed in parliament. Three days later, Neal Ascherson explained to readers of *The Observer* why Brandt's *Ostpolitik* offered a positive future for all of Europe, 'It is not just to Germany that the treaties matter. They have become the centrepiece of the whole process of settling the Cold War in Europe.'

Brandt weathered the storm, and the treaties of Moscow and Warsaw passed the Bundestag on 17 May, removing one of the most significant obstacles to the normalisation of relations between east and west. The Strategic Arms Limitation Talks (SALT) agreement was signed just a few days later, on 26 May, signalling progress in nuclear arms control between the United States and the Soviet Union. Besides all this, West Germany had enjoyed uninterrupted economic growth for over a decade and faced up to German crimes of the past with humility.

With the opportunity to host the Olympic Games for the first time since they were co-opted by the Nazi regime in 1936, West Germany projected a new self-image characterised by modernity, globalism and social liberalism. The 1972 European football champions exuded these values in appearance but also in playing style, earning international plaudits. 'The entire German team and its manager deserve a memorial,' wrote the Belgian newspaper *La Meuse*. 'They have made football the biggest attraction again.' The French sports newspaper *L'Équipe* affirmed, 'Brussels witnessed the rehabilitation of attacking football, of enthusiasm for the game, and of having fun with the ball ... Netzer is the best player on the continent.' As so often, the venerable Geoffrey Green provided perhaps the most vivid articulation of West Germany's brilliance in overcoming the Soviet Union in the final with another two goals from Müller and one from Wimmer:

'Clearly they are the most gifted national side on the continent. They are a pleasure to watch. Elegant and imaginative, they have an infinite variety to their game as they stroke the ball around in a flood of angles on the ground and in the air. It is like light being fed through a prism.'

* * *

At the end of the 1972/73 season, the second final of the UEFA Cup was contested by Shankly's Liverpool and Hennes Weisweiler's Borussia Mönchengladbach. Liverpool, the new champions of England, had beaten Eintracht Frankfurt and two East German teams, Dynamo Berlin and Dynamo Dresden, on their way to the final, while Gladbach overcame fellow Bundesliga sides 1. FC Köln and 1. FC Kaiserslautern. Liverpool won 3-0 in the first leg on 10 May at Anfield, with two goals from Kevin Keegan, aged 22. Ray Clemence saved Jupp Heynckes's second-half penalty, allowing Liverpool to travel to Germany two weeks later with a comfortable advantage.

On a rainy night in Mönchengladbach, Heynckes scored two first-half goals as Netzer again controlled the play, and Liverpool took what *The Guardian*'s Paul Fitzpatrick called 'a fierce battering'. Robert Oxby in the *Daily Telegraph* saw Gladbach's performance as a signal of 'their arrival as a side likely to become as formidable as Ajax Amsterdam', the continent's best club side who were then just days away from completing a hat-trick of European Cup wins. Two weeks later, however, the transfer of Netzer to Real Madrid was agreed, and Gladbach would have to begin anew without their most gifted player.

In the 1973/74 season, it was FC Bayern who took charge in Europe, complementing a third successive Bundesliga title with the club's first European Cup. Schwarzenbeck's equaliser at the very end of extra time in the final against Atlético Madrid forced a replay on 17 May 1974, which Bayern won with an outstanding performance that heralded an era of dominance. Under manager Udo Lattek, who had succeeded Zebec in 1970, the Bavarians overran the Spanish champions 4-0, with two goals apiece from Hoeneß and Müller. It was the perfect preparation for the home World Cup the following month, for which Schön selected seven players from FC Bayern in his squad.

England's qualification campaign for the 1974 World Cup had gone awry during 1973 and ultimately cost Ramsey his job. The damage was done in two games against Poland in June and October, but as McKinstry pointed out, the failure to qualify for the World Cup was merely the final pretext needed for the manager's opponents within the FA to oust him. The so-called blazer brigade had always sneered at Ramsey, who bristled with insecurity about his background and also treated the FA officials with contempt. His chief antagonist was the association's vice-chairman, Harold Thompson, a renowned Professor of Chemistry at Oxford University. According to those who worked with him, Thompson was a disdainful and domineering administrator, and his manner was anathema to Ramsey.

After the 1-1 draw with Poland at Wembley on 17 October, for which he was pilloried in the press, Ramsey dug his heels in and refused to resign, but his contract was up for renewal in June 1974. Thompson's campaign to oust Ramsey found support from the new FA secretary Ted Croker, who was keen to cash in on commercial opportunities and improve relations with the press, which had soured badly after the failures against Poland. The decision to remove the manager from his post was taken by an FA committee in Ramsey's absence on 14 February, and he was formally sacked on 1 May. Although there had been growing calls among press and public for him to be replaced as England manager after 1970, the manner in which he was dismissed caused consternation, as McKinstry explained:

'After years of modest, poorly rewarded service, Alf was given a meagre golden handshake of £8,000, with a pension of only £1,200 a year; to add insult to injury, when Don Revie was appointed his permanent successor, he was paid £25,000 a year, more than treble Alf's salary. Moreover, no attempt was made to utilise Alf in any other role in the FA, such as a coach, advisor or ambassador, despite his vast professionalism.'

Alan Ball, who won 66 caps under Ramsey, remarked that it was, 'The most incredible thing that ever happened in English football. The most successful manager in the history of our country was just sacked by the amateurs of the FA.'

FIFA World Cup 1974
West Germany

West Germany's campaign on home soil at the 1974 FIFA World Cup was a game of two halves. During the first group stage, the squad was riven by tension and acrimony which culminated in humiliating defeat in the only match the *Nationalmannschaft* would ever play against its East German counterpart. Things came to a head and Beckenbauer came to the fore. Thereafter, a team spirit developed that ultimately allowed West Germany to overcome Rinus Michels and his formidable Dutch exponents of 'total football' in the final. The Dutch term *totaalvoetbal* describes a tactical system of heightened positional flexibility that was associated with the great Ajax side of the early 1970s and now the national team at the World Cup.

The tournament had begun amid heightened security measures in response to the widespread activities of the Baader-Meinhof Group and even the IRA. Less than two years had passed since the terrorist attack at the Munich Olympics, in which 11 members of the Israeli Olympic team were killed by the Palestinian militant organisation Black September. The West German squad were accordingly kept under close guard, and were unsettled by the stringent measures. The secluded camp at Malente, in the far north of the country, housed 40 men in small rooms with outside washrooms and toilets, and was guarded by counterterrorism police.

It was there that a bitter pay dispute between the DFB and its senior players reached crisis point just five days before the tournament began. Throughout the night, Beckenbauer led negotiations with DFB vice-president Hermann Neuberger for individual bonuses in the event of winning the World Cup. At one point, Schön was so exasperated with the players' selfish concerns that he considered dismissing the entire squad and competing at the home World Cup with a team of reserves, an unthinkable eventuality. Similarly to his England counterpart Ramsey, Schön was left alienated by his group of modern professionals. 'For the first time,' explained Hesse, 'he realised that this was a new generation of footballers, far removed from the Fritz Walters and Uwe Seelers. He heard their words, but he could not understand what they were saying.'

The defeat to the DDR in the third group match meant that West Germany would avoid Johan Cruyff's Netherlands and the South American giants Argentina and Brazil in the second phase, but as Hesse was keen to point out, the notion that there was any deliberate strategy behind this outcome 'must rank among the most preposterous claims ever made in connection with football', since it ignores the political significance of defeat in the unique intra-German encounter. The winning goal from Jürgen Sparwasser, who had led the line in 1. FC Magdeburg's famous win over Trapattoni's AC Milan in the Cup Winners' Cup Final a month before, gave the DDR a propaganda victory and dealt a major blow to the Dresden-born Schön.

On the team's return to Malente, the dam was fit to burst. A dejected Schön locked himself in his room while the players stayed up drinking. 'Nobody could think about sleeping, and I wiped the floor with anyone who crossed my path,' remembers Beckenbauer, who brought the rabble into line that night and organised the team's transfer the following day to their new base for the second group phase. Convincing wins followed in Düsseldorf against Yugoslavia and Sweden, before what was effectively a semi-final against Poland in torrential rain in Frankfurt. The conditions stifled the free-flowing football of Polish playmaker Kazimierz Deyna and the tournament's top-scorer Grzegorz Lato, and an outstanding performance from Maier meant that Müller's late goal was enough to send West Germany into a final against the Netherlands.

Beckenbauer freely admitted that the Dutch were the best team coming into the tournament, and they had since beaten Uruguay, Argentina and Brazil to underline their claims, but he asserted that, come the final, 'We were on equal terms.' West Germany were now a different proposition with a new *Teamgeist*. As Steffen Haffner of the *Frankfurter Allgemeine* put it, 'The heat of the second group stage forged a team that knew how to fight bravely and play well.' In Munich's Olympiastadion on 7 July, the team won a second World Cup for Germany, beating the great Dutch side 2-1. Even here, a setback turned out to be a blessing in disguise. The Dutch took the lead in just the second minute when Johan Neeskens converted a penalty that his team had won before their opponents even touched the ball. Significantly, Vogts failed to touch the ball in conceding the foul too, and it was an uncontroversial decision, even if it was the first penalty to be awarded in a World Cup Final. Beckenbauer said that the early goal 'caused the Dutch to drop back and bring us into the game. Then it's difficult, once you've let the reins slacken, to re-gain the initiative.'

On 25 minutes, English referee Jack Taylor arguably initiated a bitter and enduring football rivalry between the Dutch and the Germans, when he adjudged Wim Jansen to have fouled Frankfurt forward Bernd Hölzenbein, and awarded a penalty to West Germany that was duly dispatched by Breitner. On this occasion it was highly questionable that Jansen had made contact and fouled Hölzenbein, who fell theatrically. Shortly before half-time, West Germany took the lead through the 14th and final World Cup goal from Müller. The young Gladbach midfielder Rainer Bonhof surged down the right flank to collect Grabowski's astute pass, dropped a shoulder to beat Arie Haan, and played the ball across for the Bayern striker. Müller's first touch saw the ball drop behind him but also away from defender Ruud Krol, in not too dissimilar fashion from Hurst's disputed goal eight years before. On the turn, *der Bomber* finished between Krol's legs, wrong-footing goalkeeper Jan Jongbloed.

The player who thus won West Germany the 1974 World Cup with the last of his 68 international goals was also at the centre of controversy immediately after the final, when the players' disaffection with the DFB returned to the surface and erupted. At the reception for the newly crowned world champions in Munich's city centre that evening, they were told that their wives and partners had been excluded from the banquet. Many of the players stormed out and celebrated elsewhere, and Müller retired from international duty in disgust. Breitner signed for Real Madrid for a record fee that summer and built a powerful midfield partnership with Netzer, winning two Spanish league titles and one Copa del Rey in the next two seasons. He also quit the national team, although he would be lured back some years later. Hoeneß, a butcher's son who did not mince his words, once said, 'It's amazing that we won the World Cup with such a bad federation. That must have been some team.'

12 March 1975
England 2-0 West Germany
Wembley Stadium

Don Revie was the outstanding candidate to become the new England manager in the summer of 1974, having led Leeds United to two league titles, one FA Cup, one League Cup and two Inter-Cities Fairs Cup titles in the 13 years since he became player-manager at the end of the 1960/61 season. Revie accepted the offer from the FA in July, after caretaker manager Joe Mercer had overseen seven matches.

The new era got off to a flying start in a European Championship qualifier against Czechoslovakia in October, when England scored three goals after a double substitution from Revie with 25 minutes remaining. Gone were Banks, Moore, Peters and Hurst, leaving Ball as the only World Cup winner in the squad. The new era was also signalled by England's first use of the Admiral home shirt that featured red and blue stripes from the neck to the cuffs, as well as the manufacturer's logo. The FA's pursuit of commercial opportunities after the Ramsey era was thus manifested on the field of play.

The eagerly awaited friendly match against world champions West Germany in March 1975 marked the 100th time England played at Wembley, and it also happened to be the 400th recognised DFB international. It was just the third match of Revie's tenure, yet he was already exhibiting a tendency to make changes and experiment with the team. In the three games against Czechoslovakia, Portugal and West Germany, he used 21 different players from 13 clubs and awarded five debut caps. For this match, an FA Cup quarter-final replay between Leeds and Ipswich Town on the preceding evening meant that Revie had to do without Hunter and Madeley, and could not give an expected debut to Ipswich left-back Kevin Beattie. There were thus two debutants at full-back in Leicester City's Stephen Whitworth and Ian Gillard of Queens Park Rangers. Assured of their place, meanwhile, were Liverpool team-mates Keegan and Ray Clemence, the successor to Banks in goal.

Southampton forward Mick Channon had won 12 caps under Ramsey and was also favoured by Revie, while Newcastle United striker Malcolm Macdonald, who finished the 1974/75 season as top goalscorer in the league, looked to secure a place in the side. As one of English football's so-called mavericks, Macdonald had been unable to earn Ramsey's trust but was now in irresistible form. Another flamboyant player with a similar reputation, Stoke City's Alan Hudson, was given his international debut here in the number ten shirt, a decision welcomed in *The Guardian* by the headline 'Revie gives Hudson chance at last'. Hudson claims that Ramsey had unjustly imposed a three-year suspension on him for failing to report for an under-23 international when suffering from an injury.

Three days before the game, Revie handed Ball the captain's armband, which had been worn by Hughes under Mercer and in Revie's first two matches. This was a disputed choice since Ball had been sent off five times in his career, most notably in the defeat in Poland in 1973 that precipitated Ramsey's downfall. *The Guardian*'s David Lacey relayed Revie's argument, 'With the team at an experimental stage he needs a captain with experience and infectious enthusiasm.' Lacey also remarked that the European Championship qualifiers away to Czechoslovakia and Portugal that autumn would be the true tests of the captaincy decision, but by that time Ball would be unceremoniously dropped by Revie.

On the West German side, the season would end in continental triumph for the leading clubs, with FC Bayern and Borussia Mönchengladbach winning the European Cup and the UEFA Cup, respectively. Gladbach's opponents in an all-German semi-final were 1. FC Köln, and Schön's line-up at Wembley in March thus included seven players involved in the later stages of European club competition. The Bayern players were Maier and Beckenbauer, with Schwarzenbeck on the bench, while Vogts, Wimmer and Bonhof represented the *Borussen*. Wimmer was joined in midfield by the Köln pair of Heinz Flohe and Bernd Cullmann, who between them could not muster an influence on the game to rival that exerted by Netzer three years before. Another problem for Schön was in attack, where the absence of Müller's goalscoring prowess was keenly felt. Alongside the World Cup winner Hölzenbein, he fielded the Offenbach striker Manfred Ritschel and his club-mate Erwin Kostedde, the first black footballer to play in the *Nationalmannschaft*.

In his match report, Heimann bemoaned West Germany's 'serious weaknesses in midfield, where the team lacked a game-changing personality against England, but also in the attack, which was only very rarely able to assert itself'. Another major factor that both manager and press on the visiting side were keen to point out after the match was the condition of the pitch, which due to heavy and persistent rain was a world away from the surface – described by Netzer as being 'as smooth as a billiard table' – on which they had played three years earlier. Heimann commented with subtle disdain that the West German players had expended enormous energy due to the heavy ground, to which the English were accustomed through their 'everyday experience'. Similarly, if a little more self-effacingly, Schön was quoted in the *Daily Telegraph*, 'England's win was well deserved as they adapted to the difficult condition of the pitch. Our players wanted to play, but some forgot that, before you play, you must win the ball in the tackle.'

As indicated by Schön's words, Revie's England here produced a physically strong and committed display which, but for wayward finishing, could have resulted in a bigger margin of victory. Bell opened the scoring from a Hudson free kick after 25 minutes, his volley from ten yards deflecting off Frankfurt defender Karl-Heinz Körbel and past Maier. With a quarter of the game remaining, Ball sent a deep cross into the penalty area that was met at the far post by Macdonald, who headed past a flailing Maier for his first senior England goal. Saunders afterwards affirmed, 'This was a performance none of us had a right to expect from so inexperienced an England side.' On Hudson's impressive debut he added, 'It was a long, long time since I have seen an England player so arrogantly control the middle of the pitch,' but unfortunately the subsequent reminder that Hudson's 'dedication has so often been questioned' unknowingly anticipated the premature end to his England career after just one more game.

Hudson appeared in the news following the European Championships in 2021, when he said that the treatment of the modern-day maverick Jack Grealish in Gareth Southgate's England team reminded him of his abortive international career, 'Seeing how Grealish was humiliated by so little playing time when he was the one player who might have won the tournament for our country has pushed me over the edge.' Hudson wrote to the FA to demand the permanent deletion of his England playing records, accusing the association of failing to support him after a serious accident in 1997 left him with permanent injuries. He was a King's Road icon during his early playing days with Chelsea, and the story of his England career and later life makes tragic reading. However, any adjustments to the official records would not expunge the words written in praise of his performance against West Germany on that rainy night. 'Hudson rekindles England flair and world champions go down' exclaimed the *Daily Telegraph*'s headline the next day; 'Majestic Hudson to stay' was the verdict in the *Daily Mirror*. In *The Times*, Green wrote, 'Hudson, for his part, was a *tour de force*, a mercurial player, poised, assured, polished as a nugget and even at times arrogant,' before quoting Netzer, who asked after the game, 'Who is this man Hudson and for whom does he play? He can play.'

* * *

On 28 May 1975, Revie's former club Leeds faced FC Bayern in the first Anglo-German European Cup Final. Now managed by former England full-back Jimmy Armfield after the ill-fated 44-day tenure of Brian Clough, Leeds lined up with four Englishmen alongside great players from across the British Isles, such as captain Billy Bremner, Johnny Giles and Terry Yorath. The Bayern side featured Maier, Beckenbauer, Schwarzenbeck, Hoeneß, and of course Müller, who completed another four Bundesliga seasons after quitting the national side.

The records show that Bayern won 2-0 in the Parc des Princes in Paris to lift the second of their three consecutive European Cup trophies, with Franz Roth and Müller on the scoresheet. The game is given short shrift at the FC Bayern Museum, where it is described as a 'fortuitous' win that was 'a testament to the smart tactics of coach Dettmar Cramer, and to Bayern's ability to dramatically raise their game on special occasions', since the club finished only tenth in the Bundesliga that season. Bayern fans also remember the almost immediate realisation of fears that Leeds would exhibit the violent and cynical play for which they had been renowned throughout Revie's tenure. After just four minutes, Yorath cynically fouled Swedish full-back Björn Andersson, who was unable to continue, and shortly afterwards full-back Paul Reaney was booked for another bad challenge, Yorath having escaped censure.

The historian David Downing boldly wrote, 'The game was only eight minutes old and already Leeds had sacrificed any moral claim to victory or right to expect justice from the referee.' For good measure, he later added, 'Leeds had played unimaginative English football in the worst possible spirit and had deservedly lost.' A foul by Frank Gray on Hoeneß would have far-reaching consequences. Then aged just 23, Hoeneß suffered a meniscus injury that led ultimately to his retirement from playing at 27.

Inevitably, the match is remembered somewhat differently by anyone associated with Leeds. Towards the end of the first half, Beckenbauer fouled Allan Clarke in the penalty area but the French referee Michel Kitabdjian neglected to award a penalty amid vociferous protests. Twenty minutes into the second half, Scottish midfielder Peter Lorimer stood underneath a poor clearance and struck a fierce volley through a crowd, beating Maier from 15 yards. In a scene that mirrored another controversial Anglo-German final, the referee at first appeared to give the goal but then ruled it out upon consultation with his linesman, ostensibly on account of Bremner standing in an offside position in front of the goalkeeper at the instant of Lorimer's shot. The Bayern midfielder Rainer Zoibel has said, 'It was a goal, it wasn't offside, but that often happens in football. You can't look back. You can be angry about it, you can be disappointed, but you can't let it affect you forever.'

The Leeds fans' indignation was compounded just minutes later when Roth scored with a left-footed shot from just inside the penalty area. Ten minutes from time, Müller scored with a characteristic poacher's finish at the feet of goalkeeper David Stewart to make it 2-0. The evening ended amid ugly scenes described by a regretful Saunders in the *Daily Telegraph*, 'Alas, some of the 8,000 Leeds supporters could not take this defeat as sportingly as did the footballers who had every reason to feel sorry for themselves. So yet again the once highly respected name of British sportsmanship was disgraced on a foreign field.' The episode sadly pointed the way towards yet more serious incidents of fan violence in the years to come.

* * *

The downturn under Revie's management began with the two qualifying matches in late 1975 that Lacey had warned would represent the true test of the new England team. Revie's side had not yet lost a match when arriving in Bratislava to face Czechoslovakia at the end of October, and they had beaten the world champions West Germany and the auld enemy Scotland with impressive Wembley performances. Over the next year, however, they failed to progress from the qualifying group for the 1976 European Championship, lost the 1976 British Home Championship with defeat at Hampden Park, and then lost 2-0 to Italy in a crucial qualification match for the 1978 FIFA World Cup. Revie received heavy criticism after the defeat in Rome, for which he again made several changes and displayed the indecision that would constitute his legacy as national team manager.

For Tim Vickery, Revie and England at this time laboured under an 'ideological confusion' as to how to play, in part because of the lack of time at international level to implant the collective ideas with which Revie's Leeds side had flourished. Centre-forward Stan Bowles had not played for England in two and a half years but was preferred to the Manchester City striker Joe Royle, who scored against Finland in the previous game. Central defender Colin Todd, a regular in the team since the win over West Germany, was also dropped for the crucial match in Rome. 'Once he took over England,' said Todd of Revie, 'he never gave the impression of knowing what his best team was. It was his downfall in the end because the close team spirit he worked so hard to create [at Leeds] was impossible to generate as the faces changed so much. If he had gone about the England job like he did at Leeds, I am certain he would have been a big success.'

The press began to turn against Revie, as did the architect of Ramsey's downfall at the FA, Harold Thompson. The final straw was the 2-1 defeat to Scotland at Wembley on 4 June 1977, a famous win for the visitors that ended with a pitch invasion by the Tartan Army and the indelible image of the Wembley goal frame buckling under the weight of delirious Scottish fans. Behind the scenes, the FA began plotting against Revie and reportedly targeted Ipswich manager Bobby Robson as his replacement. On 12 July, however, the *Daily Mail* ran the front-page headline 'Revie Quits Over Aggro', and the sensation of the England manager's clandestine negotiations with the United Arab Emirates became the biggest story of the summer. The indiscretions landed Revie with a ten-year ban from English football for bringing the game into disrepute, although he successfully overturned this in court.

Ron Greenwood, the long-time West Ham United manager and former secretary of the FA, was installed as caretaker manager for the three remaining matches in 1977, including the all-important final World Cup qualifiers away to Luxembourg and at home to Italy. Greenwood oversaw victories in both these games, but England agonisingly finished second in the group on goal difference. The 1966 world champions' second successive failure to qualify for the World Cup was sealed.

West Germany qualified for the 1978 World Cup in Argentina as holders, meanwhile, which meant that the *Nationalmannschaft* played no UEFA or FIFA competition matches during the 1976/77 and 1977/78 seasons. At the European Championship finals in Yugoslavia in 1976, Schön's side overcame the hosts in the semi-final with a 4-2 win in extra time, having trailed 2-0 after an hour. It was a dream debut for the Köln striker Dieter Müller, who scored a hat-trick after coming on as a substitute with only ten minutes remaining in normal time. 'We have a new Müller!' exclaimed *Kicker*. In the final against Czechoslovakia on 20 June, West Germany again went 2-0 down before mounting a comeback with goals from Müller and Hölzenbein. As their predecessors had famously done at previous tournaments, Schön's men scored a last-minute equaliser to force extra time. West Germany were building on a reputation for resilience, which at this championship gave rise to descriptions of the team as a 'machine' in the international press.

Remarkably, just five days before the final, the participating nations had decided against a replay in the event of a draw after 120 minutes, meaning that the winner would be determined by a penalty shoot-out. This was the first such event in the European Championship or World Cup, and that is not the only reason it will always be remembered. After Hoeneß became the first player to miss when he blazed the ball over the crossbar, Czechoslovakia just needed to convert their last of five regulation penalties to win. The player who stepped up to assume this daunting responsibility was the Bohemians Praha midfielder Antonín Panenka, whose impudent chipped finish over Maier has entered the footballing vernacular as the 'Panenka penalty', replicated by players around the world. More importantly, it won his country the 1976 European Championship. The Henri Delauney trophy was lifted by a player wearing the white of West Germany in Belgrade that evening, yet only because the Czechoslovak players had to a man swapped shirts with their opponents at the conclusion of a hard-fought and high-quality final.

In the 1976/77 season, the West German national team passed important milestones in terms of personnel, namely the debut of FC Bayern forward Karl-Heinz Rummenigge on 6 October 1976, and the 103rd and final international appearance by Franz Beckenbauer on 23 February 1977. Although Schön was still in charge, this period arguably marks the transition between the much-admired European and world champions of 1972 and 1974 and the new, hard-nosed generation that won another major title but few friends.

In club football, the 1976/77 season represents the high-water mark of Borussia Mönchengladbach's golden decade. While rivals FC Bayern struggled again, Gladbach won a third successive Bundesliga title, their Danish striker Allan Simonsen won the Ballon d'Or, and a successful season in the European Cup culminated in the competition's second Anglo-German final in Rome. Both Gladbach and Liverpool were appearing in their first European Cup Final after dominating their domestic leagues in recent seasons, and Liverpool took to the field just four days after an FA Cup Final defeat to Manchester United that dashed hopes of an unprecedented league, cup and European treble.

Nine players in Bob Paisley's starting line-up were English, including Clemence, Hughes, Keegan, and the veteran of the 1966 World Cup squad Ian Callaghan. The as-yet uncapped midfielder Terry McDermott opened the scoring in the first half, and Simonsen equalised for Gladbach shortly after the interval. Veteran defender Tommy Smith – of whom Bill Shankly once said he 'wasn't born, he was quarried' – restored Liverpool's lead midway through the second half with a header from a corner, and in the final stages the latest in a series of penalty appeals was met with the referee's assent, for a foul on Keegan by Vogts. The spot kick was converted by full-back Phil Neal, who would go on to become an England regular under Greenwood. Liverpool became the second English club to win the European Cup, consolidating an era of domestic dominance and European success under Paisley that eventually comprised six league titles and four major European trophies between 1976 and 1983. Gladbach won their second UEFA Cup in 1979, beating Manchester City in the quarter-final, but to this day the club has not won another league title. Defeat to Liverpool in Rome signalled the beginning of the end of the glory days under managers Hennes Weisweiler and Udo Lattek in the 1970s.

22 February 1978
West Germany 2-1 England
Olympiastadion, Munich

The 1977 European Cup Final was Keegan's last game for Liverpool. A week later, he sensationally signed for Hamburger

SV, the new Cup Winners' Cup champions following a 2-0 win over Anderlecht in Amsterdam. The club's £500,000 record transfer was the stratagem of their ambitious general manager Peter Krohn, who revolutionised HSV in the mid-1970s. Over the following three seasons, they reached the next level, winning the Bundesliga title in 1979 and finishing runners-up to Nottingham Forest in the European Cup in 1980, while Keegan became a double European Footballer of the Year for 1978 and 1979. He had already played 29 times for England by the end of his Liverpool career and won three more caps on the South American tour in the summer of 1977, which turned out to be a redundant preparatory exercise for the World Cup in Argentina. Keegan made his third appearance under the new England manager in the match against West Germany in Munich in February 1978. Greenwood had returned the captaincy to Hughes, but he was in no doubt that he needed to build a team around the Bundesliga's biggest star.

For England, this first match of 1978 was another new beginning. 'The true significance of England's failure to qualify for the World Cup,' wrote Saunders ahead of the game, 'is demonstrated by their role tonight, as sparring partners in what amounts to a work-out for the champions.' Most troublingly for English fans, Schön reportedly 'thought that meeting England was good preparation for the possibility of playing against Scotland in Argentina'. The England team featured three Liverpool players in Clemence, Neal and Hughes, and the Chelsea midfielder Ray Wilkins, who won his 11th cap at the age of 21. West Germany fielded three players from the Köln side that was well on its way to winning a famous league and cup double: left-back Herbert Zimmermann, midfielder Herbert Neumann, and the club captain and regular international Heinz Flohe. FC Bayern's Rummenigge won his ninth cap alongside Hölzenbein and the youngster Rüdiger Abramczik in the forward line. Schalke's Klaus Fischer, the established centre-forward after 1977, was missing due to illness, as was manager Schön.

West Germany's 2-1 win in Munich was snatched from the jaws of defeat, and was described on all sides as somewhat fortuitous. England took a deserved lead at the end of the first half, after Wilkins picked out the advancing Neal on the right flank with a lofted pass. Neal fed the ball to Manchester United's Steve Coppell, who looked for his club-mate Stuart Pearson in the penalty area with a high cross. The number nine rose high above Schalke defender Rolf Rüßmann and his looping header dropped into Maier's net. As the second half kicked off, commentator David Coleman made reference to the previous day's 'B' international in Augsburg, in which England had prevailed:

'Certainly our performance in the last 48 hours has increased the standing of English football by some amount. There was a feeling on the continent that we were dead and buried, but we've shown, both in the "B" international yesterday and in the first half of this match today, that we still have something to say in football terms.'

With 15 minutes remaining and West Germany still labouring, Schön replaced the ineffective Hölzenbein in attack with the MSV Duisburg striker Ronald Worm, who had scored in that match between the second-string sides in Augsburg the previous evening. In his first involvement here, Worm played a neat one-two with fellow substitute and club-mate Bernard Dietz and then struck a low left-footed shot past a wrong-footed Clemence, who should easily have made the save. 'Perhaps England were still dazed by that disappointment,' wrote Saunders, 'when they conceded the winner seven minutes later.' Manchester City defender Dave Watson fouled substitute Manfred Burgsmüller on the edge of the penalty area, and the Austrian referee Franz Wöhrer made every effort to ensure that the five-man England defensive wall stood at least ten yards from the ball. Yet as Wöhrer was still busy giving instructions, Bonhof took his chance and struck the free kick hard and low around the wall to the far side of Clemence. England's protests fell on deaf ears, and Greenwood acknowledged that it was a lapse of concentration that had cost them.

Norman Fox in *The Times* summed up the mood of the underwhelmed spectators in Munich, 'As an indication of the crowd's dissatisfaction, they gave Keegan more appreciation when he left the field with cramp than their own team at the end.' The German press was more generous in its assessment, with Heimann applauding the fighting spirit that West Germany showed when threatened with defeat. He also praised England's playing style under Greenwood, 'They built their game up from defence with many variations, let the ball run and used the space skilfully with clever passes.'

1978 FIFA World Cup
Argentina

West Germany's successful era under Helmut Schön came to an end at the World Cup in Argentina, where the team played six matches but could only win one. Having first lost his linchpin Beckenbauer to the fleeting glamour of the North American Soccer League in 1977, the absence of *der Kaiser* from the World Cup was confirmed at a DFB meeting in Munich around the England match in February. 'A comeback from Beckenbauer would only have made sense if he could participate in all our preparation matches, but [New York] Cosmos would not allow it,' explained DFB president Hermann Neuberger.

Heimann had remarked after the England game that the biggest concern ahead of the tournament was the lack of a personality that was capable of organising play and exerting a positive influence on the team. This was painfully evident in the goalless draw against Poland, remembered in the *Chronicle of German Football* as 'one of the most boring opening matches in World Cup history'. A 6-0 win over Mexico followed, with Rummenigge brought into the attack and scoring twice, but the Mexicans had lost their first match to Tunisia and represented weak opposition. After two more goalless draws, against Tunisia and, more predictably, the obdurate Italians, West Germany faced the Netherlands in the second group phase in a much-anticipated repeat of the 1974 final. Arie Haan and René van de Kerkhof scored two brilliant equalisers for the eventual finalists and the game ended 2-2, but relations between the two teams deteriorated further when substitute Dick Nanninga was sent off for dissent.

Despite the poor results, West Germany still stood a chance of qualifying for the final as they took the field in the city of Córdoba for the last time in the second group phase. At the least, the team was expected to progress to the third-place play-off – a fitting farewell match for Schön, who before the tournament had already announced his forthcoming departure. In Austria, it suffices merely to utter the word 'Córdoba' to raise a smile and conjure memories of the match which followed. The radio commentary from the Austrian commentator Edi Finger, who screamed the dialect-inflected phrase *'I werd' narrisch!'* ('I'm going crazy!') in response to Hans Krankl's late, winning goal, has since become a cornerstone of Austrian popular culture. The 3-2 upset was the country's first win against its neighbour in 47 years. In German football, it is remembered simply as *die Schmach von Córdoba*, or the disgrace of Córdoba, and it brought the curtain down on Schön's 14-year tenure as manager of the *Nationalmannschaft*.

9

Angstgegner
1982–1990

On 1 October 1982 a vote of no confidence in Chancellor Helmut Schmidt was carried in the Bundestag, and a conservative-liberal coalition headed by CDU leader Helmut Kohl was voted into power. The collapse of Schmidt's government thus represents the end of the social-liberal era in West Germany. 'The self-image and self-perception of society in the Federal Republic had altered unmistakably' during the 1970s, explained German historian Ulrich Herbert. 'It had become more Western, more European, more liberal and also more inclined to the Left.'

Yet at the beginning of the 1980s, the destabilisation of the world economy after the oil crises of 1973 and 1979, the intensification of the Cold War, and the forces of deindustrialisation and globalisation all gave rise to a collective anxiety that contrasted markedly with the optimism of 1972. Britain had crossed the political rubicon three years earlier, at the 1979 general election. According to the historian Kenneth Morgan, the 1970s in Britain 'marked a peak in egalitarianism before things fell away under the social injustices of the Thatcher era'. Moreover, great progress had been made in relation to Europe, and to Britain's place in the world, with Edward Heath's original decision to join the European Communities vindicated by an unprecedented nationwide referendum in 1975, in which over 67 per cent of votes were in favour of membership. The referendum was called by Harold Wilson, who had returned to power after winning the 1974 election. Although 'agnostic' on the European question, Wilson was keen to settle debates within his party and consolidate his authority, much as David Cameron would aim to do four decades later, although with starkly different results.

Wilson retired in April 1976 and was succeeded by his Foreign Secretary Jim Callaghan, who developed a good relationship with Schmidt. Achievements in international diplomacy were undermined, however, by domestic strife. The government's income restraint policy to battle inflation had led to increased opposition from trade unions, culminating in the so-called Winter of Discontent of 1978/79. When the public service unions took action, the whole country was affected by the strikes. Refuse went uncollected, petrol stations closed, and even burials were suspended. In January, the prime minister returned from an international summit in Guadeloupe, where Schmidt was also present, and rebuffed suggestions that Britain was in chaos. The front page of *The Sun* on the following day carried the headline 'Crisis? What Crisis? Rail, lorry, jobs chaos – and Jim blames the Press'.

The leader of the opposition was Margaret Thatcher, who now sensed an opportunity and addressed the nation in a party political broadcast. At the end of March she tabled a vote of no confidence that was carried by just a single vote, and in the ensuing general election on 3 May 1979 the Conservatives won a 44-seat majority. A new era had officially begun, but the first three years of Thatcher's premiership were very different to those that followed and for which she is remembered. In 1975 she had favoured staying in the Common Market, but as prime minister she now railed against the £1bn cost of membership and became 'increasingly suspicious of the unelected and unaccountable Brussels bureaucracy'. This was a patriotic stance which won support for Thatcher in the popular press at a time when the economy was still in dire straits. At the European Council in Dublin in November 1979, she made a lasting impression on Chancellor Schmidt, who later recalled her insistent demands of a rebate for Britain, 'After Margaret Thatcher had said for the third time that she wanted her money back – she actually said, "my money" – we postponed the whole issue. We did not want to be treated for hours as if we were the enemies of Great Britain.' The summit redoubled

Thatcher's aversion to French and German domination of the European Community, and she turned instead towards transatlantic diplomacy with the United States, particularly after the election in November 1980 of Ronald Reagan, with whom she enjoyed a close relationship.

A month earlier, Thatcher had famously proclaimed that 'the lady's not for turning', with reference to her government's economic liberalism that caused a damaging recession and soaring unemployment. Rioting followed in cities across the country in 1981, most notably in Brixton, south London, and in Toxteth, Liverpool. By late 1981, the Conservatives faced the worst poll ratings of any government since 1945, and the chances of a second term for Thatcher were slim. It was Argentina's invasion of the Falkland Islands in April 1982 which gave the prime minister a much-needed opportunity to transform her public image and political fortunes. The ensuing conflict ended in Argentinian surrender on 14 June 1982, and Thatcher had set the tone for an uncompromising decade in power.

* * *

England's qualification campaign for the 1980 UEFA European Championship in Italy was marked by sparkling performances from the two-time European Footballer of the Year Kevin Keegan, who scored seven goals in seven games. Ron Greenwood observed that since moving to the Bundesliga, his captain had 'met and overcome the challenges of playing abroad. This has made him a better man, as well as a better player.' A month before the tournament, England recorded an impressive 3-1 win at Wembley over world champions Argentina, who fielded a 19-year-old Diego Maradona. In Turin on 12 June, however, optimism around the team dissipated in air thick with tear gas, as England's first appearance for a decade at an international tournament was marred by crowd violence. Not for the last time by any means, the England manager was left to make a plea to the fans, 'Please will you behave yourselves. You are damaging the chances of the England team and the reputation of English football.' Greenwood separately told Italian journalists of his feelings towards rioting fans, 'I wish they would all be put in a boat and dropped in the ocean.'

Lamentably, this was just the start of a troubled decade in which the England team became – for all the wrong reasons – every other nation's *Angstgegner*, or feared opponent. While the extensive security measures for the subsequent match against Italy proved largely effective, England's hopes of winning the championship were dashed by a 1-0 defeat in a high-quality game. On the West German side, the long-time assistant manager Jupp Derwall replaced Helmut Schön, just as Schön had followed Sepp Herberger in 1964. At the championship in Italy, Derwall's team extended a record-breaking run of consecutive victories against the Netherlands in Naples, where a hat-trick from Fortuna Düsseldorf striker Klaus Allofs proved enough to withstand a late Dutch rally. The match is also significant as the international debut of Borussia Mönchengladbach midfielder Lothar Matthäus, the future captain and world champion who would play his last match all of 20 years later.

Derwall's side was built around Karl-Heinz Rummenigge, exceptionally the only representative of FC Bayern in the national team. Harald 'Toni' Schumacher of 1. FC Köln was a fixture in goal from 1980. Alongside Rummenigge and Allofs in attack, in the absence of the injured Klaus Fischer, was the 30-year-old Hamburg centre-forward Horst Hrubesch, a team-mate of Keegan at Branko Zebec's Hamburger SV. Hrubesch was a half-time substitute in the 1980 European Cup Final in Madrid, where Hamburg lost by a single goal to Brian Clough's Nottingham Forest. On 22 June in Rome, he quickly made up for this disappointment, winning the European Championship Final for West Germany against Belgium with a headed goal just two minutes from time. The goal displayed the striker's formidable aerial ability that earned him the nickname *das Kopfballungeheuer*, or 'the beast of heading'.

The beginning of the 1980s further demonstrated the dominance of English and West German teams in European club competition. Forest's win over Hamburg was the third of four Anglo-German European Cup finals between 1975 and 1982, and it brought the fourth successive title for an English club. Borussia Mönchengladbach had won a second UEFA Cup in 1979 and thereby qualified for the following edition despite a mid-table finish in the Bundesliga. Remarkably, all four semi-finalists of the 1979/80 UEFA Cup were Bundesliga clubs, with Eintracht Frankfurt beating FC Bayern, and Gladbach overcoming VfB Stuttgart. Frankfurt won their first European trophy on the away goals rule, following a 3-2 defeat in Mönchengladbach and a 1-0 win in the Waldstadion.

In the 1980/81 season, an Anglo-German semi-final in the UEFA Cup saw Bobby Robson's Ipswich Town beat 1. FC Köln, with the emerging England defender Terry Butcher scoring the only goal of the second leg in Germany. On the losing side was the England striker Tony Woodcock. The former Nottingham Forest player had made an impression on Köln manager Hennes Weisweiler in the European Cup semi-final between the clubs in April 1979, and he signed for Köln that summer. FC Bayern, meanwhile, experienced three years of upheaval between 1976 and 1979, finishing as low as 12th in the 1977/78 Bundesliga. Gerd Müller followed Franz Beckenbauer to the North American Soccer League, and Uli Hoeneß and Sepp Maier were both forced to retire due to injury, the latter because of a serious car accident in July 1979.

On a positive note, World Cup winner Paul Breitner had rejoined FC Bayern in 1978 and formed a formidable partnership with Rummenigge that sparked the club's recovery. The 1980/81 season was the high point for the duo affectionately nicknamed *Breitnigge*, as Bayern won the battle with Hamburg for the Bundesliga title and reached the semi-finals of the European Cup, losing to eventual winners Liverpool on the away goals rule. Breitner was voted German Footballer of the Year for 1981 and also finished runner-up to Rummenigge in the voting for the Ballon d'Or. Boosted by Breitner's return to the national team at Derwall's persuasion in April 1981, West Germany enjoyed a flawless qualification campaign for the 1982 World Cup. The success of *Breitnigge* at club level was effectively transmuted to the national team, where the pair combined with prolific goalscorer Fischer.

1982 FIFA World Cup
Spain

Derwall's win percentage of almost 66 per cent from his six-year tenure remains the highest of any German national team manager in history. Statistics do not tell the full story, however, and two incidents either side of a turgid scoreless draw with England in Madrid on 29 June 1982 are emblematic of the cold-blooded, ruthless and widely disfavoured West Germany team under Derwall's leadership between 1978 and 1984.

The first occurred in the northern Spanish city of Gijón four days before, where West Germany faced Austria in the final match of the first group phase. Derwall's side had only two points after a surprising defeat to Algeria in their first match and a good response against Chile that included a Rummenigge hat-trick. Austria had won both their matches and needed only to avoid defeat by three or more goals to secure their passage to the second phase, having seen Algeria beat Chile 3-2 the previous day. After Hrubesch put West Germany ahead ten minutes into the game, the two teams settled into a pattern of sideways passing and running down the clock towards a result that would allow both teams to progress. Algerian fans in the stands protested and waved banknotes at photographers to express their indignation at the suspected corruption on show. Derided in Spain as *El Anschluss*, and known in German as *der Nichtangriffspakt von Gijón*, or the non-aggression pact of Gijón, the game has gone down in history as one of German – and Austrian – football's darkest days.

It is important to note that while Derwall and his players were unrepentant in the face of heavy criticism following the match, German fans, ex-professionals, broadcast commentators and the press all voiced their disapproval. While Breitner labelled the crowd 'stupid' for failing to understand that progress to the next round was all that mattered to the team, and although Dr Hans Tschak, head of the Austrian delegation, was guilty of the most contemptuous, racist remarks towards the Algerians imaginable, there were many others who quickly understood the enormous price this match had cost German and Austrian football. Writing in *Kicker* after the match, Werner-Johannes Müller offered his view of the players' conduct, 'The almost icy coldness with which the German players brushed off the criticism of the 42,000 spectators in the stadium, as if it all long since doesn't affect them any more, was shocking!'

England arrived in Spain to play in the World Cup finals for the first time in 12 years following a tortuous qualifying campaign that included defeats in Bucharest, Basel, and most notably Oslo in September 1981. It was on that occasion that the commentator Bjørge Lillelien unforgettably greeted Norway's 2-1 win over England with the words 'Maggie Thatcher, can you hear me? Maggie Thatcher … your boys took a hell of a beating!' A subsequent 1-0 win over Hungary at Wembley in November was only just enough for England to secure qualification to the expanded 24-team World Cup. However, an upturn in form in the new year, together with the sixth successive European Cup win by an English club in May, when Aston Villa beat FC Bayern 1-0 in Rotterdam, meant that there was some optimism around English football ahead of the tournament. The national mood was buoyant too, since victory in the Falkland Islands was declared a mere two days before England's opening match in Spain.

The squad included talented individuals, such as the dynamic Manchester United midfielder Bryan Robson, Tottenham Hotspur's mercurial Glenn Hoddle, and striker Trevor Francis, who famously became British football's first million-pound player when he moved from struggling Birmingham City to Nottingham Forest in February 1979. In Munich's Olympiastadion on 30 May that year, Francis provided the crowning moment of one of English football's greatest achievements when he scored the goal that won Forest their first European Cup, a mere two seasons after promotion to the First Division under Brian Clough. The 1-0 win over Swedish club Malmö was Francis's first game in the competition, having been ineligible for European football for three months following his transfer.

With Robson and Francis in the starting XI, and Hoddle on the bench, England made a dream start to the 1982 World Cup. Robson scored in the first minute of the opening match against Michel Hidalgo's France, and he added another in the second half after Gérard Soler had equalised. Ipswich striker Paul Mariner completed an impressive 3-1 win a few minutes from time. Francis scored England's opener in a 2-0 win over a poor Czechoslovakia side, and he also scored the only goal in the final group match against Kuwait. Greenwood's team thus advanced to the second stage to play West Germany and Spain in a three-team group played out in Madrid, the scene of significant English victories in the past.

29 June 1982
FIFA World Cup second group stage
West Germany 0-0 England
Santiago Bernabéu, Madrid

The versatile Gladbach player Uli Stielike followed in the footsteps of Breitner and Günter Netzer when in 1977 he signed for Real Madrid, where he subsequently became a fans' favourite. It was on Stielike's suggestion that the West German players each threw five red carnations into the crowd ahead of the match against England in *Los Blancos'* famous Santiago Bernabéu Stadium, as a belated apology for the disgrace of Gijón four days earlier. Any neutral spectators would likely have preferred a display of enterprising and attacking football as a conciliatory gesture, but they had to content themselves with flowers. The negativity on show was partially attributable to the competition format, since both teams knew that defeat would likely render progress to the semi-finals impossible.

Derwall made three changes to account for the special circumstances, bringing in the Stuttgart pair Bernd Förster and Hansi Müller in midfield to nullify Coppell and Wilkins. Felix Magath and the diminutive young Köln winger Pierre Littbarski were the more attacking players who made way. Uwe Reinders, with just a few minutes of international experience to his name, replaced Hrubesch up front, and Rummenigge played with a muscle injury he had also carried in the games against Chile and Austria. It was a limited, deliberately defensive line-up, and Derwall duly made three changes again for the next game against Spain. For Greenwood, the biggest problem was the absence of Keegan due to a persistent back complaint, but with Coppell, Wilkins, Robson and Francis all in the side there was nonetheless ample goalscoring intent and ability.

England's best chance of the first half fell to Robson, but his looping header from ten yards was just kept out by an athletic save from Schumacher. Two minutes later, the labouring Rummenigge arrived a split second too late to divert a teasing cross from Breitner past Peter Shilton, and the ball flashed across the face of goal untouched. West Germany's only shot at goal in the first half came from Breitner, who beat Phil Thompson on the left flank and unleashed a fierce, curving effort from a narrow angle that Shilton parried away at his near post.

Notably in the second half, three substitutes were introduced – Littbarski and Fischer for West Germany, and Woodcock for England – who all represented 1. FC Köln. The game's most memorable moment, however, came just four minutes from full time from its most high-profile player, the European Footballer of the Year. Fed by Stielike in England's half, Rummenigge turned into space and hit a powerful, rising shot from 30 yards that beat Shilton with its swerve but hit the crossbar and rebounded all the way back to its originator, such was the force of the strike. 'It could have put England out of the World Cup if it had been six inches or so lower,' remarked commentator Martin Tyler. The best articulated summary of this disappointing match came from Stuart Jones on the eve of the teams' next encounter, when he wrote that it had been 'rendered sterile by the cold steel of *Angst*'.

After West Germany then beat the hosts 2-1 with goals from the restored Littbarski and Fischer, England knew that a win by two clear goals against Spain was needed to progress to the semi-finals. Yet Greenwood was still unable to start two of his most important creative players, Keegan and Trevor Brooking, and Coppell was now ruled out with a knee injury. The big question once again was where to find the necessary goals. Stuart Jones in *The Times* noted that 'the Germans had waited patiently until the second half before taking the initiative' against Spain, and after a toothless first half the hope for England was that the introduction of Keegan and Brooking just after the hour mark would turn the game in a similar manner.

These were sadly the only minutes Keegan ever played in a World Cup, but he came agonisingly close to opening the scoring and giving England every chance to extend their Spanish sojourn. Twenty minutes still remained when Robson's cross from the bye-line found Keegan unmarked on the edge of the six-yard box, and the former Hamburg star, now at Southampton, inexplicably headed well past the post. 'I couldn't believe it when it went wide,' said Keegan afterwards. 'No excuses, I should have buried the chance. It would have been some game then.' As it was, a second successive goalless draw showed that England's supposed advantage of knowing exactly what was required of them before their final match was an illusion. Indeed, Donald Saunders in the *Daily Telegraph* thought that 'the added need to win by two clear goals obviously inhibited them'.

With the business of the second phase concluded, and a semi-final between France and West Germany in Seville now confirmed, Derwall continued his efforts to restore relations with the public, 'After the first half I was afraid the English would attack flat out. I had cold feet until the last seconds. We owe it to the Spanish team and the Spanish crowd to be back in Madrid for the final.' Not all his players had received the memo, however, as revealed by an extraordinary *Kicker* report of Breitner's arrogance in a press conference that followed West Germany's fortunate progress to the semi-finals. In front of one of the best German World Cup reporters, Breitner even asked what such a 'mediocre journalist' could still have to write about. The reporter responded, 'I too have been asking myself for weeks what a mediocre player like you is doing at a World Cup.'

* * *

The semi-final between West Germany and France on 8 July 1982 at the Estadio Ramón Sánchez-Pizjuán is known in both countries as 'the Night of Seville'. It was one of the most extraordinary World Cup matches in history, and despite defeat, French captain Michel Platini remembers it as his 'most beautiful game', adding, 'What happened in those two hours encapsulated all the sentiments of life itself.' As with West Germany's unforgettable World Cup semi-final against Italy in 1970, the match ended 1-1 after 90 minutes and a flurry of goals were scored in extra time, but now the heightened drama of the first World Cup penalty shoot-out was added to the equation.

The key moment, however, which drew Derwall's team further into ignominy and compounded the damage done in Gijón, came after an hour had been played. French substitute Patrick Battiston had come on to replace Bernard Genghini just ten minutes earlier and now found himself advancing on goal in the path of a characteristically effective defence-splitting pass from Platini. Battiston just managed to connect with the ball on the edge of the penalty area, but he was instantaneously struck down by an appalling challenge – in truth, an assault – from the onrushing Schumacher. The goalkeeper was not even booked as Battiston lay unconscious on the ground with broken bones and two lost teeth, and the fallout of the incident in the following days even exercised Chancellor Schmidt's diplomatic skills.

A resurgent, incensed French side scored two brilliant goals in the first half of extra time to put the game seemingly out of reach. The injured Rummenigge, who had taken the decision not to play unless his team were in arrears, came on as a substitute just moments before Alain Giresse gave France a 3-1 lead. Rummenigge quickly initiated a West German recovery, picking the ball up in the centre circle and combining with Stielike and Littbarski in a flowing move that ended with a poacher's finish from the FC Bayern star just six yards from goal. In the second half of extra time, Fischer scored with a memorable overhead kick from the same distance after Hrubesch headed a deep Littbarski cross back across goal. Although Stielike was first to miss in the subsequent shoot-out, West Germany prevailed after Schumacher, the villain of the piece, saved Maxime Bossis's penalty. This was the first of four successful World Cup penalty shoot-outs for the German national team, and at the time of writing, their record in such circumstances remains unblemished by defeat.

In Madrid on 11 July, Breitner became only the third player in history to score in two different World Cup finals, but it was a mere consolation goal after Italy, the surprise vanquishers of Brazil, had taken a 3-0 lead through goals from Paolo Rossi, Marco Tardelli and Alessandro Altobelli. West Germany's World Cup record against their Italian *Angstgegner* now stood at two group-stage draws and two painful defeats, and another 24 years would pass before a chance to make amends materialised on home soil in 2006.

13 October 1982
England 1-2 West Germany
Wembley Stadium

The FA delegation was still in Madrid when chairman Bert Millichip announced Bobby Robson as successor to the retiring

Ron Greenwood, just two days after England's elimination from the World Cup. Robson had already been considered during the last days of Don Revie's tenure in 1977, when Greenwood was preferred. In the interim, he led Ipswich to an FA Cup Final win over Arsenal in 1978 and to the UEFA Cup trophy in 1981.

As the new England manager he was given a wider remit than his predecessor, with responsibility for the national coaching structure as well as the first team. Robson's first match in charge came in September, away to Denmark in the qualifying group for the 1984 UEFA European Championship. His decision to omit Kevin Keegan from the squad caused a sensation. The player, who had signed for Newcastle United at the start of the season, was offended that he first heard of the snub through the media, and the ensuing fallout with Robson meant that Keegan's England career was over at the age of 31, with 63 caps and 21 international goals. Trevor Francis scored twice in Copenhagen, but a late Danish equaliser meant that England's qualification campaign got off to a disappointing start.

For Robson's second match, his first at Wembley, England welcomed West Germany for a friendly international on 13 October. It was a significant week in the history of Anglo-German football contests, since on the previous evening, in Bremen, England's under-21 side under Dave Sexton won the third edition of the biennial UEFA European Under-21 Championship against its German counterpart, managed by Berti Vogts. The young England team had a 3-1 lead from the first leg in Sheffield and scored first at the Weserstadion to extend their advantage, but the star of the match was Littbarski, who scored a thrilling hat-trick that gave his team the chance to draw level in the tie. However, England's two goals on the night capped an 'indomitable performance' that saw them win the first of two successive European under-21 titles. Littbarski's personal reward was a trip to Wembley to play for the first team as a substitute just 24 hours later.

The West German senior squad arrived in London plagued by controversy and discord. Ahead of the previous international, a goalless draw with Belgium in Munich, DFB president Hermann Neuberger had caused a stir when he stated in an interview that the manager would leave his post after the 1986

World Cup, which Derwall immediately refuted. Rummenigge then followed in Beckenbauer's footsteps and attempted to take control, organising a vote among the players and making their support for Derwall public. In London, Rummenigge gave his thoughts on the issue of player conduct, and in particular the suggestion that the DFB would have a say in players' commercial activities, 'My advertising contracts are entirely my business. I would consider it an unreasonable invasion of privacy if the DFB involved itself in those matters.'

As they had been before West Germany's historic first win at Wembley in 1972, expectations were low, and relations with the press, public, and even the DFB, were worse still. This was the first of eight consecutive away internationals over the next 12 months, and *Kicker* jocosely suggested, 'You can't blame Derwall and his players for being happy to escape the troubles and hostilities at home.' The manager also had to make do without Stielike, Bernd Schuster and Hansi Müller, who played their club football in Spain and Italy, and he thus called upon the inexperienced Matthäus in midfield. A fit-again Rummenigge once again represented West Germany's greatest hope. Robson, meanwhile, lost his namesake Bryan to injury but fielded six others from the team that faced West Germany in Madrid. They were joined by five inexperienced players with five caps or fewer, including the debutant Gary Mabbutt. The versatile Tottenham Hotspur player was to play as a defensive midfielder alongside Wilkins, but instead made his debut at right-back as a late replacement for the injured Viv Anderson. Mabbutt 'entered the international stage almost with a swagger' and came close to making a dream start to his England career when a clearance dropped for him around 25 yards from goal, and his powerful left-footed half-volley struck the post.

Midway through the second half, England were given a warning of what was to come when Allofs found Rummenigge with an incisive through ball, but the FC Bayern star shot over the bar. A few minutes later the captain made amends with a splendid opening goal, neatly combining with the newly arrived Littbarski and then chipping Shilton with an audacious finish. Littbarski was then too much for Mabbutt to handle on England's right, and the Köln winger provided another accurate cross in a move that recalled the Night of Seville, with Rummenigge again beating his marker to the ball on the edge of the six-yard box to score. It had been 'a late but devastating demonstration of how to make chances into goals'. England substitute Woodcock scored a late consolation, but West Germany had done enough to claim their second Wembley win, a feat that no other nation from outside Britain had yet achieved.

A sour note to the evening for Derwall was the serious injury sustained by VfB Stuttgart defender Karlheinz Förster in an early challenge with Wilkins. Förster, the younger brother of his team-mate for club and country Bernd, was voted German Footballer of the Year for 1982 and was a player Derwall could ill afford to lose at this time. Without him in Belfast a month later, West Germany lost 1-0 to Northern Ireland in a qualifying match for the 1984 UEFA European Championship. After he was replaced by Hamburger SV *libero* Holger Hieronymus at Wembley, the team quickly had to readjust, with debutant Gerd Strack vacating the sweeper position to take up Förster's job of marking Paul Mariner. This was not an unfamiliar assignment for Strack, who had faced Mariner in the UEFA Cup semi-final between 1. FC Köln and Ipswich two seasons before. Nonetheless, the early change to personnel caused West Germany to play within themselves in the first half, avoiding any risks. Bobby Robson was consequently able to conclude that 'for the first hour we were the much better side', but he conceded that England were unable to match their opponents during the last half an hour.

In the English press there was criticism for Robson's experimental team selection and late substitutions. 'To ask such an inexperienced crew, with an average of only 21 caps, to subdue the Germans, with eventually eight of the side that reached the World Cup Final, for an hour must have been beyond the hopes of Mr Robson,' wrote Stuart Jones in *The Times*. Referring to the manager's triple substitution with nine minutes remaining, Frank McGhee in the *Daily Mirror* lamented what he saw as a 'desperate late gamble in an attempt to rescue a match which looked hopelessly out of England's reach'.

* * *

One of Robson's trio of late substitutes at Wembley was the Jamaican-born Watford striker Luther Blissett, who that night became the fifth black player to appear for England. Ron Greenwood had made Anderson the England national team's first black footballer in the 1-0 win over Czechoslovakia on 29 November 1978, before overseeing the short international career of Laurie Cunningham, who became the first English player to move to Real Madrid in 1979. Cunningham's erstwhile West Bromwich Albion team-mate Cyrille Regis, the player whom Blissett replaced on the field, was the third of three black players selected by Greenwood.

As David Goldblatt put it, these players had to contend with abuse that 'sprang effortlessly from a ready-made vocabulary of invective and a deep historical reservoir of ignorance and prejudice'.

Although the *Nationalmannschaft* had crossed the milestone earlier, with Erwin Kostedde in 1974 and the Hamburg midfielder Jimmy Hartwig in 1979, the wealth of talent England could now call upon from among second-generation immigrants in Britain was a fascination for German observers. On occasions the language used to express such interest was questionable, as with the headline for Arthur Rotmil's profile of the new England manager in *Kicker*, 'Robson sieht für England schwarz.' The phrase *schwarz sehen*, or 'seeing black', has negative connotations of pessimism in the same way that 'seeing red' denotes aggression, making it an infelicitous choice for an article which ponders a bright future for black English footballers under Robson's management.

Of the 12 black players eventually given their England debut by Robson, the biggest impact was made by Jamaican-born John Barnes, who moved to London at the age of 12 and began his professional career with Watford. After his England debut in Belfast on 28 May 1983, Barnes famously scored against Brazil in the Maracanã in Rio de Janeiro on a summer tour in 1984. In 1987 he joined Liverpool, where he won two league championships and two FA Cups, and in 1988 and 1990 he was voted the Football Writers' Association Player of the Year.

* * *

Margaret Thatcher's 11 years in power from 1979 to 1990 align fairly neatly, and not without cause, with English football's great depression, from the groundswell of violence in the late 1970s to the Taylor Report resulting from the Hillsborough disaster. The *annus horribilis* was 1985, when one of the worst incidents of stadium violence, at an FA Cup sixth-round match between Luton Town and Millwall on 13 March, prompted Thatcher to set up a task force to address football hooliganism.

On 11 May, 56 people lost their lives in the Bradford City stadium fire, when an antiquated wooden stand was engulfed in flames and spectators were trapped without means to escape. Less than three weeks later, on 29 May in Brussels, 39 people were killed in the Heysel Stadium disaster at the European Cup Final between Juventus and Liverpool. A skirmish by Liverpool fans from their designated area of the stadium into an adjacent neutral section that housed many expatriate Juventus fans ended in disaster when a dilapidated retaining wall collapsed and people were crushed to death. Heysel was a nightmare combination of the kind of hooliganism seen in Luton and the type of inadequacies and neglect which caused the Bradford fire, and it happened on the biggest stage in front of an international audience. David Goldblatt offered a measured articulation of the factors involved at what he calls the 'moral ground zero' of European football:

'The culpability of these Liverpool fans at Heysel is not in question, nor can their behaviour be viewed with anything other than disapproval. However, the genesis of their actions had a wider context and their actions could only have mutated into a grotesque killing field with the help of others' disastrous decisions and unforgivable neglect.'

At 6am local time the next day, FA chairman Bert Millichip received a call from the British ambassador to Mexico. Millichip had only arrived in Mexico City the previous evening for a post-season tour with the national team, but now he was summoned to London to answer to the prime minister. Thatcher was willing to act even before UEFA, who 'were pinning blame ... squarely on the English fans' on the day after the disaster. 'We have reached the stage now where football is at the crossroads,' asserted UEFA secretary Hans Bangerter. 'We cannot and are not willing to let this game be killed by irresponsible elements who have no place in football stadiums.'

On Saturday, 31 May, the FA, with Thatcher's vocal agreement, decided to withdraw all English clubs from European competition in the following season, reportedly 'to avoid the ignominy of their being expelled', but by 3 June the front pages carried the story of an indefinite ban imposed by UEFA. 'European football chiefs are determined not to allow English clubs back to European competition before the British Government has been seen to take vigorous action to end years of riotous behaviour abroad by British fans,' explained the *Daily Telegraph*. The ban ultimately lasted for five seasons, ending in 1990, while Liverpool were excluded for an additional year, which cost the club another European Cup campaign as English champions for 1989/90. Meanwhile, the hand of fate decreed that the next England international, a mere eight days after the Anglo-Italian disaster at Heysel, was a friendly with Italy in Mexico City.

12 June 1985
Azteca 2000 Tournament
England 3-0 West Germany
Estadio Azteca, Mexico City

England travelled to Mexico at the end of the 1984/85 season to participate in friendly tournaments organised as part of preparations for the following year's FIFA World Cup. While there was no Liverpool representation in the England squad for this tour, four Juventus players had joined up with the *Azzurri* after Heysel, and this meant that the game against Italy on 6 June represented an emotionally charged 'early opportunity ... to try to repair some of the serious damage done to the reputation of British sport in Brussels', albeit in front of a sparse crowd of only 8,000 in the cavernous Azteca. Perhaps the Mexican referee had in mind Robson's exhortation to prioritise goodwill to the Italians when he awarded a dubious late penalty that gave Italy a 2-1 win.

England lost 1-0 to Mexico three days later, before finally facing West Germany on 12 June. The meeting was the Germans' first of two matches in the difficult Mexican conditions, while it was England's third of three, and the players' acclimatisation would make all the difference in the match. Bryan Robson was now Bobby Robson's established captain, and Shilton, Butcher, Hoddle, and full-back Kenny Sansom were the other veterans of the 1982 World Cup squad who started, Wilkins having departed for Italy after the first two games to play for his club, AC Milan. The final stages of the 1984/85 Coppa Italia were played out between 12 June and 3 July, with the participating teams featuring some of Europe's best talents at a time of heightened popularity for Italian football that followed the national team's triumph at the 1982 World Cup. While the Italian clubs released their players to tour with the *Azzurri*, the same courtesy was not extended to their overseas stars, and Robson thus lost Wilkins and his first-choice strike partnership of Mark Hateley and Trevor Francis, of AC Milan and Sampdoria, respectively. West Germany, meanwhile, had to make do without Rummenigge, who had signed for Internazionale in 1984, and Hans-Peter Briegel, a member of the Hellas Verona side that sensationally won the 1984/85 Serie A.

After the disappointing failure to qualify for the 1984 European Championship in France, Robson had come under pressure over the previous 18 months to include fresh faces in the side, and the absences of Hateley and Francis gave him the opportunity to field two young strikers in Chelsea's Kerry Dixon and Leicester City's Gary Lineker. Newcastle United's Chris Waddle made his third start, Everton's Peter Reid replaced Wilkins in defensive midfield, and Reid's club-mate Gary Stevens won his second cap in defence. In all, three Everton players made their international debuts on this tour, indicating the growing importance of Howard Kendall's side in English football in the 1980s.

A positive 1984/85 season for Robson had ended with two underwhelming draws in Bucharest and Helsinki that retarded hitherto good progress in World Cup qualification. England also lost 1-0 in the annual encounter with Scotland at Hampden Park on 25 May, their last match before the tour. Ahead of the match against West Germany, they were thus staring down the barrel at the prospect of an unprecedented fourth consecutive defeat in official internationals, with Stuart Jones suggesting in

The Times that Robson 'and his players would be deeply hurt if they are responsible for breaking the record'.

On the opposition bench, England would find a familiar foe in an unfamiliar role. With no previous managerial experience, a reticent Franz Beckenbauer succeeded Derwall out of 'moral obligation' after the 1984 European Championship, the first major tournament in which the *Nationalmannschaft* failed to progress from an initial group phase. The beleaguered Derwall officially resigned from his post, although it was clear to everyone that he had been forced out. In Beckenbauer's first season at the helm, West Germany lost friendly internationals at home to Argentina and Hungary but won all five of their World Cup qualification matches. The last of these was a 5-1 win in Prague on 30 April, which the Czechoslovak coach Josef Masopust called 'a demonstration of modern football'.

Littbarski and Matthäus had both amassed over 30 caps, and the Hamburg veteran Felix Magath was still in midfield, the first to be substituted in the unforgiving conditions. Among the notable new faces in the side were the attacking left-back Andreas Brehme of 1. FC Kaiserslautern and FC Bayern captain Klaus Augenthaler, a commanding defensive presence in the Munich club's title-winning side that season. Irrespective of the personnel available, however, the two days that West Germany allowed themselves to acclimatise to the heat and altitude of Mexico City were never going to be sufficient for a game against an England side that had already spent 14 days there. Bryan Robson opened the scoring in the first half when Dixon diverted a lofted pass from Hoddle into his path and he finished neatly past Schumacher from 12 yards. Shortly before half-time, Brehme, who some years hence would score one of West Germany's most famous goals from the spot, saw his effort well saved by Shilton after Uwe Rahn had been brought down by Mark Wright in the penalty area.

According to Karl-Heinz Heimann, it was mental fatigue and a lack of concentration that inhibited West Germany's play in the first half, compounded by the missed penalty. Towards the hour mark and beyond, however, the physical impact of the conditions on the German players was plain for all to see. 'After spending less than 48 hours acclimatising to the heat and altitude,' observed Stuart Jones, 'they began inevitably to tire early in the second half and by the end looked physically exhausted, mentally shattered and fortunate not to suffer an even heavier defeat.'

The mistake which led to England's second goal was a hallmark of their opponents' fatigue, with Augenthaler carelessly ceding the ball in midfield to allow Butcher to advance on Schumacher and feed a pass to Dixon, who just had to adjust his feet and finish into an unguarded net. The Chelsea striker was coming off a 36-goal season in domestic football, and after 64 minutes he scored a second goal which better demonstrated his abilities. Substitute John Barnes sped to the bye-line on the left flank and provided a deep cross that Dixon met with a strong header, rising well above Hamburg defender Ditmar Jakobs. The ball looped over Schumacher and into the net to give England a three-goal lead. 'A genuine Dixon goal,' said a delighted Brian Moore in the commentary box. With the losing run over, a relieved Bobby Robson said afterwards, 'The team deserved to win for their perseverance when everybody else was looking for cracks that were not there. It was a question of keeping our confidence and soldiering on.'

1986 FIFA World Cup
Mexico

At the start of the World Cup a year later, England's primary concern was the fitness of their most important player, Bryan Robson. Before the ban on English clubs in European football, Robson had led Manchester United to a famous second-leg comeback against Diego Maradona's Barcelona in the quarter-final of the 1983/84 UEFA Cup Winners' Cup. Robson's inspirational performance in front of a sell-out crowd at Old Trafford on 21 March 1984, when he scored the first two goals in a 3-0 win, gave rise to his nickname, 'Captain Marvel'. The following season, he scored the winning goal against East Germany in a friendly international at Wembley, the last of England's four meetings with the DDR national team between 1963 and 1984. He then led England's successful World Cup qualification campaign, missing just one of the eight matches and scoring five goals, including a hat-trick in an emphatic 8-0 win in Turkey.

At the end of 1985, however, Robson was sidelined for three months with calf and hamstring injuries. On his comeback in Manchester United's FA Cup fourth-round tie at Sunderland, his frustration overcame him and he was sent off, attracting significant criticism in his capacity as England captain. Just a fortnight later, on 5 February 1986, Robson suffered an ankle ligament injury in a league defeat at West Ham United, prompting Rob Hughes in the *Sunday Times* to warn, 'If a man is to play as he should, and if furthermore he is to restore the success of English football in Mexico this summer, he must not be broken on the wheel of an English season's week-in, week-out expediency.' Robson's fortunes did not improve, and on another visit to Upton Park, this time in the FA Cup fifth round on 5 March, he dislocated his shoulder. Remarkably, Robson sustained both injuries at the same stadium and in tackling the same player, Tony Cottee. He carried the shoulder injury into England's World Cup preparations, and Bobby Robson ultimately resolved to take a gamble on his star player's fitness, starting him in the first two World Cup group matches.

It soon became clear that the captain would not last the course. After a poor 1-0 defeat to Portugal in the opening game, he had to leave the field still in the first half of a difficult match against Morocco in the searing heat of Monterrey. Moments later, Wilkins received a second yellow card for throwing the ball at the referee. The game ended in a goalless draw, and Robson's tenure as England manager, not to mention the team's World Cup campaign, seemed as good as over.

The tactical shift necessitated by the absence of Robson and Wilkins gave England a welcome new lease of life, however. For the final group match, against Poland on 11 June, Bobby Robson made four changes, bringing Reid and his Everton club-mate Trevor Steven into midfield, while Aston Villa's Steve Hodge replaced Waddle, and Hateley made way for Newcastle United forward Peter Beardsley. The formation shifted from the ineffectual 4-3-3 of the first two matches to a 4-4-2 with Hodge and Steven playing wide. Lineker was the beneficiary of England's improved play, diverting a cross from the advancing full-back Gary Stevens into the net within ten minutes, and then finishing a sweeping move that began on the left flank with Sansom and Beardsley.

Hodge in particular made a great impact, and he ran on to Beardsley's astute pass and played an accurate first-time cross behind the defence for Lineker to convert. The Everton striker completed a first-half hat-trick when he pounced on an error at a corner from Polish goalkeeper Józef Młynarczyk. As David Lacey put it in *The Guardian*, 'The clouds of doubt began to roll away from England's World Cup ambitions.' Robson's side progressed to the last 16 to face Paraguay in the Estadio Azteca, where Lineker added two more goals to his tally in another 3-0 win. This in turn set up a quarter-final in the same venue against Argentina on 22 June, England's biggest match for 16 years.

The contest was decided in a five-minute period at the start of the second half, in which Maradona scored two of the most memorable goals in football history. Even a brief visit to Buenos Aires today is enough to apprehend that the controversial first goal, for which a different verb may be more apt, is not seen as a shameful instance of cheating in Argentina, but rather a daring and impudent act of defiance in the face of not only the pioneers of football, but also the perceived occupiers of Argentinian territory in the *Malvinas*. The player himself said that it had been achieved 'a little with the head of Maradona and a little with the hand of God', immortalising the divine moniker for a deed which the English press saw as the work of the devil.

For many people watching around the world, Maradona's transgression was mitigated to some extent by the sheer brilliance of what followed three minutes later, when he skilfully eluded Reid and Beardsley in the centre circle and set off on a mesmerising dribble down the right flank that took him past Butcher, Reid for a second time, then a helpless Terry Fenwick, and finally Shilton, while riding a desperate last-ditch tackle from Butcher. As opposed to the controversial Hand of God, this is a goal which calls to mind Willy Meisl's phrase about the brilliance of Stanley Matthews allowing us to forget our differences. In an effort to save the game, Robson introduced the wingers Waddle and Barnes, and the latter provided the cross for Lineker's sixth goal of the tournament with a few minutes remaining, but England could not find an equaliser.

A more even-handed assessment amid the indignation levelled at Maradona for his handball goal came from veteran football writer David Miller in *The Times*, who pointed out, 'To become obsessed with the decision is to overlook all the other evidence which is relevant to England's defeat.' His verdict was, 'England, on the admission of their own tactics until the time they were two behind, had not the nerve nor the ability to risk attacking a suspect defence which by the finish was having its inadequacies exposed by England's belated rally.'

Following another outstanding two-goal performance from Maradona in the semi-final against Belgium, Argentina faced West Germany in the final on 29 June. Beckenbauer had made no bones about the fact that his squad lacked players of sufficient quality for a World Cup challenge, but at the start of 1986 the *Nationalmannschaft* surprisingly recorded three wins against significant opponents, at home to Brazil and the Netherlands, and away in Italy. In Mexico, Beckenbauer erred on the side of caution for the opening group game against Uruguay, fielding six defenders, only to see his side concede after five minutes. A late goal from Allofs rescued a deserved point, and the team then responded well to an opening goal from Gordon Strachan to beat Scotland 2-1. A 2-0 defeat to Denmark meant that West Germany would face Morocco in the second round, avoiding Spain. Beckenbauer waved away suggestions that his team did not play to win with his preferred Bavarian slang term *Schmarrn*, meaning 'a load of nonsense'.

As in 1982, there were internal problems in the squad, not least because the most experienced player, the now 30-year-old Rummenigge, was again hampered by injury in the run-up to the tournament. Ostensibly to protect him, Beckenbauer used the Internazionale star sparingly as a substitute in the group stage, but Rummenigge was unimpressed, alleging that the 'Cologne clique' of Schumacher, Littbarski and Allofs were responsible for his demotion to the bench. Beckenbauer, meanwhile, asserted the stringent authority he had always exuded as a player when he was insulted by Schumacher's deputy, Uli Stein. The Hamburger SV goalkeeper's jibe of *Suppenkasper*, which means something akin to 'soup buffoon', can only be understood with reference to Beckenbauer's appearances in television advertisements for the

Knorr brand in the 1960s. Stein duly became the first German player to be sent home from a World Cup for disciplinary reasons, and he never played for the national team again.

For the second-round match against Morocco, Beckenbauer fielded Rummenigge from the start, but a dour contest was only settled two minutes from time by a long-range free kick from Matthäus. Another defensively minded performance against the hosts in the Monterrey quarter-final was complicated by Thomas Berthold's red card after an hour, but West Germany endured waves of Mexican attacks and won the ensuing penalty shoot-out thanks to two saves from Schumacher and a nerveless winning spot kick from Littbarski.

In Guadalajara on 25 June, Beckenbauer's men faced a daunting semi-final against the reigning European champions, France, who were highly fancied to win the tournament after eliminating Italy and Brazil in the previous rounds. Perhaps in part because of the draining quarter-final against the Brazilians, *Les Bleus* were surprised here by a West German team that played with great commitment and self-belief. The Hamburg midfielder Wolfgang Rolff was brought in specifically to marshal Platini, and to great effect, allowing the likes of Magath and Briegel to play with more freedom. The Germans' early opening goal came by means of a goalkeeping error from Joël Bats, who let a typically fierce Brehme free kick slip underneath him. Following several crucial saves from Schumacher, substitute Rudi Völler, who had started every game before withdrawing with a thigh strain against Morocco, scored in the last minute to seal a 2-0 win and send West Germany to a record fifth FIFA World Cup Final.

Against Carlos Bilardo's Argentina in the Estadio Azteca, Beckenbauer's team again demonstrated their resilience and underlined West Germany's reputation for indefatigability. Ultimately, however, the day belonged to Maradona. Argentina's José Luis Brown opened the scoring with a header from a first-half free kick after Matthäus, detailed to mark Maradona, was booked for a tackle from behind. Shortly after half-time, Jorge Valdano finished assuredly past Schumacher to double Argentina's lead, prompting Beckenbauer to replace Magath with FC Bayern forward Dieter Hoeneß, Uli's younger brother.

With just over 15 minutes remaining, Brehme sent a corner towards the near post where Völler headed the ball on for Rummenigge to score from five yards. On 82 minutes, from another Brehme corner, Völler himself headed in to equalise for West Germany. The dramatic dénouement then swung immediately the other way when Maradona with a perfectly weighted pass from the centre circle released Jorge Burruchaga, who evaded Briegel's desperate last-ditch challenge and slotted the ball past Schumacher to win a second World Cup for Argentina.

It had been an extraordinary final. Beckenbauer was satisfied that his team had given everything and concluded, 'In 1974 we were programmed to be world champions. We simply had to win. This time we surprised everyone with our performances.' The weekly news magazine *Der Spiegel* also observed, 'The players in the German World Cup squad no longer see themselves as artists on the ball, but rather as respectable workers on the field of play.' The *Nationalmannschaft* had evidently gone a long way in Mexico to repairing the reputational damage of the Derwall era.

9 September 1987
West Germany 3-1 England
Rheinstadion, Düsseldorf

England travelled to Düsseldorf for their first match of the 1987/88 season, Robson's sixth campaign as England manager. They had won their first three qualification matches for the 1988 European Championship to be held in West Germany, and they had also achieved another famous result in the Santiago Bernabéu Stadium, in February 1987. Lineker, who signed for Barcelona after the World Cup, scored all four England goals in the 4-2 win over a Spanish side that included three of his club-mates and five Real Madrid players.

For the friendly international in Düsseldorf, Robson fielded the young Arsenal defender Tony Adams, a debutant in Madrid, alongside his north London rival Mabbutt, as Butcher was recovering from a slipped disc. The rest of the XI were members of the World Cup squad in Mexico, but Barnes was now a Liverpool player and about to become a permanent fixture on England's left, as opposed to an impact substitute. With

Bryan Robson injured and Hodge recovering from a stomach virus, the manager opted to repeat a tactic he had employed against Brazil at Wembley earlier that year, which saw Barnes and Waddle occupying the wings. Reid, who had played only once in an England shirt since the World Cup, was brought back into the side to play alongside Hoddle and nullify the threat posed by the young Schalke 04 midfielder Olaf Thon. Up front, the partnership between Lineker and Beardsley, another new Liverpool recruit, was now well established.

For the home side, Stuttgart goalkeeper Eike Immel had replaced Schumacher after the World Cup, while 20-year-old Bodo Illgner was already on the bench. Immel's club-mate Guido Buchwald, a tall and versatile player born in West Berlin, started alongside Jürgen Kohler of 1. FC Köln in defence. Strike partners Allofs and Völler had signed for Olympique Marseille and AS Roma, respectively, and were now the senior members of the team, Rummenigge having ended his international career after the World Cup. Five years after his hat-trick against England in a losing cause for the under-21 side, Littbarski was again the star player in an impressive display from a well-balanced West German side, particularly in the first half.

On 23 minutes, Littbarski put Adams on his backside with a clever turn and scored with a fine right-footed shot from 25 yards that sailed into the very corner of Shilton's net. Ten minutes later, he achieved what is known in South America as an 'Olympic goal', a goal scored directly from a corner. This was enabled by the sheer disarray on England's goal line, where Shilton, Sansom and Anderson were all entangled in hapless attempts to clear the ball. Replays suggest the ball may have come off Anderson's head for an own goal, but it was credited to Littbarski.

The opening half an hour had 'reduced England to a state of fumbling bewilderment', wrote Colin Gibson in the *Daily Telegraph*. For Stuart Jones in *The Times*, the visitors had 'been teetering on the edge of a dark abyss' and were fortunate not to concede more. Shortly before half-time, Reid committed a bad foul on Buchwald that went unpunished, and the ball broke loose for Peter Beardsley, who played a first-time pass for the unerring Lineker to score his 20th international goal in 21 starts.

England pulled away from the abyss, and Hateley made a good opportunity with his first action after replacing the ineffective Waddle, twisting Buchwald inside-out on the left flank and then forcing a save from Immel. The second-half rally enabled David Lacey to conclude that 'England's self-respect just about survived' the evening.

The match ended with a stunning goal from Wolfram Wuttke, a gifted midfielder whose career was dogged by unprofessionalism and disputes that earned him the sobriquet *das schlamperte Genie*, or 'the slovenly genius'. The litany of stories of pranks and bust-ups that followed Wuttke from Schalke 04 to Kaiserslautern, via Borussia Mönchengladbach and Ernst Happel's Hamburger SV, anticipated the more high-profile *enfants terribles* of the 1990s Bundesliga such as Mario Basler. Of his four international appearances, Wuttke reportedly said – to Günter Netzer, no less – that he had at least played four good internationals, whereas others had 50 appearances and 49 bad ones. Six minutes after Beckenbauer handed him a chance here in Düsseldorf, Wuttke received the ball from Thon on the left and unleashed a shot that was subtly deflected off Anderson's toe, causing it to arc over Shilton. Jones called it 'as explosive as a stick of dynamite' and extended the metaphor, 'The Germans had earlier been as dazzling and as brilliant as a lavish firework display and, after extinguishing England's brightest flames, they finished in spectacular fashion as if signalling that the show was about to close. Robson and his men were thankful for that.'

1988 UEFA European Championship
West Germany

Coming in the middle of English football's five-year ban from European club competition, the match in Düsseldorf was indicative of the lingering fears on the continent that attended encounters with English fans. Ticket sales for the fixture were banned in Britain, but as ever, some, supporters still made the journey and supported the team in the Rheinstadion. *The Guardian* reported that the match was 'widely seen as the acid test of West German ability to deal with hooliganism at next year's European Championship', and this was, of course, because England were the opposition.

At the tournament itself, the worst episode of violence came, with dreadful inevitability, on the night of England's exit from the group phase after three straight losses. An opening 1-0 defeat to Jack Charlton's Republic of Ireland was followed by a hat-trick from Marco van Basten in a 3-1 win for the Dutch in Düsseldorf, where England fans fought with locals in the city centre. Finally, in Frankfurt on 18 June, England lost 3-1 to the Soviet Union. It was the first time that England had been eliminated from a major tournament having not even achieved a draw, and the press reported the next day that West German police had arrested 'at least 80 English soccer hooligans in Frankfurt's worst night of violence since the European Championships began'. In Westminster, there were renewed discussions about travel bans and ID cards for supporters, while an exasperated Brian Glanville wrote in the *Sunday Times*, 'There is really no case at all, now, for keeping the England team in international competition.'

In sporting terms, the tournament was a disaster for Bobby Robson, who faced the latest in a series of tabloid campaigns to oust him. A significant example is the *Daily Mirror*'s back page from 16 June, the day after the defeat to the Netherlands, which exclaims 'Go Now! Come on, do the honourable thing, Bobby'. Underneath came the words of Nigel Clarke, 'For the sake of our international future, Robson must resign in time to give someone else a chance to build a side for the 1990 World Cup.'

Away from England's dismal experience, the tournament was one of excitement and positive play. West Germany's developing rivalry with the Netherlands had been missing one important ingredient since the controversial World Cup Final in 1974, namely a win for the Dutch. The moment finally came in the semi-final at the Volksparkstadion in Hamburg on 21 June. A stellar *Oranje* side featuring Ronald Koeman, Frank Rijkaard, Ruud Gullit and van Basten came back from a goal down after Matthäus put the tournament hosts ahead from the penalty spot. An equalising penalty from Koeman and a last-minute winner from Van Basten sent Rinus Michels's side to the final, and Koeman intensified the enmity between the sides by celebrating with Thon's shirt in a provocative, scatological gesture.

Against the Soviet Union in Munich, Van Basten's famous volley from the right-hand side of the penalty area became the enduring image of the Netherlands' first major championship win, achieved in front of thousands of jubilant orange-clad travelling supporters on German soil. For West Germany, the tournament brought a customary draw with Italy and two good wins over Denmark and Spain, as well as a new strike partner for Völler in VfB Stuttgart's Jürgen Klinsmann, the Bundesliga's top goalscorer in the 1987/88 season. Perhaps more significantly, however, the competition was a success on and off the pitch, with well-attended stadia, no red cards, and significantly less crowd disorder than expected. After the completion of the group phase, the now-retired HSV legend Felix Magath wrote in the *Hamburger Abendblatt*, 'This European Championship has developed into a real festival of football. On the pitch and in the stands. The atmosphere is outstanding, and the performances are in no way lesser than the enthusiasm. I have rarely experienced such a positive atmosphere in German stadiums.'

* * *

Perceptions of the so-called 'English disease' were tragically reinforced by the incompetence, negligence and mendacity of those responsible for the Hillsborough stadium disaster and the ensuing cover-up. At the FA Cup semi-final between Liverpool and Nottingham Forest on 15 April 1989, 94 people lost their lives, and a further three sustained fatal injuries, in a crush that resulted from overcrowding in the Leppings Lane End which housed the Liverpool supporters. On 26 April 2016, only after an unforgivable delay of 27 years, the victims' families were vindicated in their pursuit of justice when the jury at the second coroner's inquest returned a verdict of unlawful killing in respect of 96 fatalities.

In the immediate aftermath of the tragedy, South Yorkshire Police initiated a smear campaign which alleged that hooliganism on the part of Liverpool fans had been the cause of the disorder. The false narrative was disseminated by elements of the regional and national press, but most notably by *The Sun*, which published a slanderous front page four days after the disaster, under the headline 'The Truth'. The Taylor Report commissioned by

Thatcher's government criticised police failures and led to the wholesale improvement of safety standards in English football stadia during the 1990s. Yet the first coroner's inquest concluded in 1991 with a verdict of accidental death, and nobody was held accountable.

Long before the Hillsborough disaster, a schism had developed between Thatcher's government and the city of Liverpool. David Goldblatt explained how in the 1980s, Liverpool was 'demonised on the political right as the last redoubt of a lumpen-proletariat that prospered on social austerity fraud and voted for a lunatic municipal socialism'. On the significance of the football club's sustained success throughout this period, he added, 'In a city cast as an outsider in its own land, battered by the deliberately engineered economic downturns and clear-outs of the early 1980s, Liverpool Football Club was an enduring source of pride, a magnet for the energies and emotions of a public hungry for success.'

After Hillsborough, the club's fanbase was used as a collective scapegoat for institutional failings, but it has now at long last been unequivocally established, on a legal basis, that there was no evidence of wrongdoing on the part of Liverpool fans that led to the tragedy. Nonetheless, the persistent association of Hillsborough – quite apart from Heysel – with the hooliganism of Liverpool fans, and of English supporters more widely, was sadly on show once more at the 2022 UEFA Champions League Final in Paris. A report from the French sports ministry for Prime Minister Élisabeth Borne referenced the disaster in connection with policing measures to counter hooliganism. According to investigative journalist David Conn, the report 'appears to confirm many Liverpool supporters' bleakest assumptions at the final, that the heavy-handed policing they suffered, including being teargassed, was informed by prejudice about their likely behaviour'.

* * *

England's visit to Düsseldorf in 1987 had come just three months after US President Reagan stood in front of the Brandenburg Gate in Berlin and urged Soviet General Secretary Mikhail Gorbachev to 'tear down this wall!' Indeed, the match took place in the same week as a landmark political meeting of minds in the capital Bonn. On 7 September, Erich Honecker became the first East German head of state to visit West Germany. This was a crucial step in normalising relations between the two German states, although the prospect of reunification still seemed distant.

Two years later, circumstances had changed dramatically. The opening of the border between Hungary and Austria in the summer of 1989 initiated an exodus of East German refugees that the ruling Socialist Unity Party (SED) was powerless to prevent. With more and more people continuing to cross borders to the west, and amid a growing protest movement in the DDR, the SED Central Committee met on 9 November to discuss a proposed modification to the law on travel freedoms for its citizens. At a subsequent press conference, party representative Günter Schabowski read the document he had been given without knowledge of its content, and mistakenly announced that the changes applied with immediate effect. The West German ARD network duly announced on the evening news that the DDR had opened its borders, causing Berliners from east and west to gather at the Wall and demand that the gates be opened. The historian Mary Fullbrook illustrated the barely credible scenes of that evening:

'A euphoric party atmosphere rapidly developed. By midnight, people were dancing on the top of the Wall, helping each other over – in both directions – and drinking bottles of champagne, as Berliners were reunited over what was rapidly becoming merely a piece of concrete, rather than the ultimate boundary of the habitable universe.'

Chancellor Kohl subsequently exploited the heated political situation to accelerate the reunification of the two German states, which was finally achieved on 3 October 1990. By the time of the 1990 FIFA World Cup in Italy, this process was already well under way, with currency union between the two states effected on 1 July. In football, Andreas Thom, who played 51 times for the DDR national team, became the first East German player to transfer to a West German club, on 16 December 1989, when he moved from Berlin club BFC Dynamo to Bayer Leverkusen for a fee of 2.5 million Deutsche Mark. Although the *Nationalmannschaft* officially represented West

Germany in Italy, its fortunes were followed by millions of East Germans who were just months away from formal reintegration into unified Germany.

1990 FIFA World Cup
Italy

The spectre of hooliganism even extended as far as the FIFA World Cup draw, for which England were controversially made one of the six seeded teams. The organising committee made a late change to the ranking criteria that allowed them, as part of 'football's worst-kept secret', to place England above Spain, thus sending their 'malign supporters' for three group matches to Cagliari, on the island of Sardinia. 'Elba might have been better,' quipped David Miller in *The Times*. In his memoir of the 1990 World Cup, Pete Davies wrote that the secretary of the local organising committee in Sardinia told him that 'It had been known for six months in advance of the draw that if they qualified, then England would be there.' The president of the committee was Hermann Neuberger, the long-time president of the DFB. He rebuffed criticism from the Spanish delegation by insisting that England merited their position, and that the decision was 'in no way a concession to English hooliganism'. As in 1988, England's first two matches of the group phase were against the Republic of Ireland and the Netherlands. A 1-1 draw against a spirited Irish side had the tabloids spitting feathers again, with *The Sun* calling for the players to be sent home to spare the country from humiliation, but this was followed by a significant tactical switch. Robson introduced Derby County defender Mark Wright to play as a sweeper behind the central defensive pairing of Terry Butcher and Des Walker. Recalling that he 'had no intention of allowing Van Basten and Gullit to rip holes in us the way they had in Dusseldorf in June 1988', Robson later explained the thinking behind his surprising decision:

'I saw that Mark Wright had the attributes to play as a sweeper. He was tall, he could pass, he was good in the air, clever in possession and not a bad marker. The so-called "*libero*" role was perfect for him. Mark was a sufficiently accomplished footballer to be able to carry the ball out of defence and support his midfield. He was ideally equipped to work the two sectors of the pitch.'

Glanville praised Robson's initiative and remarked, not without a hint of self-satisfaction, 'Those critics who have felt for a long time that a vulnerable, four-in-line English defence should, in fact, be playing with two central markers and a sweeper may appear to have been justified.' Colin Malam in the *Sunday Telegraph* praised a 'fluid, enterprising side that deserved to take more than a point from the disappointing European champions', and the overall press response was as good as it comes for a goalless draw. The subsequent 1-0 win over Egypt was enough to send England through to the knockout stages as group winners, and there was significant relief at avoiding West Germany, who would face the Dutch.

A more dispiriting note from the game against the Netherlands was yet another injury to Bryan Robson, who would miss the rest of the tournament. For the next two matches he was replaced by Liverpool midfielder Steve McMahon, and then by David Platt of Aston Villa, who as a substitute scored a magnificent volley on the turn in the last minute of extra time to beat Belgium in the second round. The captain's absence was also less damaging to England than it had been in Mexico because of the presence of Paul Gascoigne, the precociously talented attacking midfielder who had left his hometown club Newcastle United for Tottenham Hotspur in 1988. Gascoigne turned 23 shortly before the World Cup and had already amassed 11 caps ahead of the tournament, although mostly as a substitute. After the impressive team display against the Netherlands in Cagliari, Glanville singled out Gascoigne for praise:

'This is a classically English player. Combining physical strength and courage with a refined technique, and abundant flair. He never stopped running and exerting himself, never hesitated to try to go past a man, however often and however painfully he was chopped down.'

Gascoigne was by consensus the most gifted English player of his generation, and in Italy he came to the world's attention. It was his free kick that Wright nodded in for the winning goal against Egypt, and likewise his lofted pass into the penalty area from another free kick that Platt converted against Belgium. In an incident-packed quarter-final against Cameroon in Naples, Gascoigne conceded a penalty that precipitated a five-minute rally in which England went 2-1 behind. Yet he was nonetheless instrumental in the comeback that saw England win 3-2 in extra time, thanks to two penalties from Lineker.

West Germany now awaited Robson's men in the Turin semi-final on 4 July, and for David Miller in *The Times*, whose column after the quarter-final was headed 'No evidence of any threat to West Germany', England were no match for Beckenbauer's side, whose 'attractiveness lies in their assertive pace and power rather than any fantasy'. Based in the imposing, expanded San Siro stadium in Milan, West Germany had made an impressive start to the tournament, beating Yugoslavia and the United Arab Emirates 4-1 and 5-1, respectively, before drawing with Colombia when their position as group winners was all but secured.

The outstanding player in the side was Lothar Matthäus of Internazionale, at ease in his home away from home. Against Yugoslavia in particular, he played as the archetype of the box-to-box midfielder, receiving the ball in his own half and either distributing it intelligently or surging forward, but also dependably dispossessing his opponents. Two powerful finishes from distance, the first with the left foot and the second with the right, crowned a commanding captain's performance that sent a signal to the watching world. The Inter team-mates Matthäus, Brehme and Klinsmann were again on song against the UAE, while Völler scored three goals across the first two games.

Perhaps the key moment of West Germany's campaign came in the second-round match against the Netherlands, which became the high-water mark of the football rivalry between the two nations. The incendiary atmosphere of the match was also attributable to the fact that this was a Milan derby in microcosm, with West Germany's *Nerazzurri* trio taking on the Dutch *Rossoneri* Rijkaard, Gullit and Van Basten, colleagues at AC Milan. The touchpaper was lit after 20 minutes with the infamous scene involving Rijkaard and Völler that ended in both of them being sent off by the Argentinian referee Juan Carlos Loustau. The loss of Völler from the front line affected

West Germany less than Rijkaard's absence did the Netherlands, however. Rijkaard had been playing directly against Klinsmann, who now found greater freedom against Berry van Aerle in the reshaped back line, while midfielders Littbarski and Matthäus were able to play further forward. Klinsmann opened the scoring five minutes after half-time, beating van Aerle to a Buchwald cross from the left flank. Five minutes from full time, Brehme put the game beyond the *Oranje* with a looping right-footed shot from just inside the penalty area.

The quarter-final against Czechoslovakia was West Germany's fifth successive match in the San Siro, where a first-half Matthäus penalty was followed on 70 minutes by a second yellow card for Lubo Moravčík, later of Celtic fame, who was dismissed by the conspicuously named Austrian referee, Helmut Kohl. Despite progress to the semi-final, however, Beckenbauer was incensed by the players' complacent attitude in the final 20 minutes. 'I was convinced that we had an intelligent team,' he later recalled, 'but in the last 20 minutes of the match, they played anything but intelligently.'

4 July 1990
FIFA World Cup semi-final
West Germany 1-1 England (after extra time)
West Germany win 4-3 on penalties
Stadio delle Alpi, Turin

After three group games in Sardinia, England had also played in Bologna and Naples, and those fans who could still afford to continue now made their way north-west to Turin, the home of Juventus; 'Heysel town' as Pete Davies called it in his celebrated World Cup memoir. On arrival, England fans were herded to a spartan campsite in a dilapidated stadium at Parco Ruffini, where they were left to linger and await news of their derisory ticket allocation for the semi-final. When Italy then lost to Maradona's Argentina in the first semi-final, local fans went on the rampage and attacked the English camp. Fear and tension were everywhere. 'To follow England here meant submitting to the effective deprivation of your liberty,' explained Davies. 'It meant being treated like some sort of prisoner of war, on the most limited of paroles.'

As Davies himself affirmed, however, it was all worth it. England had never gone this far in a World Cup on foreign soil. On the morning of the match, Bobby Robson simply said, 'Germany's the big one.' For this test against the side he called 'the most impressive team in the tournament', Robson again used a sweeper, as he had done against the Netherlands, Belgium and Cameroon. On this occasion it was the stand-in captain Butcher who was given the task, while Wright, with half a dozen stitches above his eye, was asked to mark Klinsmann. The wing-backs, as they are now known, were Stuart Pearce, who had played in every game at the World Cup so far, and the young Queens Park Rangers right-back Paul Parker, who had replaced Gary Stevens after the first match. Gascoigne, Platt and Waddle played in midfield and, with Barnes ruled out by a groin strain, Beardsley supported Lineker in attack.

Beckenbauer, meanwhile, brought Thon into midfield to play alongside Matthäus and Thomas Häßler, the diminutive Köln midfielder who would play for Juventus the following season. Littbarski had started the previous two games but struggled with fitness and did not even feature on the substitutes' bench. West Germany would miss his creativity in midfield, especially in opposition to Gascoigne. All the while, the mood in the English press was of hope rather than expectation. 'So much lies in the Germans' favour tonight,' remarked Lacey, 'that you have to allow for the possibility that, in a World Cup which has so consistently scorned the obvious, England might win.' Beckenbauer's respectful platitudes towards England – 'still a great football nation' – were widely quoted, but Völler was less generous, observing, 'The English play the same game they played 20 years ago.' It was Stuart Jones in *The Times*, however, who saw into the future:

'The World Cup semi-final here tonight features West Germany against England, the masters against the novices, the efficient against the spirited, the practised against the spontaneous. Logically, it should be a mismatch. In reality, it could remain as balanced as finely tuned scales.'

England made a flying start with a succession of early corners and good build-up play. Any doubts that they could be competitive on this stage against the formidable West Germans were dispelled by half-time, although England were helped in part by playing against ten men for some time after Rudi Völler sustained an injury on the half-hour mark. He was eventually replaced by Werder Bremen's Karl-Heinz Riedle, who had also played in the suspended Völler's stead against Czechoslovakia. West Germany grew into the game in the second half as Augenthaler came forward with the ball, and the midfield three of Matthäus, Häßler and Thon began to take more risks.

Just before the hour mark, Häßler was brought down outside the penalty area by a robust challenge from Pearce. BBC commentator John Motson was quick to mention Brehme's free kick from a similar position against France in the Guadalajara semi-final four years earlier, and the Inter full-back duly shaped up to hit another fierce left-footed shot. Another man who was wary of the threat was Parker, who raced out to block Brehme's attempt as soon as Thon had nudged the ball to his team-mate. Brehme's strike cannoned off Parker, looped high into the Turin sky, and dropped behind a bewildered Shilton into the England net. Shortly after the goal, Beckenbauer introduced Stefan Reuter to relieve Häßler, who was still suffering from his close encounter with Pearce. Trevor Steven replaced Butcher to enable England to revert to a 4-4-2. England may well have had a penalty when Waddle was fouled by Augenthaler in the area, but Brazilian referee José Roberto Wright waved play on.

The goal England certainly deserved came ten minutes from full time, when the otherwise excellent Jürgen Kohler failed to deal with a long ball from Parker and it landed at the feet of Lineker, who shook off Augenthaler. The Tottenham Hotspur striker hit a half-volley across Illgner and into the bottom corner of the net to equalise. An emotional Bobby Robson, who had already confirmed that he was stepping down from his role after the tournament, flashed a broad smile on the England bench, embodying the mood of millions at home. Once again, these two great rivals were going all the way.

Where Lineker had been characteristically ruthless with his finish, Klinsmann at the start of extra time missed unexpectedly after Augenthaler had found him in the penalty area with a clever lofted pass. To England's relief, his miscued shot flashed past Shilton's far post. In England, the extra time period is remembered for the sight of Gascoigne's reaction to being booked for a lunging tackle on Berthold. His earlier yellow card against Belgium meant that he would now miss the next game through suspension, and the prospect of sitting out the World Cup Final brought him close to tears. As in 1966 and at many points since, the Germans' dramatisation of the effects of a foul was called into question by the English commentator, in this case Motson, 'I've got to choose my words carefully here, but having seen a bit of the Germans I do have to report again that the player tackled, who goes down, sometimes gives the impression he's been absolutely crippled.'

The first half of extra time ended with more drama when Waddle found himself in space on the left edge of the penalty area and unleashed a low left-footed shot that struck the base of Illgner's far post, the rebound only just eluding Platt's instinctive dive to meet it. A few minutes later England had the ball in the net from a Waddle free kick, but the referee had blown his whistle for offside as the cross came in for Platt to head past the goalkeeper. Replays suggest that with the benefit of modern technology, the goal would have stood. With just two minutes remaining, Buchwald's shot from 25 yards hit the upright. The drama of this pulsating contest appeared to know no end, but a winner would now be determined by means of a penalty shoot-out. Davies remembers the scene at the end of 120 minutes, 'Applause rang out round the whole of the magnificent arena, pure and wholly merited by both sides. In the centre circle, players from both sides shook hands, put arms round each others' shoulders, and exchanged congratulations on the game.'

As difficult as it may now be to envisage, England at this point were free of any penalty shoot-out trauma, as this was their first in World Cup or European Championship competition. As we have seen, West Germany had experienced the scenario in 1976, 1982 and 1986, winning the last two. After three successful penalties from each side in Turin, Pearce stepped up and saw his shot down the middle saved – Robson had specifically chosen him as his most dependable penalty-taker for the often decisive fourth kick. Thon then converted West Germany's fourth, which meant that Waddle had to score to keep England in the contest, but he blazed his kick high over the crossbar. By the narrowest of margins, West Germany reached their third successive World Cup Final, their sixth in all.

Colin Gibson in the *Daily Telegraph* reminded readers that England 'had been told by one newspaper [*The Sun*] that they were not fit to represent their country and that they should be brought home. Those words should be choking a few people this morning. For England have nothing to be ashamed of in defeat.' He added that Bobby Robson 'should, like the rest of the country, be proud of the night that England rebuilt their footballing image'. The magnificent contest, Gascoigne's brilliance and vulnerability, and particularly the manner of the defeat, all helped to ensure that, as Robson later put it in his autobiography, 'No England supporter will ever forget the drama of Turin. It's one of those games that is imprinted on the memory of life.'

* * *

It says everything about the rehabilitation of the *Nationalmannschaft* under Beckenbauer that Rob Hughes in the *Sunday Times* could assert the following on the morning of the World Cup Final on 8 July 1990, 'For the good of football, for a future on which to build the sport that transcends more boundaries than politics or religion, we need West Germany to beat Argentina tonight.' True enough, the article which contained this sentiment was largely a diatribe on the perceived moral failings of Maradona and his Argentina team, but it is hard to imagine anyone outside West Germany – and many within – calling for Derwall's team in 1982 to succeed in this way, especially considering Hughes's wish for the Germans' 'effervescent attacking game of the first round to return'.

Argentina had collected 20 yellow cards in six games on their way to the final, and four players had met the same fate as Gascoigne and were now suspended. To Hughes, Bilardo's team by this point were 'like the faded eyes of old men: the Argentinian sparkle has gone, and they cling with crotchety ill-will to the crown'. Maradona, moreover, was suffering with a 'blood clot the size of a golf ball' in his left ankle, making him significantly less mobile than he had been in Mexico. West Germany, by contrast, were a picture of confidence. Glanville quoted the manager as saying, 'This time, Matthäus himself can be Maradona, not the anti-Maradona' he had been in 1986, and this in part because the great man would now be marked by Buchwald. Beckenbauer also expected that the host nation's defeat to Argentina, and the presence of two Roma players, Völler and Berthold, in the West German line-up would bring the crowd at the Stadio Olimpico behind his team.

The Argentinians' negative tactics in the game itself then ensured this was the case. Half-time substitute Pedro Monzón was sent off for a reckless tackle on Klinsmann on 65 minutes, and Argentina retreated further into a siege mentality. With just five minutes remaining, two nations on the cusp of unification held their collective breath when a penalty was awarded for a foul by Roberto Sensini on Völler. With Matthäus unwilling to shoot because of problems with his boots, Brehme took responsibility and opted for placement as opposed to power. The ball nestled in the inside netting to give West Germany a deserved 1-0 win. Brehme joined the famous names Max Morlock, Helmut Rahn, Paul Breitner and Gerd Müller on the list of players to have scored in a victorious World Cup Final for West Germany.

A famous evening in Rome concluded with an indelible image in German sporting and cultural history. It was the sight of a satisfied and pensive Franz Beckenbauer, alone on the pitch in the darkened Stadio Olimpico, with hands in pockets and a winner's medal around his neck as his players celebrated wildly in the background. He had become just the second man, after Brazil's Mario Zagallo, to win the FIFA World Cup as both a player and a manager.

10

Football Comes Home

1991–1996

In April 1994, the new England manager Terry Venables was preparing for a friendly international against Germany as one of his earliest assignments in the role. The former Barcelona and Tottenham Hotspur coach had been appointed by the FA on 28 January, following the unsuccessful three-year tenure of Graham Taylor. Venables was passed over for the top job in 1990, when Taylor was chosen as Bobby Robson's successor, but he now came recommended by former England full-back Jimmy Armfield. Nonetheless, the FA's decision to turn to Venables at the start of 1994 was under scrutiny, since the previous year had been one of crisis and controversy for the man born in 1943 in Dagenham, Essex, the same town as Alf Ramsey. Following a dispute with chairman Alan Sugar in the boardroom at White Hart Lane in May 1993, the popular Venables was sacked as chief executive, prompting an outcry among fans and journalists. Sugar famously later remarked, 'I felt as though I'd killed Bambi.'

At the time of his appointment with England, Venables was consequently pursuing legal action against Sugar for unfair dismissal, and against the BBC's *Panorama* programme for libel. Rob Hughes in *The Times* called it a 'dangerous liaison' that could yet cost the FA 'everything in terms of respect and probity'. Venables was a charismatic and clubbable 'personality manager' noted for getting the best out of players, in part because he had played the game at a high level and had appeared for England, unlike Taylor. He also benefited from a good relationship with members of the press, which was all the more important in the wake of *The Sun*'s merciless campaign to oust Taylor. David Lacey in *The Guardian* employed cockney rhyming slang in a nod to Venables's East End background when he wrote that the rigours of the England job would compare favourably to his ongoing legal battles, 'In fact, after the last nine months this should be a piece of cake for Tel-Boy. And after all, he does have the Currant Bun on his side.' Meanwhile, in an article in *The Observer* in 2004, Bill Borrows wrote of Venables, 'To watch him glad-hand the press pack behind closed doors ... is to witness a conscious suspension of critical acuity and a corruption of the distance between journalist and subject.'

The failure under Taylor to qualify for the 1994 FIFA World Cup, together with England's status as hosts of the 1996 UEFA European Championship, meant that Venables faced two and a half years without a competitive international. 'Our target is 1966,' he announced on the day of his unveiling. When someone pointed out the error, he said, 'Oh, what a Freudian slip.'

After an initial 1-0 win over Denmark at Wembley, Venables was due to take his England side to Berlin to face the Germans. However, if the English FA was preoccupied about issues of respect and probity around its new manager, these concerns were as nothing compared to the political storm which embroiled the DFB ahead of this fixture. The match was originally scheduled to take place in Hamburg, yet at the end of January the city's interior minister Werner Hackmann had informed the DFB that he was not willing to host the occasion. The reason for the rejection was the polemic proposed date of 20 April, the 105th anniversary of the birth of Adolf Hitler. This attracted interest from neo-Nazi agitators in both countries and, as a result, also that of anti-fascist demonstrators. The years following German reunification and the fall of the Soviet Union had seen a rise in neo-Nazism in Europe, and football was exploited in Britain as well as in Germany to spread messages of hate and intolerance. Hackmann estimated that 10,000 far-right extremists would descend on Hamburg, and the DFB's decision simply to move the game to Berlin caused an exasperated Hughes in *The Times* to ask, 'How did football administrators, not to mention the forces of law and order, come to the conclusion that violence would not travel the autobahn from Hamburg to Berlin?'

To make matters worse, the match in the capital would be played at the Olympiastadion, the venue for Hitler's 1936 Olympic Games and the England team's Nazi salute in 1938. Hughes called it an 'unpardonable blunder', writing on 2 April when the DFB still unaccountably held the line that it was 'not responsible for things that happen outside the stadium'. DFB president Egidius Braun was quoted in Berlin's *Morgenpost* as saying that a cancellation would be 'a climbdown for democracy'.

It was left to the English FA on 6 April unilaterally to call off the fixture. While that meant a loss in terms of advance ticket sales through the England Travel Club, the FA also had to consider the potential cost of English fans' involvement in disturbances in Berlin, given that a UEFA tournament on home soil could be jeopardised. *The Times* in its leading article was adamant that the decision to cancel the match had been correct, 'Any criticism in Germany that cancelling the match is giving in to extremism is misplaced. It is demonstrably more important to take action to avoid trouble than to go ahead with a game in the sure knowledge that trouble is planned.'

The same article also stated that because 'Hitler's birthday is not a familiar date to most ordinary Germans ... the football authorities can be forgiven for not realising that a match on April 20 was inappropriate'. Gerhard Fischer and Ulrich Lindner, the authors of a landmark study on German football's relationship with National Socialism, have shown that this was a naïve notion, however:

'There was a suspicion that this was not just the work of a few dolts who had swapped football cards during history class at school, but people with strong convictions who were pursuing a political project: the reconciliation of former wartime enemies with Germany's past.'

DFB spokesman Wolfgang Niersbach, who would become president of the association in 2012, compounded matters by referencing an international Jewish conspiracy in response to criticism from the United States, 'Eighty per cent of the American press is in Jewish hands. Events in Germany are noted there with seismographic precision.' Niersbach gave his source for this assertion as the German Tourism Association, which was later exposed as housing far-right extremists who peddled anti-semitic tropes. Fischer and Lindner quote a response to Niersbach's remark from the *Morgenpost*:

'It is alarming that the press spokesman is prepared to repeat the age old nonsense about the Jewish-dominated, and therefore anti-German, American press. Could it be that there are not only intellectually challenged people at work here, but also some that are forever living in the past? Reasonable suspicion has been established.'

One prominent German voice in favour of the game's cancellation was that of Franz Beckenbauer, then manager of FC Bayern München, who called it a 'very sensible decision' and added, 'No football match is worth rioting or even injuries.' All things considered, the concluding words of *The Times*'s leader on 7 April are the most apposite, 'In such a situation the very definition of the match as "friendly" is deeply ironic. Far better, as has happened, to scrap the whole idea.'

* * *

Among the less judicious pronouncements of Beckenbauer's career was his claim immediately after the 1990 World Cup Final in Rome that, because reunification would bring East German talent into the fold, the *Nationalmannschaft* would be 'unbeatable for many years to come'. It may have been a flippant comment in the moment of triumph, but it certainly increased the pressure on Beckenbauer's successor Berti Vogts. Later that week, former international Hans-Peter Briegel wrote in his *Kicker* column, 'We should forget Beckenbauer's remark as soon as possible to allow Berti Vogts to work in peace. As nice as it would be, there can be no question of a German monopoly of football in the 1990s.'

After unification on 3 October 1990, the first home international match came against Switzerland in Stuttgart on 19 December. The venue and the opposition recalled the West German team's first postwar international in 1950, also at the Neckarstadion. Dresden-born Matthias Sammer became the first footballer from the former DDR to represent the new all-German national team. He was replaced after 75 minutes by Bayer Leverkusen's Andreas Thom, the 1988 East German Footballer of the Year, who scored just a minute after coming on. A fourth goal from Matthäus shortly before full time capped a perfect evening to celebrate German reunification on the football field.

Another East German player to feature for Vogts was Thomas Doll, now of Hamburger SV, who replaced the injured Matthäus at half-time of a European Championship qualifying match away to Wales on 5 June 1991. After an hour of the game in Cardiff, Thomas Berthold was sent off for kicking out at Welsh captain Kevin Ratcliffe, and a few minutes later the great Liverpool striker Ian Rush scored a memorable goal in Welsh football history that secured a 1-0 win against the world champions. Beckenbauer's promised era of invincibility had come to an end after 11 months.

11 September 1991
England 0-1 Germany
Wembley Stadium

Graham Taylor's first defeat as England manager, after nine wins and three draws during the 1990/91 season, came against Germany at Wembley. Gary Lineker, Trevor Steven, David Platt, and Paul Parker were the survivors from Bobby Robson's 1990 World Cup team. The tearful hero of Turin, Paul Gascoigne, was absent throughout the 1991/92 season as he recovered from the serious injury he sustained in the 1991 FA Cup Final between Tottenham Hotspur and Nottingham Forest. Gascoigne ruptured cruciate ligaments in his right knee in lunging at Forest defender Gary Charles just 15 minutes into the game, and he would sadly never be the same player again, although flashes of brilliance remained. Among the new faces were the Arsenal right-back Lee Dixon, Manchester United central defender Gary Pallister, and Dixon's club-mate Alan Smith in attack.

The visitors fielded an experienced side that featured no fewer than five players representing Italian clubs, as well as the substitute Jürgen Klinsmann, still at Internazionale. There were two significant new names in the line-up, with Stefan Effenberg of FC Bayern making his second senior international appearance, and Eintracht Frankfurt's Andreas Möller, who had played a limited role as a substitute at the World Cup, playing alongside Matthäus in midfield. For Germany the game represented an important chance to re-group after defeat in Cardiff, since their next appointment in qualification for the European Championship was against Wales in Nuremberg, now a must-win game.

The match at Wembley was decided by a single goal that came on the stroke of half-time. Under pressure deep inside his own half and facing back towards his goal, Matthäus turned to play an audacious and accurate long pass to Möller in the centre of the field, who drove forward into space before releasing Thomas Häßler on the right flank. With that chance apparently snuffed out, Matthäus played another perceptive through ball for Doll, who sent a cross into the six-yard area from the left flank. With Pallister, Tony Dorigo and David Batty all static, the unmarked Karl-Heinz Riedle scored with an easy header – a goal made and scored by Lazio players. It was enough to give the *Nationalmannschaft* a third win at Wembley after 1972 and 1982, and a first as a united Germany. The team would return just under five years later in dramatic circumstances.

1992 UEFA European Championship
Sweden

At the 1992 UEFA European Championship in Sweden, Taylor's management of England began to unravel, and the criticism he received in the press at times reached hysterical levels. After England were eliminated by a 2-1 defeat to the hosts in Stockholm, the game in which Taylor infamously left Lineker on the bench and denied him the chance to score a then record-equalling 49th goal for England, *The Sun* ran the headline 'Swedes 2 Turnips 1'. The following day, the same newspaper superimposed a turnip on a picture of Taylor's head, under the headline 'Go Now'.

Germany, meanwhile, lost the latest renewal of the rivalry with the Netherlands in Gothenburg but nonetheless progressed to the semi-finals, thanks to an unexpected favour from Scotland. The defeat to the Dutch is notable for Vogts's mitigating half-time substitution that saw Matthias Sammer take up the sweeper role, as this was a position in which he would thrive some four years later. Germany's 3-2 win over the hosts in the Stockholm semi-final featured Häßler's best performance for the national team as he led the midfield in the absence of the injured Matthäus. Häßler's early converted free kick and two goals from Riedle ensured passage to an expected showdown with the *Oranje* in the final in Gothenburg on 26 June.

Yet the Netherlands were surprisingly beaten on penalties by Denmark, a late entrant to the tournament following Yugoslavia's disqualification due to the outbreak of war. The Danish underdogs then pulled off another upset and completed one of European football's most sensational achievements in winning the continental title. John Jensen's first-half strike was a shock from which Germany never recovered, and Kim Vilfort's goal 12 minutes from time, as well as countless brilliant saves from Peter Schmeichel, gave Denmark a 2-0 win over the world champions. Two years after winning the plaudits of the international press in Italy, the *Nationalmannschaft* was humbled by a team displaying the very qualities which Germany under Vogts were perceived to lack. 'They have been notable for their fair play and have put a premium on teamwork, supporting each other tirelessly,' remarked David Miller about the Danes. 'They have earned their title and have taught everyone in the game some old, if forgotten, lessons.'

* * *

One young journalist in the *Daily Telegraph* sought to foreground the political significance of Germany's defeat, with reference to the Danish referendum on 2 June 1992 in which voters had narrowly rejected the Maastricht treaty. This was the foundation document of the European Union, which had been signed in February that year but still required formal ratification by each of its 12 signatory nations, including Denmark. *The Telegraph*'s front-page piece, entitled 'Denmark ratifies its footballing dream', quoted Danish Foreign Minister Uffe Ellemann-Jensen as greeting the result with the Wildean quip, 'If you can't join them, beat them.' The article went on to speculate, 'For the Danes, it was a grudge match, no doubt. When they rejected Maastricht, it was at least partly because of their strong aversion, ill founded or not, to being dominated by Germany in a united Europe.'

The author, then aged 28, had already cultivated a reputation as a leading Eurosceptic writer in the British press, to the extent that his employer Conrad Black would later affirm, 'He was such an effective correspondent for us in Brussels that he greatly influenced British opinion on this country's relations with Europe.' The journalist's name was Boris Johnson.

By the mid-1990s, the fear expressed at a united Germany's supposed domination of the new European Union was pervasive. Around the time of the cancelled match in Berlin in April 1994, an essay from the economist Alan Walters appeared in *The Times* under the headline 'Germans' stealthy plan to become bankers of Europe'. Walters wrote that the Maastricht treaty was designed to fix exchange rates to the Deutschmark, allowing the German Bundesbank to 'be the *de facto* central bank of Europe and the mark its currency'. He quoted the Thatcherite minister Nicholas Ridley, who had claimed that the project of economic and monetary union of the EU was 'a German racket designed to take over the whole of Europe'.

On the day of the European Championship semi-final in 1996, the Eurosceptic politician John Redwood, who had battled John Major for the Conservative party leadership in 1995, wrote a piece entitled 'Stand up to Germany, on and off the field'. He argued that the England v Germany fixture 'invites us all to think again about the problem of Germany'. Expressing his anxiety that Chancellor Kohl's united Germany was in a position to 'bully' other western European governments, Redwood wrote, 'He offers us the favour of joining Germany's idea of a federal European state before it is too late. Britain must say no. The only answer, were Germany ever to bully us, is to stand up to it.' He also took the opportunity to criticise the leader of the opposition for his stance of seeking a close relationship with Europe, 'The picture of [Labour leader] Tony Blair alongside Chancellor Kohl revealed the naivety of new Labour standing in the shadow of the new Germany.'

19 June 1993
United States Cup
Germany 2-1 England
Pontiac Silverdome, Pontiac, MI
In the summer of 1993, both England and Germany travelled to the United States to participate in the US Cup, a four-team

tournament organised by the US Soccer Federation as part of preparations for the 1994 FIFA World Cup. England arrived with their chances of qualification for the main event already hanging in the balance, following a disastrous 2-0 defeat away to Norway in which 'the wit, the fluidity, the movement of the Scandinavians was all too much' for them. Taylor had gambled at short notice on playing a back three in Oslo, and his discomfited players produced a lacklustre end-of-season display.

In the final match of the subsequent US tour, England faced Germany on 19 June. The venue was the Pontiac Silverdome, just outside Detroit, Michigan, which gave this match the distinction of being the first international played indoors on natural grass. Conditions inside the arena were hot and humid, and Germany, this time with three players in the side from Italian clubs as well as Klinsmann, now in France with AS Monaco, fared better than England in the 'steamy, stultifying climate under the Silverdome's roof'. Effenberg opened the scoring midway through the first half, turning inside Pallister before finishing between the legs of goalkeeper Nigel Martyn. England's equaliser shortly thereafter was a fine goal, albeit with Effenberg down hurt and the German players appealing to the referee to stop the game. Good combination play in the penalty area between Manchester United midfielder Paul Ince and John Barnes led to an opening for Ince to play the ball across the six-yard box for Platt to score. Platt had moved from AS Bari to Juventus the previous summer and enjoyed a strong 1992/93 season with England, in which he scored eight goals and played mostly as captain.

The winning goal came from the irrepressible Klinsmann shortly after half-time, when he pounced on a rebound after a shot had struck the post. The player who really deserved to score was the young FC Bayern defender Christian Ziege, who made his senior international debut at the US Cup. For his outstanding performance in the Silverdome, Ziege received a coveted grade one in *Kicker* magazine's individual match ratings, which reflect the German educational grading system on a scale of one to six, and was identified as the long-term successor to Andreas Brehme in the left-back position.

* * *

Anglo-German encounters in European club competition at the beginning of the 1990s were rare but on occasions spectacular. In the first round of the 1992/93 European Cup, which became the inaugural UEFA Champions League from the group stage, Leeds United travelled to Baden-Württemberg and lost the first leg of their tie with VfB Stuttgart 3-0. Leeds scored four goals at Elland Road in an effort to overturn the deficit, but Stuttgart's single away goal was enough to see the German side through. After the second leg, however, a default 3-0 victory was awarded to Leeds when Stuttgart were found to have fielded more than the permitted three foreign players. The resultant 3-3 aggregate score necessitated a third match on neutral territory. This was played on 9 October in Barcelona's Camp Nou, where the sparse attendance meant that 'the atmosphere was akin to holding a private dinner party in the Albert Hall'. Leeds eventually won the protracted tie when substitute Carl Shutt, replacing Eric Cantona, scored the winning goal with his first action. The team returned to a heroes' welcome but lost the British battle with Rangers in the next round, 4-2 on aggregate.

In the second round of the UEFA Cup in the following season, FC Bayern were drawn against Norwich City, who had finished third in the inaugural season of the Premier League and now embarked on their debut European campaign. Norwich caused a sensation on 19 October 1993 by becoming the first English club to win in Bayern's Olympiastadion, albeit thanks to two Welsh goalscorers in Jeremy Goss and Mark Bowen. The 2-1 victory in Munich is still counted among the greatest moments in the club's history, while the opening goal, a stunning volley from Goss, was voted the club's greatest goal of all time in 2008. Goss scored again in a 1-1 draw in the second leg at Carrow Road, securing progress to the third round, where Norwich lost 2-0 on aggregate to Internazionale.

1994 FIFA World Cup
United States of America
The US Cup defeat to Germany was England's sixth consecutive match without a win, leaving Graham Taylor on borrowed time, although still with slim hopes of qualification for the World

Cup. With a re-energised and inspirational Paul Gascoigne in the side, England convincingly beat Poland at Wembley in September 1993. The victory provided a chance to qualify for the United States by means of a win over the Netherlands, given that England's final qualifying fixture was against minnows San Marino. Gascoigne, who for Rob Hughes in *The Times* was 'both the orchestrator and the idiot', received a booking that would keep him out of the all-important match in Rotterdam on 13 October.

A close contest with the *Oranje* hinged on a moment at the start of the second half, when Platt was hauled down by Ronald Koeman on the edge of the penalty area. Despite being the last defender, Koeman received only a booking from German referee Karl-Josef Assenmacher. Furthermore, Tony Dorigo's resultant free kick was clearly blocked from fewer than the requisite ten yards, but when Koeman's subsequent free kick from a similar position was likewise charged down, Ince received a yellow card. Given a second chance, Koeman guided the ball over the wall with his instep to catch goalkeeper David Seaman unawares. Six minutes later, with Taylor and England still ruing the injustice, Dennis Bergkamp beat Seaman with a low shot from 20 yards to double the hosts' lead and all but ensure England's absence from the 1994 World Cup.

Taylor said he felt 'totally cheated' by the referee, but while England were unfortunate on the night and played 'as valiantly as they could against a superior team', the result merely confirmed the widely held impression that the England manager was out of his depth. Taylor and the FA would be further derided for their perceived amateurism in the wake of the landmark television documentary *Graham Taylor: An Impossible Job*, which provided unprecedented access behind the scenes of England's failed qualification campaign. The final humiliation came in Bologna, where a win over San Marino by a margin greater than seven might still have allowed England to qualify if results elsewhere went their way. Although England's 7-1 win proved inconsequential, Davide Gualtieri's goal for the Sammarinese after just eight seconds was the emblematic, embarrassing moment that brought Taylor's ill-fated tenure to a close. He resigned a week later.

As reigning world champions, Germany delivered a series of disjointed and underwhelming performances in difficult climatic conditions at the tournament in the United States. A narrow win over Bolivia at Chicago's Soldier Field in the opening game was followed by a 1-1 draw with Spain in the same stadium. In the third group match against South Korea at the Cotton Bowl in Dallas, Germany appeared to have hit their stride as they led 3-0 at half-time. With the Koreans mounting a comeback after the interval, however, the German team 'unaccountably fell apart'. On 75 minutes, Vogts bowed to vocal pressure from the travelling German fans and substituted the Fiorentina midfielder Effenberg, who made an infamous obscene gesture towards the crowd and was duly kicked out of the squad, the second German international after Uli Stein to be sent home from a World Cup in disgrace.

For the last-16 match against Belgium back in Chicago, Vogts rung the changes and brought back the veteran of 1986 and 1990, Rudi Völler, now of Olympique Marseille. The decision paid off as Völler scored twice in a 3-2 win, and Germany progressed to a quarter-final in New Jersey. On 10 July at Giants Stadium, a shock defeat to Bulgaria consigned the *Nationalmannschaft* to its earliest World Cup exit since 1962. After Matthäus put the favourites ahead from a dubiously awarded penalty at the start of the second half, the positive performance against Belgium was proven to have been a false dawn. Bulgaria shocked the football world with two quick-fire goals from the great Hristo Stoichkov and Yordan Letchkov. A flat-footed Bodo Illgner was blamed for the defeat, forcing Vogts to admit that he had made the wrong decision when he retained the Köln goalkeeper in the face of growing calls for the promotion of his deputy, Andreas Köpke of 1. FC Nürnberg. The match against Bulgaria was the final international in the careers of Illgner, Völler and Brehme, signalling a break from the generation which became world champions in Rome. Matthäus, a man with a prodigious ego who has long been given to referring to himself in the third person, was accused by Vogts of making selfish demands, of leaking stories to *Bild*, and of making light of his injuries to the detriment of the team. While Matthäus never formally quit the national team, it was clear that he was unlikely to play for Vogts again.

* * *

On 29 July 1994, Tottenham Hotspur chairman Alan Sugar made a significant contribution to Anglo-German relations by signing Jürgen Klinsmann from Monaco for £2m. Klinsmann, who turned 30 the next day, had a single-season impact on the English game that can only be apprehended in the context of his reputation among English football fans on the day he signed. Simon Barnes in *The Times* explained how Spurs supporters, who were already coming to terms with a six-point deduction and expulsion from the FA Cup (both later reversed) for financial irregularities, had now 'been asked the impossible: they have been asked to love Jürgen Klinsmann'. In Barnes's rather hyperbolic estimation, the former VfB Stuttgart and Internazionale striker was 'with the possible exception of Diego Maradona, the greatest hate figure in world football. He is regarded first and foremost as football's supreme conman: a man whose principal skill is for deceiving referees and winning penalties.'

A week later, after Klinsmann's first press conference in which he inquired whether there were any diving schools in London, perceptions were already shifting. Barnes now described 'a footballer of rare charm and intelligence. He handled his arrival press conference with effortless quantities of both. And all in English, of course. Nothing insular about Klinsmann.' At Hillsborough on 20 August, Klinsmann scored the fourth goal in a 4-3 win over Sheffield Wednesday and celebrated by diving extravagantly in front of his team-mates, reportedly on the suggestion of Teddy Sheringham. In his first match at White Hart Lane four days later, he scored with a bicycle kick from the edge of the six-yard box, and so it continued. Klinsmann finished the season with 29 goals in all competitions and was voted Footballer of the Year by the Football Writers' Association, becoming the second German player after Bert Trautmann to win the coveted award.

Ten years after his arrival in England, journalist Andrew Anthony wrote in *The Observer* that 'no one has had a greater impact in the course of a single year' on the Premier League. After moving back to Germany – much to Sugar's chagrin – to join FC Bayern in the summer of 1995, Klinsmann finished second behind George Weah of AC Milan in the voting for that year's Ballon d'Or. He returned to Spurs at the end of his career, for a six-month loan spell in 1998. In the penultimate game of his illustrious club career, Klinsmann scored four goals in a 6-2 win away to Wimbledon that secured Tottenham's Premier League status at the conclusion of a torrid season.

1996 UEFA European Championship
England

England's captivation of the Wembley crowd, and indeed the nation, during Euro '96 hinged on two minutes of play towards the end of their second group match, against Scotland on 15 June. The opening game against Switzerland had ended in disappointment when a first-half goal from Blackburn Rovers striker Alan Shearer, who ended a 12-game scoring drought in an England shirt, was cancelled out by a penalty from Kubilay Türkyilmaz just seven minutes from full time. Since the groups had been drawn in Birmingham the previous December, however, there was only one match that mattered to all England fans, and that was the meeting with the auld enemy Scotland. The game extended a rivalry that already stretched back 124 years, but it was the first time the two nations had ever faced each other at a FIFA or UEFA tournament.

Early in the second half, Shearer met Gary Neville's cross from the right flank to score his second goal of the competition, and a wave of excitement swept across Wembley in the summer sunshine. With 12 minutes remaining, however, memories of points dropped against Switzerland resurfaced when Tony Adams fouled Gordon Durie to concede a penalty. 'It's a replica of last week,' remarked ITV commentator Brian Moore. Scotland had surprisingly drawn with the Netherlands in their opening match, and they now looked set to secure another precious point against their great rivals. What followed in the next 90 seconds transformed an international football tournament into a cultural phenomenon. As Scotland captain Gary McAllister stepped up to take the penalty kick, the ball moved slightly on its spot, and his fierce shot came off Seaman's left elbow, deflecting high over the crossbar. At the ensuing corner, a free kick was given for a foul on Adams by Colin

Hendry. Seaman duly cleared the ball long into Scotland's half, while the England fans' cheers at the reprieve were still ringing around the stadium. Sheringham controlled the ball and laid it off to Darren Anderton on the left flank, who played a first-time pass into the path of Gascoigne. At that very moment, time stood still.

* * *

Towards the end of his three-year stint in Italian football, the incompatibility between Gascoigne's lifestyle and the stringent professionalism of Serie A had become an insurmountable problem. Under the exacting management of Zdeněk Zeman at Lazio in the 1994/95 season, the disaffected Gascoigne lost fitness and played only a handful of games, and in the summer of 1995 he returned to Britain with a move to Walter Smith's Rangers. In Scotland, Gascoigne found a new lease of life, scoring 19 goals in his first season with the Glasgow club as they won the league and cup double.

A bleached-blond, rejuvenated Gascoigne was soon back in the England side under Venables, but his inclusion came at a price, since wherever Gascoigne went, trouble was sure to follow. Certainly, Venables and the FA could have done without the coincidence of Gascoigne's 29th birthday falling on the day after the team's final playing commitment of their pre-tournament tour to the Far East in May 1996. With 'Gazza' as ringleader, and only assistant coach Bryan Robson to supervise them, several players went on a drinking binge in Hong Kong that culminated in reports of damage to the aircraft on their flight home to London Heathrow. The news of inebriated players bringing the England national team into disrepute just days before the start of a major tournament on home soil was manna from heaven for tabloid editors such as Piers Morgan, who had been hired by the *Daily Mirror* in 1995 at the age of just 30. On 29 May *The Mirror*'s front page exclaimed 'Drunken England Stars' Plane Shame'. On 31 May, *The Sun* ran a front-page photograph of a drunken Gascoigne, with fellow squad members Sheringham and Steve McManaman also prominent, under the headline 'Disgracefool: Look at Gazza … a drunk oaf with no pride'.

Details emerged from the last night in Hong Kong, including the infamous 'dentist's chair' in which the players were administered free-poured tequila. By Saturday, 1 June, one week from the opening match, the *Daily Mirror* ran a damaging story about Gascoigne's private life on the front page, as well as quotes from Alf Ramsey on the back page under the headline 'I will not go to Wembley if this man plays'. Inside, another headline screamed 'Collect your boots and get lost, Gazza!' Venables held his nerve, however, and confirmed Gascoigne's place in his final 22-man squad. These were the circumstances which put the troubled genius Gascoigne under the microscope and engendered a siege mentality among the England squad at their base in Burnham Beeches. When later asked by *Kicker* journalists to provide his thoughts on Germany's semi-final opponents, Klinsmann praised Venables for his handling of the situation, 'It was impressive how he coped with the fierce attacks from the tabloid press at the start of the tournament.'

* * *

Back in the hot Wembley sunshine of 15 June, Gascoigne's run into space saw him receive Anderton's lofted pass around 25 yards from goal, but he was advancing into a narrowing gap between defenders Stewart McKimmie and Hendry. The ball had bounced just once at his left side and Gascoigne now resolved to flick it with his left foot over his head and behind him, bamboozling Hendry entirely. In the blink of an eye, Gascoigne turned and adjusted himself as he watched the ball loop down on to his right foot, with which he then unerringly volleyed past Andy Goram at his near post. Lying on the ground in rapturous celebration, Gascoigne was mobbed by his team-mates and given a 'dentist's chair' soaking from a water bottle, in a provocative riposte to his critics. An ecstatic Wembley crowd greeted the sensational goal, the win over old rivals, and the talisman's sporting rehabilitation all at once. On Monday 17 June, the *Daily Mirror* featured an apology to Gascoigne on its front page, 'Over the last two weeks the *Daily Mirror* may have created the impression that England soccer star Paul Gascoigne is a fat, drunken, loutish imbecile who should have been kicked out of the team before the start of Euro '96. It has now come to our attention that he is in fact a football wizard capable of winning the tournament single-handedly.'

These were the most glorious scenes the England national team had delivered at Wembley since 1966, and there was more to come. In the third and final group match, against the Netherlands on 18 June, England produced an unforgettable performance in a 4-1 win. Shearer scored the first penalty of his international career midway through the first half, and the hosts then dismantled Guus Hiddink's shell-shocked Dutch side in a 15-minute spell after half-time. 'I can't recall hearing such noise at Wembley for an England international for many, many a year,' remarked commentator Martin Tyler as fans began to adopt the lyrics of 'Three Lions', the song written for the tournament, chanting 'football's coming home'. Shearer and Sheringham both scored twice in an effective partnership at the head of a pragmatic but well-balanced 4-4-2 formation that featured Ince and Gascoigne in central midfield, McManaman and Darren Anderton on the flanks, and a back four of Adams, Neville, Stuart Pearce, and the relatively inexperienced Gareth Southgate, who had only made four international appearances before the tournament. Even Patrick Kluivert's late consolation goal for the *Oranje* was a positive for England fans, as it allowed the Netherlands to progress from the group at Scotland's expense on the criterion of goals scored.

In the quarter-final on 22 June, England were forced to confront the demons of Turin in the penalty shoot-out which followed a goalless draw with Spain. After Gascoigne's spectacular moment of individual brilliance against Scotland, and the exhilarating team display against the Dutch, England now had gutsy resilience to add to the developing narrative of their campaign. The successful penalties and subsequent emotive reactions, especially from Pearce, who had missed in Turin, were further flashes of bravura that galvanised the England team ahead of the semi-final.

Germany's campaign in England began in difficult circumstances. With Klinsmann suspended for the first group match, against the Czech Republic at Old Trafford on 9 June, Vogts then lost Jürgen Kohler to a cruciate ligament injury just a quarter of an hour into the game. In the absence of Matthäus,

Matthias Sammer of Borussia Dortmund played in the sweeper position, while Häßler, Möller and Werder Bremen veteran Dieter Eilts made up the midfield trio. English referee David Elleray booked six German players and four Czechs, but Germany prevailed thanks to first-half goals from Ziege and Möller. Against Russia on 16 June, the returning Klinsmann partnered Oliver Bierhoff in an all-new strike partnership, and Germany won well with a goal from Sammer and two from Klinsmann after Russia had a man sent off.

Germany were themselves reduced to ten men in the final group match, against Arrigo Sacchi's Italy on 19 June, when Thomas Strunz was dismissed on the hour mark. Goalkeeper Köpke was the man of the match, saving a Gianfranco Zola penalty and consigning the *Azzurri* to early elimination from the tournament by securing a goalless draw. Sammer later called this Italy side 'tactically the best team I have ever played against', remarking that even the best and most advanced tactics are no guarantee of sporting success.

A hard-fought quarter-final against a Croatia side featuring the likes of Davor Šuker, Zvonimir Boban and Slaven Bilić followed on 23 June, Germany's fourth successive game in Manchester. Klinsmann's first-half penalty was cancelled out just after half-time by a well-taken goal from Šuker, following an error in possession from substitute Steffen Freund. Igor Štimac was sent off for a second bookable offence just five minutes after the equaliser, and the outstanding Sammer then demonstrated his value in attack when afforded space, scoring the winning goal from six yards. On a negative note, the reason for Freund's introduction before half-time was a calf injury to Klinsmann, and VfB Stuttgart forward Fredi Bobic was also withdrawn with a dislocated shoulder. Klinsmann was the only striker in the squad who had scored in the competition, and he had also been captain and leader of the team for the last two seasons. His absence was a major blow to Vogts ahead of a semi-final against the hosts in the heady atmosphere of Wembley.

A War of Words I

On Monday, 24 June, after three days of anti-Spanish headlines in the previous week, Piers Morgan and the *Daily Mirror* turned their attention to England's semi-final opponents. The infamous front page – with its instruction to 'cut out and stick in your window' – featured pictures of Pearce and Gascoigne with superimposed army helmets and the headline, 'Achtung! Surrender – For you Fritz, ze Euro '96 Championship is over.' Yet while this is the image that has left its mark, it was by no means an isolated misstep.

The whole edition was an elaborate and ill-conceived attempt to draw parallels between the European Championship semi-final and the Second World War. Many of the 44 pages were filled with anti-German rhetoric in various contexts. Twenty-six years on, it reads, mercifully, like a museum piece of hysterical xenophobia. Morgan himself took responsibility for the front-page editorial entitled 'Mirror declares football war on Germany', and feebly cast himself as Neville Chamberlain, even attempting to reconcile his fatuous declaration with the newspaper's then current stance of promoting British integration in the European Union. On 28 May, *The Mirror* had responded to internal debates about Europe in John Major's Conservative government with the following proclamation on its front page:

'The most stupid war of modern times has been launched by a few senseless fanatics. It is being fought over the future of Britain in Europe. Yet there is nothing to fight over. For if Britain was outside Europe, it would not have a future. Today *The Mirror* starts the fightback – with our own campaign. We will tell the British people the truth. And the truth is this: if we ever cut ourselves loose from our partners across the Channel, we would become an isolated, irrelevant island.'

Four weeks later, Morgan now wrote as part of his jingoistic invective, 'You can imagine what a bitter blow it is to me that all my struggle to win peace has failed. It is the *Daily Mirror* that has been at the forefront of efforts to establish peaceful and productive relations with our European partners.' On the back page, meanwhile, the headline 'Who do you think you're kidding Mister Hitman?' and the strapline 'We are not fooled, Fritz!' accompanied a story about supposed dissimulation from the German camp regarding Klinsmann's injury. This was a reference to 'Who do you think you are kidding, Mister Hitler', the theme song of the popular British sitcom *Dad's Army*, originally broadcast on the BBC from 1968 to 1977. Page two presented news of *The Mirror*'s 'surrender offer' by telephone to the German Embassy in London, alongside a report from Justin Dunn entitled 'The *Mirror* invades Berlin', which informs readers, 'We have decided to teach the Hun a lesson … We have come fully armed with a special St George flag and thousands of leaflets bearing the warning, "Achtung! Surrender! Remember 1966!"'

The illustrations on the facing page included a photograph of Dunn standing next to an East German Trabant car, with the caption 'Filthy hun – Dunn commandeers an East German Trabant, notorious for its pollution'. Elsewhere, on pages four and five, there were gleeful reports of *Mirror* journalists' 'daring raid' on Germany's team in order to place beach towels on the seats next to the hotel swimming pool, given that 'for decades, we Brits have suffered as the early rising Germans have won the holiday battle to grab the pick of the sunbeds'.

Predictably, all this puerile nonsense masquerading as journalism caused uproar, at a time when the tabloids enjoyed massive circulation figures and a significant influence on the cultural narrative. The *Daily Mirror*'s front page of the following day featured a photograph of Klinsmann accepting a gift hamper from a *Mirror* journalist by way of reconciliation, while Morgan offered his own insincere apology. Later that day, Klinsmann was asked by a broadsheet journalist about the behaviour of the English tabloids:

'The fact that it is the British media and population that have come out in protest against that sort of reporting speaks for itself and I am very grateful for that. The team can easily shrug it off and smile about it but I am afraid there is a knock-on effect on the 7,000 German fans at Wembley so I hope the atmosphere will remain calm and peaceful.'

The belligerent anti-German tone had been set back in April, when *The Sun* and the *Daily Mirror* competed in a preposterous campaign to 'repatriate' the ball used in the 1966 World Cup Final, which they saw as the rightful property of Geoff Hurst and England. The ball could be seen on a photograph under the arm of Helmut Haller, West Germany's top goalscorer at that tournament, as he shook the Queen's hand after the final at Wembley. Haller had taken great care to bring the ball home with him and subsequently gave it to his son Jürgen as a birthday present. This was no mystery, but in the heat of the mid-90s tabloid circulation war, Haller was branded a thief, and Morgan and Stuart Higgins, editor of *The Sun*, moved heaven and earth to reach him first.

Haller later recalled how two men in trench coats stood at his front door at 7am and told him, 'You're not going anywhere now, we're watching you!' He was at first fearful, but when he realised that they were journalists from *The Sun* who would offer money for the coveted souvenir, he arranged to meet them later that day in more comfortable surroundings. By lunchtime, two *Mirror* hacks had also arrived, and the bidding war began. 'Of course, none of these people cared about English football fans, let alone the country,' Haller continued. 'Each newspaper was on the scent of the story of the year. They just wanted to market the greatest symbol of success in English football for themselves.'

With the agreement of Haller and his son, the ball was brought back to England to much synthetic acclaim in the victorious *Daily Mirror*, and presented to Hurst, whose own account of the episode constitutes an entertaining chapter in his autobiography, *1966 and All That*. According to Hurst, *The Mirror*, with the help of sponsors including Richard Branson, had agreed to pay £80,000 for the ball, beating *The Sun* and a German TV station to the prize. It is now held at the National Football Museum in Manchester, where it is 'displayed courtesy of Eurostar, Mirror Group and Virgin'.

Morgan later wrote of his declaration of football war that 'the nation suffered a catastrophic sense of humour failure', but a pre-tournament editorial in the popular independent football magazine *When Saturday Comes* expertly articulated the real problem behind all the jocular jingoism:

'It isn't funny; in fact, it stinks. The biggest odour comes not from the casual bigotry, but from the hypocrisy, because if there's any trouble during Euro '96, on whatever scale … you can be sure that the front pages of the *Mirror* and *The Sun* will be screaming of the nation's disgrace … You can guarantee, though, that among all the opinions offered by their reporters, columnists and leader writers, there will be not even the slightest hint of a suggestion that the blind chauvinism of the tabloids helps create the atmosphere in which such events take place.'

Christoph Wagner, who undertook a comprehensive survey of the press coverage of the Anglo-German football rivalry in the 20th century, cites an article from Bernhard Heimrich in the *Frankfurter Allgemeine Zeitung* as a significant example of the German response to the English press in 1996. Wagner explains how Heimrich 'argued that much of the nationalistic hype could be explained by a British identity crisis arising from the growing tensions within the United Kingdom between the English, the Scots, and the Welsh which were then becoming apparent' in the context of contemporary political debates about the devolution of power from Westminster. Wagner also argues that greater historical distance from 1945, and increased national sentiment after 1990, now enabled the German press to level a response at its English counterpart, 'As the passing of time lifted the burden of war guilt from German shoulders, there was no longer any requirement to accept the negative stereotyping that featured so prominently in the *Daily Mirror*'s tasteless tabloid war on Germany.' Responses such as Heimrich's, meanwhile, 'pointed to insularity and nostalgia as an explanation for the excesses of English newspapers, singling them out as the worst press in Europe'.

26 June 1996
UEFA European Championship semi-final
Germany 1-1 England (after extra time)
Germany win 6-5 on penalties
Wembley Stadium

In the broadsheet newspapers, the focus was on Germany's sporting threat, in particular that posed by Sammer. 'He glides out of so-called defensive positions with a freedom that not even Beckenbauer exploited in such athletic fashion,' wrote Rob Hughes in *The Times*. 'He attacks all the way, often advancing ahead of his forwards, often showing an eye for goal that would make Alan Shearer proud.' The rumour that Klinsmann would make the starting XI after all was widespread, with *The Guardian*'s Martin Thorpe reporting that Sheringham had called his former Spurs team-mate to ask about his injury. 'He rang to ask how I was doing because he saw the game and the injury and he still hoped that I could play tomorrow night, but I told him that would not be the case,' said Klinsmann.

Meanwhile, Gary Neville's booking against Spain meant that he was suspended, and his younger brother Phil was widely expected to deputise at right-back. Henry Winter in the *Daily Telegraph* lent his support to this idea on account of the threat posed by Ziege on Germany's left, but he acknowledged 'a strong school of thought that believes Phil Neville is too inexperienced', adding, 'This line of reasoning continues that England should go to a three-man defence with David Platt remaining in midfield alongside the returning Paul Ince,' who had missed the quarter-final through suspension. This was indeed the gamble Venables took for England's biggest match at Wembley in 30 years. The back three of Stuart Pearce, Gareth Southgate and captain Tony Adams played behind Ince, Platt and Paul Gascoigne, with Steve McManaman and Darren Anderton on the flanks, and the partnership of Teddy Sheringham and Alan Shearer up front. It was a bold and attacking selection that included six offensively minded players.

With only 15 outfield players available, Vogts selected Stefan Kuntz as a lone striker in Klinsmann's absence. FC Bayern's creative midfielder Mehmet Scholl, who had come into the side for the Croatia game, played in the number ten position. A midfield three of stand-in captain Andreas Möller, Dieter Eilts and Steffen Freund started ahead of Thomas Helmer and Markus Babbel in defence, with the in-form Sammer in the sweeper position and Christian Ziege and Stefan Reuter on the flanks. Reuter was the only German player who had also appeared in the World Cup semi-final in Turin, while Pearce, Gascoigne and Platt were the three English survivors.

Playing in a colour that was officially termed indigo-blue and which will forever be seen as an infelicitous choice, England made a fast start in front of the excitable Wembley crowd of over 75,000. After just 90 seconds, Ince hit a dipping volley from 35 yards that Köpke punched over the crossbar. From the resultant corner, Gascoigne played a ball to the near post that was flicked on by Adams for Shearer to head in from close range for his fifth goal of the tournament. Barely two minutes were on the clock, and the stirring pre-match atmosphere became more intense still as 'Three Lions' enjoyed some of its most jubilant refrains yet.

Seaman had not been tested in the English goal when Germany equalised on 15 minutes. Helmer advanced from defence and found Möller, who was quickly attended by Adams and Gascoigne but managed to play a pass back to Helmer, now in the penalty area. The Bayern centre-back played a low left-footed cross on the turn through Southgate's legs, and Kuntz ghosted in behind Pearce to stab the ball into the net. For 15 minutes after this goal, Germany played on the front foot and penned England back, albeit without clear-cut chances to show for their positive play.

Around the half-hour mark, England began to grow into the game again by playing long passes in behind the German defence. From one of the resultant corners, Anderton's cross fell behind Sheringham in the penalty area, but the Spurs striker was nonetheless able to volley on target where Reuter blocked off the line. Shortly before half-time, good combination play from Platt and Anderton on the right flank resulted in a cross for Shearer, who throughout the game was dominant in the air against Babbel and Helmer. On this occasion his header flashed just inches wide of Köpke's right-hand post.

At the very beginning of the second half, Reuter suffered the psychological blow of a booking that would keep him out of the final with a suspension, and he would now have to take additional care in his duel with McManaman. England enjoyed a good spell of possession, although they were unable to get close to the opposition goal. On the hour mark, Eilts beat Platt on the left, where England indeed lacked a full-back presence, and cut the ball back from the bye-line, but Helmer skewed his finish over the crossbar. Vogts introduced Häßler for Scholl with a quarter of an hour remaining in an effort to shore up midfield, where Gascoigne in particular was finding space. Ten minutes from full time, after an altercation with Pearce, Möller received his second booking of the tournament and knew, like Reuter, that he would be suspended for an eventual final.

For the fourth time, and the second time at Wembley, the two rivals headed for an additional period of play, although with a notable difference on this occasion. This was the first major international tournament to adopt the short-lived 'golden goal' rule, by which the first team to score in extra time was immediately declared the winner. The three knockout matches at Euro '96 which necessitated extra time had all ended in a penalty shoot-out, and the golden goal was thus still an elusive, largely unknown quantity that significantly heightened the drama of this semi-final after 90 minutes. Just three minutes into extra time, England came agonisingly close to putting the new rule into effect when Anderton struck the post. The chance came when Platt found McManaman behind the German back line, and the Liverpool winger cut a pass back into the six-yard box. The ball just escaped the diving Köpke and reached Anderton, who strained to divert it towards goal but had arrived perhaps half a step too soon to finish accurately. On the television coverage, the scene was followed by a famous image of Venables with his head in his hands.

Any concerns that the new regulations would precipitate a timid and defensive half hour of play were quickly dispelled as the game flowed from end to end, and both teams had chances to finish the contest. Six minutes in, a major reprieve came for England as Hungarian referee Sándor Puhl blew his whistle just as Kuntz headed a Möller corner past Seaman and into the net. The Beşiktaş striker was adjudged to have pushed Southgate in the back while jumping for the ball. The almost intolerable tension then reached an inimitable crescendo after a heavy touch from Häßler on Germany's right allowed England to take possession. The ball found its way to the withdrawn Sheringham, who looked up and played an excellent long pass over Shearer's shoulder on the right side of the penalty area. With his first touch Shearer played a tantalising cross behind the German back line and along the face of goal. All the while, Gascoigne had made a surging run into the danger area, fending off Freund. As with Anderton's earlier chance, the ball narrowly eluded the flailing goalkeeper and then rolled, in a mind-bendingly dramatic moment that toyed with perceptions of time and space, past Gascoigne's outstretched left foot, two yards from goal.

In the second half of extra time, Vogts brought on Werder Bremen forward Marco Bode and Bayern's Thomas Strunz to use all his permitted substitutions, while Venables notably chose not to make any changes to his side over the 120 minutes, despite the presence of strikers Robbie Fowler and Les Ferdinand on the bench. The dreaded penalty shoot-out, a repeat of Turin, was drawing ever closer. When it came, Ince sat in the centre circle with his back to goal, unable to watch. England, who have since built up such an unfortunate reputation when it comes to penalties, in fact scored all ten of their regulation kicks across two shoot-outs in this tournament. They retained the same order that had prevailed against Spain, with Shearer followed by Platt, Pearce and Gascoigne. Pearce further exorcised his Turin demons and greeted the fans with a thumbs-up, and Gascoigne rallied the crowd with more impudent gestures.

After Häßler, Strunz, Reuter and Ziege all converted, Sheringham and Kuntz made it ten out of ten, which meant that players who had not volunteered now had to step up. The first to do so was Southgate, who saw his kick saved by Köpke low to his right side, and who thus followed Stuart Pearce and Chris Waddle to an unwanted destiny. Möller then stepped up and hit a fierce shot into the top of Seaman's net before reeling away to celebrate in front of the German fans. With hands on hips, he cocked his head to the left and momentarily stood still in front of a bank of photographers, perfecting an emperor-like pose that has gone down as an enduring image of German arrogance. Möller later said that he met Gascoigne two days after the match and was asked to explain himself, 'Paul Gascoigne asked me, "Why did you celebrate like that?" I said I don't know, it was a reaction, I was very proud after the penalty because we were in the final and we beat the English team in their own stadium, it was a sign of [pride].'

One spectator at Wembley that evening who welcomed Germany's victory was Alastair Campbell, press secretary to the leader of the opposition Tony Blair. After 17 years of Conservative rule in Britain, Labour enjoyed a sizeable lead in the polls at this time and were expected to win the next general election, which Major was obliged to call by May 1997. At the semi-final, there was some anxiety that if England beat Germany and went on to win the tournament, the national team's success could swing the political narrative in the government's favour.

Campbell, who was born in Yorkshire to Scottish parents, told *The Guardian*'s Simon Hattenstone in 2021:

'I was at the Germany game with Tony Blair. John Major was in the front row, Tony was in the second row and I was at the back with this Scottish Special Branch guy. Being absolutely frank, I wanted Germany to win, mainly because the Tories were so desperate for England to win it. As we got out of the ground Tony said to me can you at least try to look a little bit pissed off. I got in the car and punched the roof and said, *"Jetzt sind die Tories absolut gefuckt mein Kapitän."*'

* * *

With Möller suspended and Klinsmann restored, Germany played with two strikers and numerous players short of fitness in the final on 30 June, against a talented Czech side featuring Pavel Nedvěd, Patrik Berger and Karel Poborský. The Czechs took the lead after an hour through a contentious Berger penalty, and threatened to repeat the achievement of their Czechoslovak predecessors, who beat West Germany to the title in 1976. Yet it was substitute Oliver Bierhoff, making only his eighth senior international appearance, who made a name for himself at Wembley and won a third European Championship and sixth major trophy for the *Nationalmannschaft*. His second, golden goal just five minutes into extra time came from an unfortunate error by Czech goalkeeper Petr Kouba, who was unable to hold the Udinese striker's surprise shot on the turn from the edge of the penalty area and helplessly watched the ball bounce into the net behind him.

The outstanding Sammer, whose performances as *libero* were reminiscent of Beckenbauer, was voted Player of the Tournament, and later that year he also won the Ballon d'Or, the fifth – and to date last – German player to do so. For his performance in the semi-final against England, *Kicker* awarded Sammer a grade one, noting how he 'broke out of defence almost every time he won the ball to push his team forward'. His career was sadly curtailed by injury, however, and Vogts would have to do without him at the World Cup two years later. In his capacity as sporting director at the DFB, Sammer later remarked that the win over England was the greatest game he could remember.

In the prestigious setting of Wembley, Germany were champions of Europe once more, and Klinsmann duly collected the trophy from Queen Elizabeth II, in the presence of Prime Minister John Major and Chancellor Helmut Kohl. In *The Telegraph* the following day, Henry Winter paid tribute to Germany's captain:

'Few could begrudge England's semi-final conquerors their golden moment, their score-settling session with history. If Tony Adams could not lift the European Championship trophy, who better than Klinsmann? ... A lifelong admirer of Wembley, a man almost in tears when Tottenham Hotspur failed to reach the 1995 FA Cup Final, fulfilled one of his greatest ambitions when he strode up those 39 steps to receive the Henri Delauney Trophy from The Queen.'

At one distant end of the stadium, the travelling German fans sang a last refrain in faultless English, 'Football's coming home.'

11

Fear and Loathing

1998–2001

With the exception of Sam Allardyce, who only took charge of the national team for one game in 2016, Glenn Hoddle is the only permanently appointed England manager not to have faced Germany or West Germany during their tenure. Hoddle's reign as successor to Venables was marked by a courageous draw in Rome on 11 October 1997 that secured qualification to the 1998 FIFA World Cup. At the tournament in France, Hoddle benefited from the young Manchester United talents David Beckham and Paul Scholes, both aged 23, and teenager Michael Owen, who scored one of the greatest goals in World Cup history against Argentina in the second round.

Stuart Pearce, David Platt and Paul Gascoigne were the only members of the Euro '96 team who did not feature. Gascoigne harboured hopes of inclusion in the squad until just days before the tournament began, when he was dropped amid more tabloid revelations about his conduct and private life. He would never play for England again, and of those writers who disagreed with Hoddle's decision, Matt Dickinson put it best in pointing out that some members of the squad 'will be doing football's equivalent of carrying the drinks tray this summer. Gascoigne, meanwhile, may be helping himself to the drinks cabinet. It is a shameful waste and a needless one.'

England were eliminated from the last 16 in a thrilling and tempestuous match against Argentina in Saint-Étienne, where Beckham was infamously sent off after kicking out at Diego Simeone in front of Danish referee Kim Milton Nielsen.

England's World Cup campaign ended once more in penalty shoot-out heartache, when Paul Ince and David Batty failed to convert, but the emergence of Owen, still only 18, had been a major positive. When Hoddle was dismissed in February 1999, he had the highest win percentage of any England manager since Alf Ramsey, and optimism abounded around the young players in his squad. Crucially, however, Hoddle had alienated the press, and he unwisely told Dickinson in a *Times* interview at the end of January that 'the gloves are off' where his relationship with the media was concerned.

Even without the revelations of his controversial religious beliefs, his days were surely numbered, but his comments in that same interview about reincarnation, and his stated view that disabled people are paying for sins in a past life, accelerated his departure. By 17 February, the FA named Kevin Keegan, then manager at Fulham in England's third tier, as Hoddle's successor, although at first only on a part-time basis for four games.

The 1998 World Cup was the end of the road for Berti Vogts, whose ageing team – labelled '*Dinosaurus germanicus*' by Agence France-Presse – performed feebly on their way to a quarter-final defeat by the great Croatia side that would eventually finish third. The humiliating 3-0 loss in Lyon, capped by a solo goal from Davor Šuker, was a disaster for German football which compounded serious off-field problems. A week after scenes of violent disorder had preceded England's opening match against Tunisia in Marseille, French police made around 100 arrests amid organised hooligan skirmishes around Germany's group-stage encounter with Yugoslavia in the northern city of Lens. After the match, a *gendarme* named Daniel Nivel was brutally assaulted by a group of German men in an attack that left him with life-altering injuries. Photographs and video footage showing Nivel lying helplessly on the ground in a pool of blood hit the front pages and news bulletins in Germany, causing uproar. Chancellor Helmut Kohl called the incident an 'absolute disgrace for our country', and DFB president Egidius Braun said, 'This is the darkest hour of my life.' Braun later set up the Daniel Nivel Foundation to combat football hooliganism and support its victims. In November 1999, a 28-year-old man was sentenced to ten years in prison for Nivel's attempted murder, and three other men were also jailed for grievous bodily harm.

The incidents in France were indicative of a growing problem at the end of the 1990s, when hardened groups of organised hooligans, driven out of stadia by improved policing, safety reforms and the commercialisation of the game, adopted new strategies of evading surveillance and arrest. Some of the most dangerous such groups from England and Germany were on a collision course whose terminus was decided on 12 December 1999, when the two countries were drawn to face each other in the city of Charleroi, south of Brussels, in the group stage of the UEFA European Championship. Four days earlier in Japan, England and Germany were also drawn together in group nine of UEFA qualification for the 2002 FIFA World Cup. As a result, there would be an unprecedented series of three competitive Anglo-German internationals in a 15-month period. Coming in the midst of a crisis period for German football and a wave of English hooliganism abroad, this was the height of the rivalry when measured in terms of fear and loathing.

* * *

Between 1996 and 2002, German football provided seven finalists in the three major UEFA club competitions, with Borussia Dortmund and FC Bayern winning the Champions League in 1997 and 2001, respectively, and Schalke 04 claiming the UEFA Cup in 1997. Bayern had also won the UEFA Cup the previous year, beating Nottingham Forest 7-2 on aggregate in the quarter-final before overcoming Zinedine Zidane's Bordeaux in the final. Meanwhile, the penultimate season of the Cup Winners' Cup ended in an Anglo-German final between Chelsea and VfB Stuttgart in Stockholm on 13 May 1998. Chelsea won their second European trophy thanks to a goal from Gianfranco Zola, one of the Premier League's most popular foreign imports at the end of the 1990s. The losing Stuttgart side featured Fredi Bobic and veteran Thomas Berthold, and was managed by Joachim Löw, then aged 38.

English football's major force in Europe was Alex Ferguson's Manchester United, five-time Premier League champions in the 1990s. After winning the 1991 Cup Winners' Cup, their first continental title since 1968, Ferguson had set his sights on the European Cup, and by 1997 his team reached the semi-finals, where they lost 2-0 on aggregate to Ottmar Hitzfeld's Borussia Dortmund. In the 1998/99 season, United and FC Bayern, now managed by Hitzfeld, were drawn together in the group phase, in which they played out a 2-2 draw in Munich and a 1-1 stalemate at Old Trafford.

The two clubs famously met again in the final at Barcelona's Camp Nou on 26 May 1999. United had beaten rivals Arsenal to the Premier League title by a single point on 16 May, and then won the FA Cup Final against Newcastle United on 22 May. In Barcelona they thus had the chance to complete a historic treble, but the new Bundesliga champions scored after just six minutes through a Mario Basler free kick and controlled the game. The astonishing dénouement, in which United substitutes Teddy Sheringham and Ole Gunnar Solskjær both scored from successive corners in injury time to win the match, secured Ferguson's legacy and had a profound effect on FC Bayern. Two seasons later they re-scaled the summit and won their fourth European Cup thanks to Oliver Kahn's heroics in the penalty shoot-out against Valencia in Milan. On their way to the San Siro, Bayern exacted a measure of revenge, beating Manchester United 3-1 on aggregate in the quarter-final.

A War of Words II

In 2003, the linguistic scholars Hywel Bishop and Adam Jaworski published a study of the British press reportage of the England v Germany match at Euro 2000. Their methodology was Critical Discourse Analysis, which examines the link between discourse and power, and how discourse reproduces and maintains social relations. Crucially, the legacy of linguistic theory shows us that discourse – be it spoken, written, visual, or else – 'is both socially constituted and socially constitutive', which brings us back to the hypocrisy of the tabloid newspapers.

The study showed in granular detail how the English 'nation is imagined in terms of its past through the invocation of a variety of historical sporting and military references'. At the European Championship in Belgium, an added frisson to the usual Second World War rhetoric was generated by the proximity of the

Charleroi venue to Waterloo, scene of one of Britain's greatest military victories, even if at that battle in 1815, the Germans – or rather, Prussians – fought alongside the Duke of Wellington to defeat Napoleon Bonaparte. *The Sun* nonetheless leveraged the symbolism of military conflict, 'Kevin Keegan's lionhearts will be roaring into battle against Germany today – after spending the night at Waterloo.' In *The Times*, meanwhile, the author and biographer Hunter Davies wrote, 'They say don't mention the wars, but really you have to. England-Germany conflicts have been woven into our souls for 100 years now. And since those two big victories in 1918 and 1945, there haven't been many times England has got one over Germany.'

As Bishop and Jaworski noted, in such formulations 'the history of the two nations becomes a conflation of two temporal narratives: the military and sporting'. Perhaps the most famous and enduring example of this came from Vincent Mulchrone in the *Daily Mail* on the day of the 1966 World Cup Final, 'Germany may beat us at our national sport today, but that would be only fair. We beat them twice at theirs.' This sentiment was later reflected in the chant, sung to the tune of 'Camptown Races', which was popularised after England's victory, 'Two world wars and one World Cup.' Another significant example came from the great Hugh McIlvanney in 1970, ahead of the World Cup quarter-final in León, in an *Observer* article entitled 'Echoes of previous battles that sound in the blood':

'Football matches between these two countries have as much to do with atavism as with athletic skills. When the English and the Germans meet on any competitive field, echoes of previous battles, more distant and more bitter than the Wembley final of 1966, sound in blood. This may be regrettable but it is inescapably real and there is no doubt the unique tensions that pulse beneath the surface of these occasions have always done more damage to Germany than to England.'

These words were published on the morning of 14 June 1970, when West Germany still had only beaten England once, in a game which McIlvanney could barely bring himself to acknowledge. Thirty years on, after a string of German footballing successes against England, it was no longer clear who, if anyone, benefited from these 'unique tensions'.

In Charleroi, a no-tolerance policy from Belgian riot police resulted in hundreds of arrests across the weekend of 16–18 June, and UEFA threatened England with expulsion from the tournament. After readily adopting militaristic symbolism and the language of 'us' and 'them' to promote 'the idea that the football team is on a mission to protect the nation from its enemies', the newspapers were then quick to distance themselves from the serious violence that unfolded on the streets of Charleroi and Brussels. Bishop and Jaworski demonstrated the linguistic strategies employed to achieve this, such as the use of quotation marks to call violent fans' motives into question – 'more than 500 England "supporters" arrested'; language such as 'scum' and 'dregs of our society' to describe those involved; the listing of attributes and behaviours apparently shared by all such like-minded people; and references to hooligans as 'a minority', often in the same space as warnings that the problem is now widespread and uncontrollable – 'A tiny minority spoiling it for the rest of us? Don't you believe it. A tidal wave of sewage follows England abroad and it is high time it was stopped.'

As Bishop and Jaworski were careful to point out, the right-wing tabloid press in Britain 'draws on similar metaphors used in reference to the perceived threat of "illegal immigrants" and "asylum seekers" flowing uncontrollably through the borders of the nation and threatening its integrity', and this tendency has lamentably only grown since their study, most notably in the run-up to the 2016 referendum on EU membership.

The *Sunday Mirror*'s front page of 18 June 2000, the day after England's gritty win over Germany, featured an exemplary juxtaposition of nationalist rhetoric with the 'othering' of violent supporters. The headline 'The Great Escape' linked the sporting victory to the mass escape from the Stalag Luft III prison camp in 1944, as famously depicted in the 1963 film of the same name, while the sub-heading 'Now let's beat the thugs' was accompanied by the words 'England fans shame the nation'. Politicians were also blamed for their inaction, as in Oliver Holt's piece in *The Times*, 'The Government's culpability is all the more serious because it has backed England's bid for the 2006 World Cup energetically, but by failing to take preventative measures such

Captains Eddie Hapgood (left) and Fritz Szepan shake hands at White Hart Lane, 4 December 1935

England v Germany, 4 December 1935. The Nazi flag flies from the roof of White Hart Lane

Post-match banquet at the Park Lane Hotel, London, 1 December 1954. From left to right: Stanley Matthews, Fritz Herkenrath, Jupp Posipal, and Billy Wright

Sepp Herberger, Reichstrainer *1936–42;* Bundestrainer *1950–64. Pictured in 1959*

Alf Ramsey, England manager 1963–74. Pictured in 1965

Decorative Royal Shrovetide ball presented to the West German team for their on-field performance and fairness at the 1966 World Cup German Football Museum

The protagonists at kick-off of the 1966 World Cup Final. From left to right: Linesman Tofiq Bahramov, West German captain Uwe Seeler, referee Gottfried Dienst, and England captain Bobby Moore

The ball bounces on the goal line after Geoff Hurst's shot hit the crossbar behind Hans Tilkowski in the West German goal. A goal is awarded to give England a 3-2 lead in extra time in the 1966 World Cup Final

England players seek shade and water ahead of extra time in the stifling heat of León, Mexico, during the 1970 World Cup quarter-final

Günter Netzer (left) and Helmut Schön at the UEFA European Championship quarter-final, first leg at Wembley, 29 April 1972

Lothar Matthäus (left) consoles Paul Gascoigne after the World Cup semi-final in Turin, 4 July 1990

Helmut Haller greets Queen Elizabeth II with the match ball under his arm after the World Cup Final at Wembley, 30 July 1966. The ball was recovered by the Daily Mirror *shortly before Euro 96*

Sharing the pain: Stuart Pearce with Gareth Southgate after England's penalty shoot-out defeat to Germany at Wembley, 26 June 1996

England manager Kevin Keegan trudges off the wet Wembley turf after a 1-0 defeat to Germany in the last game at the old stadium. He resigned shortly afterwards

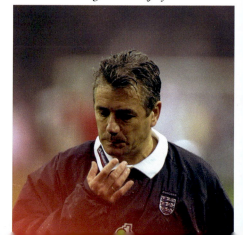

Jürgen Klinsmann lifts the European Championship trophy in front of the Queen at Wembley

Michael Owen celebrates during England's emphatic 5-1 win in Munich in qualification for the 2002 World Cup, 1 September 2001

The ball bounces clearly over the line from Frank Lampard's volley past Manuel Neuer in the German goal during the 2010 World Cup last-16 match in Bloemfontein, South Africa

Bedlam at Wembley Stadium after Harry Kane scores England second goal in a 2-0 win over Germany in the last-16 of the European Championship, 29 June 2021

as the withdrawal of passports of known hooligans it has made the bid's Achilles heel into a gaping target.' Notably, England's direct rival in the bidding process was Germany, and the lessons learned there after the World Cup in France gave English writers some notion of what could be done to prevent the scenes they witnessed in Belgium. The *Sunday Express*, for example, noted that 'other countries, such as Germany, have ruthlessly effective measures in place to prevent troublemakers from travelling to sensitive matches'.

17 June 2000
UEFA European Championship group stage
England 1-0 Germany
Stade du Pays de Charleroi, Charleroi

After Vogts stepped down as *Bundestrainer* on 7 September 1998, Jupp Derwall's former assistant Erich Ribbeck was appointed his successor, with ex-international Uli Stielike as his right-hand man. Ribbeck had originally been considered for the job back in 1978 upon the resignation of Helmut Schön, and he was now 61, retired in Tenerife. Furthermore, it was clear to everyone that he was far from first choice for the DFB, who were left unduly surprised by Vogts's resignation and had to scramble for a replacement.

Qualification for Euro 2000 was only narrowly secured by means of a goalless draw against Turkey in Munich, a result described by Ribbeck as an 'away point' on account of the sizeable Turkish support in the Olympiastadion. The tournament in the Low Countries came too soon for future star Michael Ballack, then aged 23, to have made a significant impression at international level, and one of the few players of the new generation who had broken through, Jens Jeremies of FC Bayern, caused controversy just two months before the tournament. In an interview with *Kicker*, Jeremies described the current state of the national team as '*jämmerlich*', or pitiful. Asked whether progress had been made, he continued, 'The fundamental problems remain. If you look at the team over the last five years, how many impressive performances have there been? You can count the high points on the fingers of one hand. Nothing has changed or even improved.'

The confusion in Ribbeck's approach is evidenced by his split from Stielike a month before tournament, when he made Horst Hrubesch his new assistant. Germany's continuing over-reliance on older players was best illustrated by the inclusion of Matthäus, aged 39, who had left FC Bayern earlier that year to join New York MetroStars in Major League Soccer. Matthäus laboured in the *libero* position in Charleroi, despite having sustained a muscle injury at the pre-tournament training camp in Mallorca. Overall, the assessment of Ribbeck's team offered in the *Sunday Times* a week before the competition proved accurate:

'For once, the temptation to write off the Germans is irresistible. They go into the finals weighed down by criticism and stricken with self-doubt. Above all else, it is the dearth of young talent that threatens to unhinge their title defence and send them home early.'

England went into the match in Charleroi having surrendered a two-goal lead in a 3-2 defeat to Portugal in their first match, in Eindhoven on 12 June. After Paul Scholes and Steve McManaman both scored before 20 minutes had been played, a comeback from the eventual group winners, masterminded by the Fiorentina playmaker Rui Costa, put Keegan's side under yet greater pressure going into their second game. For this all-important and much-anticipated meeting with Germany, Keegan introduced the experienced and pugnacious Martin Keown and Dennis Wise, both aged 33. Wise joined Ince, Scholes and Beckham in midfield, while Keown played in central defence alongside Tottenham's Sol Campbell, eight years his junior but already with three more England caps. The Neville brothers occupied the full-back positions, and Michael Owen, now aged 20, partnered captain Alan Shearer in attack. The Newcastle United striker had announced in February that he would step back from international duty after the European Championship to allow England to plan for the future, and after the result against Portugal, he knew that defeat in Charleroi would spell a sad end to his international career.

In a wider sense, there was also a 'now or never' element to England's perspective on the match, considering that almost 34 years had passed since the 1966 World Cup Final and England had only beaten the *Nationalmannschaft* twice in the intervening years. Both the match at Wembley in 1975 and the Mexican encounter in 1985 were also of little consequence. Counting the Germans' two penalty shoot-out successes as victories, an official record between the two nations that had reached 7-0 in England's favour in 1966 now stood at 10-9 to Germany since 1930. Although it is an assessment largely informed by subsequent results and the benefit of hindsight, it does seem that Keegan and England overcommitted to this perceived summit meeting with Germany, at the expense of the rest of their Euro 2000 campaign.

The game was won by a second-half Shearer header that came from the most prominent weapon in this England side, a Beckham set piece. The Manchester United star had been the target of foul personal abuse from a small section of the England support at the Portugal game, prompting him to respond with what we might call an 'Effenberg salute' at the final whistle. Keegan supported his player, however, claiming that it was the worst abuse he had ever heard, 'If David Beckham is getting even 50 per cent of what was said in Eindhoven some days of his life, I think he handles it fantastically well.'

In Charleroi, Beckham was effectively kept in check on the right flank by Christian Ziege, but he repaid his manager's faith with a trademark swerving cross behind the German back line from a free kick in an unpromising position. The ball eluded central defenders Jens Nowotny and Markus Babbel, reaching an expectant Shearer on the far side of the six-yard box. The England captain scored with a diving header from a standing position past Oliver Kahn, by now Germany's undisputed number one. With the lesson of the naïve defeat to Portugal in mind, Keegan responded quickly to his team taking the lead and replaced Owen on the hour mark with a notable substitute winning his second cap, the 20-year-old Liverpool midfielder Steven Gerrard. It is an indictment of Keegan's management that, with the likes of Beckham, Scholes and Owen in the side, German journalist Rainer Holzschuh could still conclude, 'It is a long time since such a weak English team has been sent into competition, without the usual fire, without creative elements.'

Nonetheless, England's landmark win, or more precisely Germany's defeat, was greeted with enthusiasm in the English press. 'Some of the devastating and disturbing self image the

German media inflicted on their team must now be redefined as enlightenment,' wrote Rob Hughes in the *Sunday Times*. 'They are bad, and they know they are.'

In the afterglow of victory over the Germans, England perhaps did not yet know that about themselves, but it became all too clear three days later, when they were eliminated from the tournament by a last-minute penalty that gave Romania a 3-2 win. While it may be comparatively dull amid all the English euphoria and German soul-searching, Joe Lovejoy's assessment in his *Sunday Times* match report probably best reflected the on-field reality of this contest, 'In practice, there are no really bad German teams, whatever the pundits may say, and England are not strong enough to approach any match with certainty at this level. As ever down the years, it was always going to be close.'

* * *

Less than three weeks after England's win on the field in Belgium, Germany scored a major victory in Zurich, winning the right to host the 2006 FIFA World Cup. While the reasons for the failure of England's bid were manifold and complex, Geoff Hurst, who campaigned vigorously for the FA with the full support of Tony Blair's Labour government, wrote in his autobiography that the violent scenes at Euro 2000 'finally put England's bid beyond salvation'. Hurst explained, 'We'd always realised there was a risk of hooliganism at Euro 2000 but the fact that this took place just three weeks before the voting for the 2006 World Cup is what proved to be so damaging.'

The successful German campaign was the latest triumph in the glittering career of Franz Beckenbauer, then vice-president of the DFB. He subsequently became the chairman of the World Cup organising committee, overseeing a tournament that was an enormous success on and off the field. However, in late 2015 the *Kaiser*'s integrity was called into question in the wake of an investigation by weekly news magazine *Der Spiegel*, which alleged that bribes were paid to secure votes in the bid process. The story referred to a slush fund containing money paid by former Adidas CEO Robert Louis-Dreyfus, 'It appears that both Franz Beckenbauer … and Wolfgang Niersbach, the current head of the DFB, and other high-ranking officials were aware of the fund by 2005 at the latest.' DFB officials subsequently acknowledged a payment made to FIFA but claimed that this 'had no connection to the awarding of the World Cup'.

On 4 March 2016, the lawyer presenting an independent report commissioned by the DFB affirmed that there was no evidence of vote-rigging in the award to Germany, 'Although we cannot rule it out completely.' Later in 2016, the Office of the Attorney General of Switzerland opened a criminal investigation into the dealings of Beckenbauer, former DFB presidents Theo Zwanziger and Wolfgang Niersbach, and former DFB secretary general Horst Rudolf Schmidt, but all these cases ended without a verdict after the Swiss statute of limitations expired in 2020. Likewise, FIFA announced on 25 February 2021 that its independent Ethics Committee could not prosecute Beckenbauer, Zwanziger and Schmidt because of the expiry of the limitations period.

7 October 2000
FIFA World Cup qualification
England 0-1 Germany
Wembley Stadium

Measured against the low bar set in Charleroi, Germany produced an impressive and highly praised performance under new manager Rudi Völler in the last England international to be played at the old Wembley Stadium. This was Völler's third match in charge, following a 4-1 friendly success against Spain and an opening 2-0 win over Greece in World Cup qualification. He abandoned the use of a *libero* and played a 3-4-3 formation in these matches, earning plaudits for his style of play. Germany won 1-0 at Wembley thanks to an intelligent and slightly fortunate free-kick goal from Liverpool midfielder Dietmar Hamann just a quarter of an hour into the game.

The reinvigorated performance and impressive tactics tailored to the opposition caught the eye every bit as much as the result, however. In *Kicker*, the team was described as 'completely transformed' from the disastrous showing at the European Championship. Left-sided midfielder Marco Bode dropped into defence out of possession to form a back four, and he combined with Michael Ballack on the left flank to nullify the threat posed by Beckham. Hamann was outstanding in defensive midfield, earning *Kicker*'s highest grade for his overall performance as well as his quick-thinking goal. Mehmet Scholl, who suffered as an isolated lone playmaker in Charleroi, dropped behind Bierhoff and was Germany's most conspicuous creative player. *Kicker* journalist Karlheinz Wild concluded enthusiastically:

'The German XI built on what they had shown in the previous two games. The victory in England brought a significant step forward in terms of playing style, which was possible because the system has been modernised, and because every player is fully committed. This makes it fun – for the players as well as for the spectators.'

Hamann's goal came from a free kick 35 yards out, his low shot skidding on wet ground to deceive David Seaman, who was still trying to organise a two-man wall when the ball was struck. The conditions were of the sort in which any effort at goal was worthwhile – Beckham had numerous attempts from distance – and England failed in the basic task of delaying the kick while getting organised. Hamann later said that after the ball hit the net, he was at first unsure whether the referee had allowed his quick free kick to stand.

With just five teams in the qualifying group, England had sat out the first matchday in September and thus needed a win to join Germany and Finland on three points and ensure they were not cut adrift at this early stage. The farewell event for the famous stadium was dubbed 'The Final Whistle' by the FA, and the impending demolition of Wembley's iconic twin towers, the dreadful conditions and the course of the game all conspired to produce one of English football's most melancholy days. The afternoon ended with the incongruous scenes of fireworks and ticker tape in failing light, England fans calling for the manager's head, and celebrating German players covered in mud.

In the *Sunday Times*, Rob Hughes questioned how the visitors were allowed to 'squelch England's apology for a side into the turf'. To a large extent, the answer lay in Keegan's experimental selection and tactics. England started the game employing a midfield diamond with Gareth Southgate at its base, and in the first half they were overrun by Germany's five men in the middle. According to Joe Lovejoy, Keegan had devised his plan in the expectation that

Germany would play with two strikers ahead of Scholl, and was caught unawares when Carsten Jancker failed a late fitness test. Yet Keegan waited until half-time before resolving to abandon the experiment. He introduced Newcastle United's Kieron Dyer into midfield, with Southgate withdrawing into a three-man defence, and with numerical parity in midfield England delivered a better second half. The damage had been done, however, and the tactical error had been patently obvious for all to see, even if England only conceded just the once, from a set piece.

As Keegan made the long, sorry and sodden walk to the old Wembley tunnel at full time, with abuse raining down on him, he knew his time was up, and he promptly resigned in the dressing room. In his interview with Sky Sports immediately following the decision, he spoke with notable magnanimity:

'I think I've had more than a fair chance. I have absolutely no complaints, and I have no complaints against the media either, I think they've given me a fair run, which is all you can ask for in this day and age when you're in my position, so absolutely no one to blame but myself. I did it to the very best of my ability … but I'm just not the man to take it that stage further and I know that, and I've got to be true to myself first and foremost.'

A footnote to the game was the England fans' clamours of 'stand up if you won the war', to which Hughes offered an articulate response, 'Has it come to this? Has England no virtue other than this dull and dangerous mockery? Could the loudmouths not see, as they ridiculed the German anthem at the beginning, that to such a nation this boorish behaviour can do nothing but stir the determination?'

* * *

The *Nationalmannschaft*'s fifth win at Wembley came at the time of an unseemly, high-profile scandal for German football remembered as the 'Daum affair'. Its context was a heated rivalry at the top of the Bundesliga. Under manager Christoph Daum, Bayer Leverkusen had finished second to FC Bayern in three of the previous four seasons. Indeed, earlier in 2000, the *Werkself* suffered the heartbreak of losing the league title on goal difference, having started the final matchday with a three-point lead. After the shock of the national team's performance at Euro

2000, the DFB looked to appoint Daum as Ribbeck's successor, but his club would only agree on the condition that he remain with Leverkusen for the 2000/01 season, enabling them to find their own replacement. As a solution, Rudi Völler, then sporting director at Leverkusen, agreed to coach the national team for one season only, and in this capacity he oversaw the impressive win over England on 7 October.

Just days earlier, Daum's long-time rival Uli Hoeneß, general manager at FC Bayern, had reacted to persistent rumours about Daum's private life, which linked him with cocaine use, by stating that he could not become *Bundestrainer* if the allegations were proved true. A furore developed which culminated in Daum agreeing voluntarily to submit a hair sample for laboratory testing to prove his innocence, while Hoeneß was assailed from all sides by criticism of his conduct. On 20 October, Daum received a positive test result and was forced to quit his post as Leverkusen manager with immediate effect, vindicating Hoeneß. The standing agreement between Daum and the DFB was summarily cancelled. At a press conference in Cologne on 12 January 2001, Daum finally admitted he had consumed cocaine. Völler, meanwhile, acted as interim coach at Leverkusen until the club appointed Berti Vogts in November, and at the same time he accepted the role of DFB *Teamchef* on a permanent basis. This was a designation first used for Franz Beckenbauer in 1984 to circumvent the issue of his lack of coaching qualifications, and which essentially means 'head coach', while *Bundestrainer* is analogous to the English term 'manager'. When asked if the scandal had affected preparations for the game at Wembley, Oliver Kahn responded, 'Perhaps it's not even a bad thing that this issue is in the foreground. Then we can play our football, and they can fight their battles.'

1 September 2001
FIFA World Cup qualification
Germany 1-5 England
Olympiastadion, Munich

By the time of England's visit to Munich for the return fixture with Germany in World Cup qualification on 1 September 2001, Völler was beginning his second season at the helm of the

Nationalmannschaft, and England were a drastically transformed proposition. Even before Keegan's resignation, rumours abounded that the FA would turn to a foreign manager to succeed him, 'the success of Arsène Wenger [at Arsenal], and others, in the Premiership having overcome the xenophobic tendency'. The man eventually appointed was the Swede Sven-Göran Eriksson, aged 52, who had enjoyed a successful managerial career in Portugal and Italy, most notably winning five major trophies with Lazio between 1997 and 2000.

After taking over in January 2001, Eriksson guided England to three wins in World Cup qualification, rehabilitating the campaign. Under Eriksson, England played in an uncomplicated 4-4-2 formation, with David Seaman still in goal at the age of 37, Gary Neville and the Arsenal youngster Ashley Cole at full-back, and Rio Ferdinand partnering Sol Campbell in the centre of defence. Manchester United pair David Beckham and Paul Scholes were fixtures in midfield, as was Steven Gerrard when fit enough to play. The left side of midfield posed Eriksson a significant problem, however. At first he selected Steve McManaman, who had moved to Real Madrid in 1999, but at the start of the 2001/02 season it became clear that the former Liverpool star would not find favour with Eriksson, and he made his last England appearance against Greece in October. In Munich, the position was taken by Liverpool's Nicky Barmby, who had played in fits and starts for England since 1995, often as a substitute.

Up front the manager looked for a long-term partner to the outstanding Michael Owen, and he opted for his club-mate Emile Heskey. Owen was later awarded the 2001 Ballon d'Or in recognition of the three major trophies he won with Liverpool in the 2000/01 season. Indeed, just a week before England played in Munich, Liverpool contested the 2001 UEFA Super Cup with FC Bayern in Monaco. The Liverpool side featured Gerrard, Heskey, Owen and Jamie Carragher, a substitute in Munich, as well as Dietmar Hamann. The Bayern starting XI featured only two Germans, Oliver Kahn and Thomas Linke, while Carsten Jancker was used as a substitute. All three played against England eight days later, as did Hamann. Liverpool's dominant first-half performance in a 3-2 win, which included goals from Heskey and Owen, gave some indication of what was to follow in Munich.

Given the famous and often mythologised England victory that followed, it is important to outline the circumstances in which it transpired. Going into the match, England had amassed ten points from five games and were six points adrift of Germany, who had played a game more. Significantly, a win for the home side would seal qualification for the tournament in Japan and South Korea, leaving England, Greece and Finland to fight for a play-off place. A FIFA draw on the eve of the match confirmed that the team to finish second in this group would face Ukraine in the two-legged play-off in November, which removed fears of a possible tie with the likes of Portugal or the Netherlands. As David Lacey put it in *The Guardian*, 'Now England know that if the main parachute fails to open they should still enjoy a reasonably soft landing.'

Winning the group, and thereby qualifying automatically, was still a possibility for England, but only if they could become just the second team in history to record a win over Germany in World Cup qualification, not to mention the first international team to beat the hosts in Munich since Yugoslavia in 1973. The task was formidable, and the opponents were quietly confident after a convincing win in Budapest two weeks earlier, although Völler would have to make do without Jens Jeremies and Mehmet Scholl due to injury. Michael Ballack, who would be named German Footballer of the Year in three of the next four years, was making only his 18th senior appearance and was recovering from a broken toe. In attack, the much-maligned Jancker was joined by the Swiss-born Oliver Neuville, in a little-and-large partnership.

Ironically, it was the diminutive Neuville who headed the ball down for his much taller strike partner to score the opening goal after just six minutes. Campbell and Ferdinand could only stare at each other and ask whose responsibility it had been to mark the Bayern frontman, because neither of them had come close. Five minutes later England were level. Endeavouring to keep the ball in play after a Beckham set piece had been cleared by Linke, Gerrard played a high pass back to Neville, who noticed that the German back line were slow to push out towards him and duly headed the ball back into the danger area. Barmby then bravely knocked the ball down near the penalty spot as

Kahn was rushing out to meet it, and Owen took full advantage to equalise. 'It's the Germans' turn to stand like statues,' said the BBC's John Motson.

On 21 minutes, Neuville from the right flank found Sebastian Deisler in wide open space in the penalty area as Ferdinand and Campbell were both dealing with Jancker. The young Hertha Berlin prospect, who suffered with the intolerable expectation placed on him as German football's *Wunderkind* in crisis, missed from just eight yards, unable to sort his feet in time to divert Neuville's cross past Seaman. A few minutes later Linke sought treatment, ostensibly for concussion. It is unclear when he had hit his head, but he was moving gingerly at this time and his signals to the medical staff indicated a head injury. Linke quickly rejoined play, but it seems highly likely that he was suffering from concussion, and this mitigates to some extent his serious errors which facilitated England's third and fourth goals, even if Owen would always have posed him problems in the manner he had already done in Monaco.

England were gaining confidence midway through the first half and were given an eminent opportunity to take the lead on 28 minutes when they were awarded an indirect free kick inside the penalty area because the uncharacteristically erratic Kahn had picked up a back pass. Beckham relished the chance to hit a dead ball from less than 12 yards out, but his shot hit Marko Rehmer, the last player in an eight-man German wall stationed on the goal line. While England looked threatening going forward, particularly from Beckham's long passes for Owen, it was Germany who then played better towards the end of the first half.

On 45 minutes, Schalke 04 left-back Jörg Böhme drew an excellent low save from Seaman after combining neatly with Jancker. Referee Pierluigi Collina added three minutes, during which the England players were content to keep possession in midfield. Only the irrepressible Beckham, a major injury doubt in the preceding week, saw the opportunity to get more out of a half of football that appeared to be as good as over. The captain took the ball and found his club-mate Neville on the right flank with another lofted pass, and when the ensuing chance was cleared he was first to the ball again, drawing a tired foul from

Nowotny near the touchline. Beckham ran to collect the ball and indicated to Collina that he was keen to take the free kick in the few seconds still available. After his initial right-footed cross was cleared by Hamann, Beckham crossed again with his left, and Ferdinand headed the ball back into space where Gerrard was waiting, fully 35 yards from goal. The young Liverpool midfielder, playing his sixth game for England, chested the ball down and fired a trademark half-volley into the bottom corner for a memorable first international goal. Collina's half-time whistle came immediately, and Gerrard's well-timed sucker punch made all the difference in what was hitherto a fairly even contest.

Beckham was again instrumental when England extended their lead just three minutes into the second half. He beat Böhme to a loose ball in the right channel and, with his back to goal and two German players in attendance, played a left-footed cross for Heskey that many a winger would struggle to emulate using their stronger foot in ample time and space. Heskey knocked the ball down for Owen, abandoned by the wretched Linke, and moments later it was 3-1. If not before, the travelling supporters, including around 6,000 official ticket holders, now began to sense that something special was afoot.

Even now, however, this was not a match where one team dominated the other and played its game at will. In the 18 minutes between the visitors' third and fourth goals, the England players endured some nervous moments, even as their fans sang with delirious fervour. Towards the hour mark, all the attacking came from Germany. In a moment which betrayed his surprising lack of confidence in heading for a tall striker, Jancker inexplicably headed the ball back for Ballack when he had again broken free from Campbell and should have scored himself from five yards out. When Ballack blazed his ensuing volley high and wide, it rendered Jancker's decision maddening as well as puzzling.

All the while, Beckham continued to lead his team with tireless pressing and harrying of the opposition, but England's fourth goal, on 66 minutes, was a Liverpool affair. Gerrard won the ball well in midfield from the clearly discomfited Ballack and played an accurate through ball inside Linke for Owen. By this point, it was impossible to think that anything but another goal would result, so lively and sharp was Owen on this famous night. Motson perfectly summed up the mood of all England fans watching their team win in Germany for the first time since 1965, 'This is getting better and better and better!' The fourth goal was the precise moment that a bad game turned into an abject, chastening experience for the *Nationalmannschaft*, the heaviest postwar home defeat. Völler immediately replaced Ballack with the young Kaiserslautern striker Miroslav Klose, but the attempt to salvage something from the contest led only to another goal on the counter attack from the now supremely confident opposition. Scholes combined with Heskey to complete the rout, but for jubilant England fans everywhere the evening had only just begun.

* * *

Hat-trick hero Owen rightly took the headlines following England's sensational win in Munich, but it was Beckham who provided the golden moment at the end of the World Cup qualification campaign to ensure that the win over Germany would count for something of immediate sporting significance. After England won their game in hand against Albania on 5 September, Eriksson's side kicked off the final match, against Greece at Old Trafford on 6 October, level with Germany on 16 points. Völler oversaw a frustrating goalless draw against Finland in Hamburg, but news filtered through that Greece were surprisingly leading 2-1 in Manchester. As things stood, Germany would win the group and qualify automatically, condemning England to a play-off with Ukraine after all.

Uncertainty reigned after the final whistle in Hamburg as players and staff sought confirmation of the result, while in Manchester, the England captain stood over the ball with 92 and a half minutes on the clock. 'I got to the TV just as David Beckham was about to take the free kick and I looked straight up to see how many minutes had gone,' said Deisler. 'I realised it must be the last chance and when the ball went in, it was such a dreadful feeling that I can't find the words to describe it.'

With one kick, England were on their way to the World Cup, and the rehabilitation of David Beckham in the hearts and minds of English football fans was complete.

12

Worlds Apart

2006–2010

In the summer of 2006, the Federal Republic of Germany threw open its doors for a 32-team FIFA World Cup attended by almost 3.5 million people. The accompanying motto was *Eine Zeit, um Freunde zu finden*, or 'A time to make friends'. The nation, and the world in which it was finding its role, had changed momentously since 1990. Helmut Kohl's 16-year chancellorship ended in 1998 amid soaring unemployment, particularly in former East Germany. The old epithet 'the sick man of Europe', which had been levelled at the United Kingdom in the 1960s and 70s, was now used to describe Germany's struggling economy after reunification.

A new coalition between the SDP and the Green party took power with Gerhard Schröder as chancellor, and in 2002 this government retained a narrow majority to win a second term. Schröder espoused the 'third way' political doctrine which sought to reconcile centre-right economic policies with centre-left social policies. In this sense, the SDP's move to the centre mirrored that of 'New Labour' in Britain, which had enabled Tony Blair to win a landslide majority in 1997.

However, a notable divergence between the two leaders emerged in foreign policy after the 11 September 2001 terrorist attacks on the United States. This event marks the beginning of a new era characterised by uncertainty, neatly summarised by the historian Mary Fullbrook, 'The predictable dangers and threats of the old Cold War in a world divided between two superpowers were replaced by an unstable multi-polar world, with unpredictable flashpoints and new forms of ideological and religious conflict.' While Blair cultivated Britain's 'special relationship' with the United States and took his country into a controversial war in Iraq, Schröder in fact used his opposition to the impending invasion to bolster his 2002 election campaign.

By 2005, the conservative CDU party had regrouped and identified Angela Merkel as its challenger to Schröder in the general election. A close result precipitated three weeks of hard bargaining which in turn delivered Germany's first female chancellor, at the head of a CDU-SPD grand coalition. Merkel had grown up in East Germany, and as chancellor she thus embodied the transformation that the Federal Republic had undergone since unification. She would oversee more profound developments in Germany's character and international reputation.

Among the Schröder government's earliest statutes was the reform of the German citizenship law first passed in 1913. The amendment guaranteed automatic dual citizenship for children born in Germany to immigrant parents, and in the context of football this meant that young players from different cultural backgrounds could more easily represent Germany from an early age. Miroslav Klose and Lukas Podolski, born in Poland in 1978 and 1985, respectively, are from so-called *Aussiedler* families. This term applies to ethnic Germans who moved from former communist states in eastern Europe to settle in Germany. These two players represented the *Nationalmannschaft* in a cultural environment that more readily accepted their Polish backgrounds when compared to the experiences of Pierre Littbarski, Jürgen Grabowski, or even Fritz Szepan down the years.

A prominent example of the representation of Germany's increasingly multi-ethnic society in football is Mesut Özil, born in Gelsenkirchen in 1988. His grandfather was a Turkish *Gastarbeiter*, which is the term used for the 867,000 workers who moved to West Germany between 1961 and 1973 as part of a recruitment scheme agreed between the German and Turkish governments. In 2007, Özil renounced his Turkish citizenship and elected to represent Germany. He became the poster child of cultural integration in modern Germany after starring at the 2010 FIFA World Cup in South Africa, and was voted the national team's best player for five of the following six years. The cultural historian Kay Schiller wrote:

'To an extent still unthinkable a decade ago, Özil, both a German citizen by birth who renounced his Turkish citizenship even earlier than required by the citizenship reform legislation and a practicing Muslim who recites the Quran before matches, is celebrated as a shining example of the successful integration of a Turk into German society.'

These words were published in 2015, and the furore three years later over Özil's close relationship with Recep Tayyip Erdoğan, the president of Turkey, which caused the player to quit the national team citing racist abuse and a lack of support from the DFB, substantiates Schiller's warning within the same article that an acceptance of a multi-ethnic society is not the same as an endorsement of multiculturalism. A focus on integration 'prioritises assimilation into German culture and suggests no more than cultural peculiarities are tolerated as long as they do not threaten the predominance of German culture', wrote Schiller. The treatment of Özil, for which the DFB at least subsequently apologised, would seem to suggest that political anxieties about Erdoğan undermined some of the principles on which the association, and by extension the nation, prides itself.

* * *

After successfully negotiating the qualification play-off with Ukraine to which they had been condemned by England, Rudi Völler's Germany surprisingly reached the final of the 2002 FIFA World Cup in Japan and South Korea. The playing style at the tournament won few friends, with French sports newspaper *L'Équipe* remarking after the narrow and controversial quarter-final win over the United States that 'you have to be German to appreciate it'. Thanks in large part to commanding goalscoring performances in midfield from Michael Ballack and a string of career-defining goalkeeping displays from Oliver Kahn, an unfancied German side earned the right to face Brazil in Yokohama on 30 June 2002. The misfortune of precisely these two star players meant that the *Nationalmannschaft* were no match for their formidable opponents, as Ballack missed the final through suspension, and Kahn, around whom an aura of invincibility had grown over six and a half games, made the fatal error which gave Brazil the lead after 67 minutes through top goalscorer Ronaldo. Luiz Felipe Scolari's side won 2-0 to claim a fifth world title for Brazil, while Germany lost a World Cup final for the fourth time.

After a goalless draw in European Championship qualification in Reykjavík on 6 September 2003, Völler gave an infamous interview to the broadcaster ARD in which he reacted furiously to the pundits' claims that his team had reached a 'new low'. For the beleaguered Völler, it was unclear why Germany should be expected to 'clearly master' the Icelanders, then top of the qualification group, away from home. A series of bad results culminated in Völler's resignation following elimination from the group stage at Euro 2004, where a German manager did lift the title, but not in the national team's colours. Otto Rehhagel had sensationally led Greece to victory and was thus tipped to replace Völler as *Bundestrainer*, but he rejected the offer and remained with the Greeks. Less than two years from a World Cup on home soil, the DFB was faced with another problematic and consequential decision to make.

England had meanwhile experienced a period of great excitement but also weighty expectation in the years following the famous 5-1 win over Germany at the start of Sven-Göran Eriksson's tenure. At the 2002 World Cup, England drew two matches in a competitive group but famously beat Marcelo Bielsa's Argentina by means of a David Beckham penalty in Sapporo. The 3-0 win over Denmark in Niigata in the second round was England's joint-biggest victory in a knockout match at a World Cup or European Championship, and this was only bettered by the recent 4-0 win over Ukraine in Rome during Euro 2020. A resultant groundswell of optimism then grew when Michael Owen gave England a first-half lead against Brazil in Shizuoka, but Paris Saint-Germain star Ronaldinho, then aged 22, added to Rivaldo's equaliser with an audacious long-range free kick that caught David Seaman off his line.

At the 2004 European Championship, Beckham, Paul Scholes, Gary Neville and Sol Campbell were all aged 29, and the younger Steven Gerrard and Frank Lampard were paired in midfield for the first time at a major tournament. Although

Scholes would retire from international football after the competition, this was a so-called golden generation of English players for which a glorious destiny at the forthcoming World Cup in Germany was now widely envisaged. In Portugal, England appeared unperturbed by succumbing to the brilliance of Zinedine Zidane at the very end of their opening game against France, subsequently beating Switzerland and Croatia to progress. 18-year-old Everton striker Wayne Rooney was the most exciting English player to emerge since Paul Gascoigne, and here he scored four goals in two matches to set the tournament alight.

England went into their quarter-final against the hosts in Lisbon on 24 June with the likes of Germany, Italy and Spain already eliminated, and with the irresistible Rooney playing alongside Owen, who scored after just three minutes. By the unscientific measure of the fevered excitement generated amid this combination of circumstances, this was probably the closest England had been to winning a major trophy since 1996, and it was certainly closer than any England team would come in the 12 years thereafter. Less than half an hour into the game, however, Eriksson was forced to withdraw Rooney, who had sustained a fractured metatarsal bone in his right foot in a seemingly innocuous collision with Portuguese defender Jorge Andrade. The evening ended in bitter disappointment for England, who were denied an ostensibly legal last-minute winner from Campbell by Swiss referee Urs Meier and were then eliminated in a penalty shoot-out for the fourth time in 14 years.

2006 FIFA World Cup
Germany

In the mid-19th century, the German writer Heinrich Heine composed 'Deutschland. Ein Wintermärchen', or 'Germany. A Winter's Tale', a satirical epic poem which imagines a journey through German lands in the period known as *Vormärz*, before the revolutions of 1848 and 1849. Heine's works were censored in Germany, and he lived as an exile in France after 1831, but a journey to his homeland in 1843 inspired this now celebrated work, in which he criticised the chauvinistic nationalism and reactionary politics of German society. Heine saw himself as a patriotic critic, writing out of love for the fatherland, but his works were abhorred by the Nazis, as much because of his Jewish background as his political opinions. In an earlier play, Heine's Muslim character Hassan speaks the following lines in reaction to the burning of the Quran, 'That was but a prelude; where they burn books, they will ultimately burn people as well'.

Ein Wintermärchen employs the imagery of winter allegorically, in opposition to revolutionary spring or glorious summer. The filmmaker Sönke Wortmann adapted this title for his documentary on the journey of the *Nationalmannschaft* at the 2006 World Cup, which he called *Deutschland. Ein Sommermärchen*, or 'a summer fairy tale'. Wortmann was able to invert the sentiment in Heine's title in this way because the tournament was seen to have instigated a wave of benevolent patriotism and national pride, in contradistinction to aggressive nationalism. Professor of Cultural Studies Gregory Paschalidis explains how the tournament transformed Germany's self-image:

'There was a striking distance between the official restraint in the face of the 1954 "Miracle of Berne", or even at the 1974 World Cup Final in Munich, and the public expression of national pride marking the 2006 event. Focused on the bounded character of "soccer nationalism", the German media rehabilitated the flag and the national hymn, encouraging a therapeutic experience of rebirth into a shared national identity. The outbreak of this highly emotional "new German patriotism" prompted a nationwide debate about the relaxed, unabashed relationship of contemporary Germans with their national symbols and their national identity.'

The World Cup was also a turning point in foreigners' attitudes to Germany, not least the English. Surveying perceptions of Germany in the British press ahead of the tournament, the scholars Jonathan Grix and Chantal Lacroix observed, 'Germany's rich cultural history and her spectacular rise from ruins during the post-war period rarely figure in foreigners' perception of modern-day Germany, especially it seems in Britain.' By contrast, in the decade between the World Cup in Germany and the United Kingdom's decision to leave the European Union, there was a proliferation of such positive commentary about Germany in the British media. For many

275

years before 2006 and during the competition itself, the German federal government, FIFA, the DFB and stakeholders from business, culture and civil society all collaborated to rehabilitate the country's image, and were successful in doing so.

Although it was Marcello Lippi's Italy who lifted the World Cup trophy in Berlin's Olympiastadion on 9 July 2006, the performances of the *Nationalmannschaft* were indispensable in bringing about the cultural phenomena described above. These positive sporting displays were in turn the result of an expeditious coaching revolution that had taken place in just two years since the 2004 European Championship in Portugal. The men who had eventually been entrusted with the incomparable responsibility of leading the hosts in 2006 were Jürgen Klinsmann, Oliver Bierhoff and Joachim Löw. Based in the United States at the time of his appointment, Klinsmann brought a forward-thinking, energetic and positive outlook to the role of head coach, while entrusting Bierhoff with public relations in the new role of team manager. Assistant coach Löw, meanwhile, was the tactical brain of the triumvirate, exhibiting ideals of progressive, attacking football that he shared with Klinsmann.

Wortmann's film captured the priorities of the staff in interviews, with Löw explaining:

'From a tactical perspective, German football lags behind strong nations such as Italy and Spain, or some of the South Americans. We have always placed great importance on so-called German virtues, but these are now basic requirements if you want to keep up with the competition. To say that we want to return to these German virtues is the wrong approach, because it's a prerequisite to have strong runners and play at a high tempo, everyone can do it. And since we're not as technically gifted as the Brazilians or the Argentinians, it's important for us to be well organised, and it's important that the coaching staff and everyone around the team stays positive and shows plenty of enthusiasm.'

During the course of the tournament, this enthusiasm was transmitted to the German public, particularly after the dramatic injury-time winner in the team's second match. Much like Gascoigne's moment of inspiration at Wembley ten years earlier, this goal elevated the mood and carried the host nation into the knockout stages, as Klinsmann attested, 'I think Oliver Neuville's goal against Poland was the moment that the fans and the team closed ranks. From then on, we were on a wave of euphoria, happiness, and positive thinking.'

The wave ultimately washed up in the semi-final, another extraordinary night of high drama against *Angstgegner* Italy in Dortmund on 4 July. Full-back Fabio Grosso followed in the footsteps of Marco Tardelli in 1982 when celebrating his stunning goal, in the last minute of extra time, which sent Italy to Berlin. The manner of the 2-0 defeat – Italy added a second with almost the final kick – was intensely painful, but it was clear that the revitalised *Nationalmannschaft* would have plenty more to play for in subsequent years. Bastian Schweinsteiger and Lukas Podolski were both just 21, Philipp Lahm was 22, Miroslav Klose 28, and the captain Michael Ballack still 29. Klinsmann left the stage after Germany won the third-place play-off with Portugal, and in time-honoured fashion he entrusted these players to his assistant, ushering in the era of Joachim Löw.

Supported by legions of fans who made the journey to Germany in unprecedented numbers by plane, train, automobile and camper van, the England squad to some extent were guilty of conducting themselves as world champions *avant l'heure*. The intense media hype, the FA's liberal approach to matchday preparation, and the fixation of many fans with winning the World Cup on German soil all conspired to render England's performances underwhelming and anti-climactic. With Rooney's reported pronouncement on returning from injury that the 'big man is back in town', and the media circus around the players' wives and girlfriends at the team hotel in Baden-Baden, the German press sneered at the perceived unprofessionalism and dissolute behaviour of the English. 'We became a bit of a circus,' admitted Rio Ferdinand later. 'Football almost became a secondary element to the main event. People were worrying more about what people were wearing or where people were going than the England football team.'

The obvious exception to the on-field disappointment was the opening goal in the third group-stage match, against Sweden in Cologne on 20 June. The sensational dipping volley from

35 yards came from Joe Cole, the talented Chelsea midfielder chosen by Eriksson to play on England's problematic left in this tournament. Ahead of the second-round match against Ecuador, hooliganism compounded England's image problems as hundreds of fans were arrested in Stuttgart city centre, and many thousands more proudly sang the wartime song 'Ten German Bombers' *en masse*. A bemused German public watched on, but for some in England, as for example the journalist and broadcaster Tony Parsons, much of this behaviour was justified, 'Less than a lifetime ago the Germans inflicted untold misery on the world. If English football fans choose to deal with that a mere 60 years later by holding their arms out and pretending to be Lancaster bombers, I would suggest that the Germans are getting off quite lightly.'

In a poor contest at the former Neckarstadion, a trademark Beckham free kick was enough to overcome Ecuador and progress to the quarter-finals, where England renewed hostilities with Scolari's Portugal. A disappointing encounter in Gelsenkirchen was marked by Rooney's dismissal on the hour, after he kicked Ricardo Carvalho in the groin during a tussle for the ball, and again England were taken to extra time having lost the player on whom so many hopes were hung. Defeat in the subsequent penalty shoot-out, in which only Owen Hargreaves could score, meant that England had lost five of the six penalty competitions they had contested, three in the FIFA World Cup and two in the UEFA European Championship.

* * *

Eriksson had announced at the end of January 2006 that he would leave his post following the World Cup in Germany. The search for his replacement lasted for three months, with Sam Allardyce and Alan Curbishley linked to the job, as well as foreign candidates such as Ottmar Hitzfeld and Guus Hiddink. The FA also pursued Scolari, the architect of England's three quarter-final exits with Eriksson, but the Brazilian ruled himself out in late April citing concerns about intrusion into his private life by the English media.

On 4 May, Steve McClaren, manager at Middlesbrough for the past five seasons, was finally appointed, effective from 1

August. FA chief executive Brian Barwick was at pains to tell the assembled media that McClaren was his and the FA board's first and unanimous choice, but the long selection process and public pursuit of Scolari suggested otherwise. With Middlesbrough, McClaren won the League Cup in 2004 and then secured a second successive season in Europe by finishing seventh in the 2004/05 Premier League. His most impressive achievement was to guide the club to the 2006 UEFA Cup Final, in a campaign which unfolded contemporaneously with the FA's manager search. On their way to the final in Eindhoven, Middlesbrough beat VfB Stuttgart in the first knockout round, the first leg coming just days after that club's appointment of Armin Veh, who would lead them to the Bundesliga title the following season. A week after being named the next England manager, however, McClaren's Middlesbrough lost 4-0 in the final to Sevilla, who that evening began their enduring love affair with the UEFA Cup trophy.

On assuming his duties with England, McClaren faced a daunting seven-team qualification group for the 2008 UEFA European Championship which included Croatia, Russia and Israel. The campaign suffered its first setback with a goalless draw against Macedonia in front of 72,000 fans at Old Trafford, and four days later England lost in Zagreb when a Gary Neville back pass bobbled over goalkeeper Paul Robinson's foot and rolled into the net for a gruesome own goal. In March 2007, a goalless draw in Israel was followed by 45 minutes with no score away to Andorra, in a game played in the Estadi Olímpic in Barcelona. Although England went on to win 3-0, the cacophony emanating from the travelling supporters as McClaren and his players left the field at half-time – in only his ninth match in charge – pointed the way to a sad end to his tenure later that year.

At the end of the season, the FA proudly inaugurated England's new national stadium at Wembley. On 11 May 2007, Bobby Charlton unveiled a bronze statue of Bobby Moore outside the stadium, at the end of the famous Wembley Way promenade that is today called Olympic Way. This marked 'the return of the national game to its true and proper home' after seven seasons in which England's home international matches were played around the country, and FA Cup and League Cup finals were staged at Cardiff's Millennium Stadium.

With a capacity of 90,000, the new Wembley became the largest stadium in the UK and the second-largest in Europe, after Barcelona's Camp Nou. Its most striking architectural feature is the 133m-high arch above the North Stand, the longest single-roof structure in the world. The arch is visible from across London but also serves to bear much of the weight of the stadium roof, ensuring that no supporting pillars are needed. Inside, guests on the stadium tour are welcomed to the Crossbar Reception, where the original crossbar from the 1966 World Cup Final is prominently displayed.

The first England international played at the new national stadium was a 1-1 draw with Brazil on 1 June, when the life of Alan Ball, who had passed away on 25 April at the age of 61, was celebrated before kick-off. The game also marked Beckham's return to the side after a 335-day absence. The Real Madrid star had been dropped by McClaren and was then frozen out by his club manager Fabio Capello in January, when he announced his planned move to Los Angeles Galaxy in Major League Soccer. Beckham subsequently played his way back into the side and helped *Los Blancos* claim their first league title in four seasons. Now the embattled England manager also recalled the 32-year-old, and McClaren was immediately rewarded when a Beckham free kick led to John Terry's headed opening goal. England were denied a win on this historic occasion by an injury-time equaliser from the Werder Bremen midfielder Diego.

22 August 2007
England 1-2 Germany
Wembley Stadium

The six-year interval between England's 5-1 win in Munich and this game at the new Wembley was the longest period without a senior international between England and Germany since the match in Nuremberg in 1965, which ended a nine-year hiatus. Germany visited with a record of five wins over England at the old Empire Stadium – 1972, 1982, 1991, 1996 and 2000 – as well as memories of the European Championship Final win against the Czech Republic in 1996. On this occasion they became the first team to beat England in their new home, with a 2-1 win over McClaren's side.

For the first time, England played in white against a German team in red shirts, one of the less popular legacies of Klinsmann's modernising period at the helm. Löw was forced by circumstance to field an experimental side, handing a debut to Schalke 04 left-back Christian Pander and moving Philipp Lahm to defensive midfield, prefiguring the FC Bayern full-back's later positional switch under Pep Guardiola. Of the many absences through injury at this time, the most notable was that of the captain, Michael Ballack, who underwent an ankle operation at the beginning of May and would not play for the national team again before February 2008.

Pander endured a torrid introduction to international football when he was beaten by the young Micah Richards on England's right and could only look on as the Manchester City full-back fed the ball to Lampard in the area. The Chelsea midfielder beat Jens Lehmann at his near post to score his ninth goal for England, with less than ten minutes on the clock. It was not enough, however, 'to divert England from what is increasingly becoming inevitable disappointment', as Martin Samuel put it in *The Times*.

After 25 minutes, Germany were fortunate to equalise thanks to a grave error from Paul Robinson. The Tottenham Hotspur goalkeeper could only parry a long-range shot from Thomas Hitzlsperger, formerly of Aston Villa, and the ball found its way to the veteran Bernd Schneider on the right touchline. Schneider's dangerous return cross deceived Robinson, who misjudged its flight and could only palm the ball clumsily to the feet of a grateful Kevin Kuranyi. Five minutes before half-time, Pander scored a sensational goal to atone for his earlier error and gave Germany the lead. The debutant advanced from defence and received the ball in midfield from Lahm, whereupon he unleashed a fierce left-footed drive from 25 yards that arrowed into the top corner. It was his first and only international goal. Robinson again might have done better, as he was standing outside his six-yard box when the shot was struck. He was substituted at half-time for David James, ten years his senior, and only made four more appearances for England.

The cover of the printed programme at Wembley for this game featured a quote from Michael Owen, 'Let's see if anyone can beat us here.' Germany did so with a patched-up, experimental side that earned significant praise. For former international Thomas Häßler, for example, the night demonstrated how Germany could now afford to lose a player of the calibre of Ballack and still perform. 'Joachim Löw is tactically very imaginative,' remarked Häßler. 'Qualification for the European Championship is not in doubt, I think, if we can continue to be this focussed.' As Martin Samuel noted, 'Germany closed the old place down by inflicting defeat and, considering the rivalry between the nations, will have been mighty pleased to enter the record books at the reconstructed site, too.'

2008 UEFA European Championship
Austria and Switzerland

McClaren lasted for only six more games in the job after defeat to Germany. Three consecutive 3-0 wins at Wembley at first eased fears that England would fail to secure one of the two automatic qualification places for Euro 2008, but a daunting trip to Moscow and a home match against group leaders Croatia still remained. On an artificial surface in the Luzhniki Stadium on 17 October, England looked set to secure qualification when Rooney scored a brilliant first-half goal that today would be ruled out by VAR for a marginal offside. In the second half, however, 'England crumbled to defeat in four panic-stricken minutes.' Rooney naively conceded a penalty, converted by Roman Pavlyuchenko, and then England lost all composure, lunging wildly at the ball from all directions as Russia retained possession and searched for the winning goal in a febrile atmosphere. The moment came when Robinson parried Aleksei Berezutski's shot and Pavlyuchenko beat Sol Campbell and Joleon Lescott to the rebound. Nonetheless, England were still given one more reprieve, when Israel scored an injury-time winner to beat Russia on 17 November.

This result meant that England went into the final qualification match, at home to Croatia four days later, in the knowledge that a single point would secure second in the group and take them to the finals. On the eve of the match, Martin

Samuel in *The Times* praised McClaren for his courage in dropping Robinson and, more surprisingly, Beckham in favour of Scott Carson and Shaun Wright-Phillips, 'He needs one point against Croatia to take England to the finals and, if he gets it, he will be able to add a penchant for forthright decision-making to his CV.' As it transpired, the night could hardly have gone worse for McClaren. With just eight minutes played, his new goalkeeper inexplicably allowed a long-distance shot from Niko Kranjčar to slip through his hands, and just five minutes later Ivica Olić put Croatia 2-0 up. After Lampard converted a dubious penalty early in the second half, it was inevitably the half-time substitute Beckham who rallied the team and provided the accurate cross for Peter Crouch to equalise to the great relief of the Wembley crowd. Yet when Mladen Petrić then beat the hapless Carson with another speculative shot, England's recovery was undone, and even Beckham could not avert the defeat. *The Guardian*'s Kevin McCarra summed up the manager's anguish, 'McClaren therefore has the worst of all outcomes, seeing the man he had left out proving him wrong without, in the end, saving his skin.' The headline said it all: 'Hopeless, hapless, helpless'.

At the European Championship in Germany's neighbouring Alpine nations, Löw's team embraced a litany of mountain-climbing metaphors and ascended one step further than they had in 2006, reaching the final in Vienna. The tournament brought more excitement and euphoria at home, particularly during the knockout stages, when the *Nationalmannschaft* succeeded where Eriksson's England had failed and eliminated Scolari's Portugal in the quarter-final with a sparkling performance. An in-form Podolski began the tournament on the left of midfield but was then moved forward to partner Klose, with the ineffective Mario Gómez making way, while the versatile Lahm was moved from the right to the left full-back position after defeat to Croatia in the second group-stage match. For the game against Portugal, Löw changed his formation from a 4-4-2 to a 4-2-3-1, with Klose playing ahead of Podolski, Ballack and Schweinsteiger.

In the semi-final against Turkey on 25 June, their second successive late-night thriller in the border town of Basel, Germany were severely tested by Fatih Terim's side on a dramatic night for fans of both sides at public viewing events in cities across Germany. The tension escalated somewhat when a power failure at the host broadcast centre in Vienna caused a six-minute cut in transmission during the second half, when the score was 1-1. German television's Béla Réthy was subsequently obliged to commentate via telephone over delayed pictures from Swiss television, and fans thus heard Klose's 79th-minute goal before they saw it. In injury time with the scores level at 2-2, it was Lahm's time to shine when he cut in from the left flank, played a one-two with Hitzlsperger, and burst into the penalty area to finish emphatically past goalkeeper Rüştü Reçber.

In Vienna's Ernst-Happel-Stadion on 29 June, Spain initiated a four-year era of dominance in international football by winning the first of three consecutive titles. A first-half goal from Fernando Torres was enough for *La Roja* to prevail in a final which they controlled throughout with their consummate possession game. Three-time European champions Germany had now also lost three finals in the competition, and *Kicker* conceded that 'against the totally superior Spaniards, the myth of tournament specialists was no longer of any use, and neither was the team spirit or the reformed system'.

* * *

England's first failure to qualify for a major tournament since the 1994 World Cup meant that McClaren's tenure as head coach was over after just 18 games. Derided for his use of an FA umbrella in the wet conditions at Wembley, he was branded 'A wally with a brolly' by the *Daily Mail*. Subliminal or not, there was a cultural link in this vein of mockery to Prime Minister Neville Chamberlain, whose trademark umbrella became an emasculating symbol of appeasement after the Munich crisis of 1938. At the start of John le Carré's novel *Absolute Friends*, the protagonist Ted Mundy defends his use of a bowler hat as a tour guide in Germany, 'Well, what's the alternative, I mean to say? You can hardly ask a thoroughbred Englishman to tote an *umbrella* like the Japanese guides, can you? Not here in Bavaria, my goodness, no. Not 50 miles from where our own dear Neville Chamberlain made his pact with the devil.' Mundy then goes on to explain 'how in German eyes, Neville Chamberlain's rolled-up umbrella remains, *to this very day*, the shameful emblem of British appeasement of *Our Dear Führer*, his invariable name for Adolf Hitler'.

If this was the image the FA sought to leave behind in their search for McClaren's replacement, they could scarcely have chosen a man with a more uncompromising and exacting reputation than Fabio Capello, appointed on 14 December at the age of 61. The former AC Milan manager had nine months in the job to prepare for England's return to competitive action, and in September 2008 the qualification campaign for the 2010 FIFA World Cup began with a statement result in Zagreb, a 4-1 win over Croatia that featured a hat-trick from Arsenal's Theo Walcott, then aged 19. England's final game of an encouraging, albeit truncated, calendar year came on 19 November in Berlin, where they had not played in 36 years and had never lost.

19 November 2008
Germany 1-2 England
Olympiastadion, Berlin

A month before England's visit to the capital, internal ructions in the German national team were made public, calling Löw's authority into question. The scorer of Germany's first goal at Wembley the year before, Kevin Kuranyi, absconded after he was dropped for the World Cup qualification match at home to Russia on 11 October, and Löw declared that the Brazilian-born striker would not play for him again. A few days later, Ballack gave an interview to the *Frankfurter Allgemeine Zeitung* in which he criticised the manager and suggested that there was a lack of loyalty and respect from the coaching staff for senior players. While Ballack agreed that Kuranyi's reaction was unacceptable, he said he could understand the striker's frustration. From Ballack's perspective, performances at Euro 2008 had been of a good standard, and he saw no justification for the recent criticism levelled at himself or the likes of Miroslav Klose and Torsten Frings. For Ballack, Löw's attempts to freshen up the side and introduce young talent after the tournament threatened the existing hierarchy in the squad, of which he, as experienced captain, was of course at the top. Löw immediately hit back,

'As a coaching team, we will not let ourselves be accused of a lack of respect. There seems to be a feeling within our ranks that respect automatically comes with the guarantee of a regular starting place.'

With Ballack missing after further surgery on his ankle and Frings still not recalled, an inexperienced midfield partnership of Simon Rolfes and Schalke's Jermaine Jones faced England in Berlin. René Adler made his third appearance in goal, between Lehmann's retirement from international football after Euro 2008 and the later emergence of Manuel Neuer.

Capello, meanwhile, was inundated with withdrawals from his squad for this so-called friendly international, with Gerrard, Lampard, Rooney, Walcott, Ashley Cole and Joe Cole all among the names reporting absent with injury. Kevin Garside in the *Daily Telegraph* wrote that his German counterparts in the press were bemused at the team news emanating from the England camp, 'The German imagination has yet to wrap itself around the notion of a foreign manager, let alone the idea that a player might consider saying no when called upon.' Capello fielded Jermain Defoe alongside debutant Gabriel Agbonlahor of Aston Villa in attack, with Gareth Barry and Michael Carrick in the centre of midfield, and Stewart Downing and Shaun Wright-Phillips on the flanks. England's wealth of options on the right of midfield caused the *Daily Telegraph*'s Henry Winter to reflect, 'Maybe the English public can now be weaned off their obsession with David Beckham.'

One player praised for his commitment to the cause was Capello's captain at centre-back, John Terry, who was keen to stress the importance of the venue and the opposition which awaited England. 'This match is massively important, especially coming here,' said Terry. 'Losing to Germany 15 months ago at Wembley is still at the back of my mind, losing in front of our home fans. The history between the two sides and how much it means to the fans back home tells you it means an awful lot to us.' The occasion was also marked by the display of a banner thanking England 'for inventing the Beautiful Game', and the presentation of the players to Bert Trautmann and Geoff Hurst before kick-off. As Winter observed, 'Hurst's presence on the team plane, around the hotel and in the stadium delighted

Capello's players and, amusingly, alarmed some of the Germans he encountered inside the Olympic Stadium.'

A poor German performance raised many more questions than it answered, and the press expressed its disappointment at the defeat to the visitors' 'emergency XI', which kept England's unbeaten record in Berlin intact. West Ham United defender Matthew Upson opened the scoring midway through the first half, when Adler failed badly in an attempt to clear Downing's corner with a punch. Just after the hour, substitute Darren Bent had the chance to take the game away from Germany when he received a through ball from Barry and rounded the goalkeeper, but he then lost his footing when facing an open goal. Immediately afterwards at the other end, Terry and substitute goalkeeper Carson were involved in a hideous misunderstanding that allowed the Leverkusen striker Patrick Helmes to take advantage and equalise. Terry was clearly enraged by the incident, and it was no surprise when the captain scored 20 minutes later to give this makeshift England side a well-deserved victory. Terry rose well above Schalke defender Heiko Westermann to head Downing's long free kick past goalkeeper Tim Wiese, another half-time substitute.

The praise for the manager in the English press was fulsome. 'Twelve months into the job, Capello has turned us all into dreamers,' wrote Garside, ending his effusive report with a look ahead to the World Cup, 'Confidence was always the issue, Capello reminded us afterwards. There is no shortage now. Up for the cup anyone?' His colleague Winter remarked with enthusiasm, 'Willed on by fans who outsang the locals, determined to seize this opportunity, eight understudies and three regulars derided as England B tore into Germany.' In *The Times*, Oliver Kay noted that 'as poor as Germany were, this is a result to be treasured', and summarised the impact that the England manager had made in his first year in charge:

'Who could have imagined last November, as they capitulated against Croatia at Wembley while the helpless McClaren sought refuge under an umbrella, that within 12 months England would be top of their World Cup qualifying group, having beaten Croatia 4-1 in Zagreb, and, with a weakened XI, claimed the prized scalp of Germany?'

All of these writers neglected to mention that Germany had also fielded a second-string side. The more phlegmatic Giles Smith in his *Times* television review wittily remarked that the presence of new faces in the England side lent a new dimension to the now five-year-old and still intractable debate about the compatibility of England's first-choice midfielders, 'Never mind whether Gerrard and Lampard could play together – could they both not play together? Could Gerrard be comfortably not accommodated alongside an absent Lampard? Could there ever be room in an England team for neither of them?'

* * *

On 29 June 2009 in Malmö, Sweden, Germany faced England in the final of the UEFA European Under-21 Championship. The match is a notable Anglo-German final in its own context, but it is especially significant because Horst Hrubesch's side that night included six future world champions: Manuel Neuer, Benedikt Höwedes, Jérôme Boateng, Mats Hummels, Sami Khedira and Mesut Özil. The teams had drawn 1-1 in the group stage, and England had beaten Finland and Spain to qualify, then saw off Sweden via a penalty shoot-out to reach the final and generate excitement at the prospect of a first under-21 title since 1984. In Malmö they were comprehensively outclassed, however, as Germany won 4-0.

Stuart Pearce's England side included Walcott, with eight senior caps already, and Micah Richards, who played 11 times under McClaren. Other notable members of the team were James Milner, who went on to win 61 senior caps, and the captain Mark Noble, who never played a full international but made over 400 Premier League appearances for West Ham before retiring at the end of the 2021/22 season.

Meanwhile, future England number one Joe Hart was suspended and watched from the stands. His replacement Scott Loach could do nothing about the fine goal from MSV Duisburg forward Sandro Wagner, a brilliant curling shot from the edge of the penalty area, but he completely misjudged Özil's earlier free kick from more than 35 yards. Özil had also provided the assist for Gonzalo Castro's opening goal in the first half. 'Some players have done well out here,' noted Henry Winter, 'but England boasted nobody of the class of Özil.' Germany were European under-21 champions for the first time, while at the same time holding that title at under-17 and under-19 level. These were the fruits of the DFB's extensive restructuring of football education under Gerhard Mayer-Vorfelder, president of the association from 2001 to 2006, in response to the senior team's failure at Euro 2000.

* * *

German football was struck by sudden tragedy on 10 November 2009, when the experienced Hannover 96 goalkeeper Robert Enke took his own life at the age of 32. He had made eight senior international appearances and was set to be the number one choice for the World Cup in South Africa. In a tearful press conference, Enke's widow Teresa revealed that he had been hiding a long-term battle with depression, in part because he feared losing their adopted daughter if his illness was revealed. DFB president Theo Zwanziger vowed that German football would 'use all its capabilities to find an answer to the question of how a young athlete celebrated by so many as an idol could land in such a situation'. Joachim Löw, meanwhile, paid tribute to his former player, 'We lost a friend, we deeply mourn Robert Enke. I feel completely empty. He was a great guy. He had incredible respect for others. We will miss him, as a top-class sportsman and an extraordinary man.' The DFB, the German Football League (DFL) and Hannover 96, in co-operation with the Ministry of Health, subsequently established the Robert Enke Foundation, which contributes to the education, research and treatment of depression.

In the 2009/10 season, Chelsea won the English Premier League and FA Cup double for the first time, under manager Carlo Ancelotti. Away from these triumphs, incidents involving two Chelsea players would significantly impact the World Cup preparations of both England and Germany. On 5 February 2010, Capello decisively stripped John Terry of the England captaincy in response to allegations published at the end of January that Terry had an affair with Vanessa Perroncel, the ex-girlfriend of his England team-mate and former club colleague Wayne Bridge. According to Matt Hughes in *The Times*, 'It was not the affair with Perroncel ... that convinced Capello to sack Terry, but a combination of allegations and rumours surrounding his behaviour, personal relationships and business dealings.' Capello handed the captaincy to Rio Ferdinand, who in turn suffered a knee ligament injury in England's first training session in South Africa and was ruled out of the tournament. This resulted in Steven Gerrard leading the side at the World Cup, as he would again as first-choice captain in Brazil four years later.

Meanwhile, the extensive debates in Germany about Michael Ballack's role in Löw's World Cup side were ended when he was injured in Chelsea's FA Cup Final win over Portsmouth on 15 May. Ballack was aggressively fouled by Kevin-Prince Boateng, older brother of Jérôme. Mere moments earlier, Ballack had raised a hand to Boateng's face in a *contretemps* off the ball, and it seemed to many observers that the subsequent tackle was an act of vengeance. An additional layer of controversy around the incident came from the observation that Boateng was set to represent Ghana, who had been drawn in the same World Cup group as Germany. Ballack later condemned the challenge, saying, 'I've seen it on TV and it didn't look a good tackle and when I was on the pitch, I knew it would be really difficult to carry on. I tried, but it wasn't possible.' The injury sadly ended Ballack's international career after 98 appearances and 42 goals between 1999 and 2010.

2010 FIFA World Cup
South Africa

The finals were a disaster for England, Capello and the FA. Not for the first time, England made a fast start, with Gerrard scoring after just four minutes in the opening match against the United States in the city of Rustenburg. Yet, after all the problems with Robinson and Carson, England's goalkeeping woes deepened when Robert Green, in just his 11th senior international appearance at the age of 30, made a dreadful mistake and spilt Clint Dempsey's innocuous shot, causing it to roll agonisingly into the net behind him.

In the supposedly inspirational setting of Cape Town, England then delivered a wretched, insipid performance to draw 0-0 with Algeria. Oliver Kay wrote that the players' 'fear of failure could almost be smelt from the back of the stands', and to compound matters, Rooney was captured on camera criticising the England fans as he and his team-mates left the field to a chorus of heavy criticism.

England had just two points after two games and stood with their backs to the wall, surrounded by negativity. Something had gone badly amiss for the team that, but for one ill-fated night in Ukraine, qualified for the World Cup with a string of convincing performances, scoring 34 goals in ten matches. There were growing calls for Capello to abandon his rigid and pragmatic 4-4-2 system, but those who accompanied the team in South Africa would later reflect that the biggest problems with England's approach were to be found off the field. In their choice of the Royal Bafokeng Sports Campus outside Rustenburg as team base, the FA overcompensated for the excesses of Baden-Baden four years earlier and erred on the side of caution and seclusion. Together with Capello's disciplinarian approach, the arrangements not only gave rise to boredom and frustration among the players, they also alienated the media and damaged England's reputation. In his book *Fifty Years of Hurt*, Henry Winter quoted former England international John Barnes on the lessons of Rustenburg:

'Who takes these decisions? It's not only just about experiencing life. It's more to do with the perception people have of you. They believe we're arrogant anyway because we're English, and then you're actually proving it by demanding better protection, better hotels, nicer training facilities, whereas everyone else is getting on with it. We are detaching ourselves from the brotherhood of football at World Cups.'

Capello made a small concession on the eve of the final group-stage match, against Slovenia in Port Elizabeth, allowing his players 'to relax by enjoying a beer'. An improved performance ensued, in terms of body language as much as anything else, and Defoe's first-half goal secured the all-important three points. As so often in the gloriously unpredictable context of the World Cup, however, there was a spanner in the works elsewhere. In Pretoria, the United States were drawing with Algeria and desperately seeking the goal they needed to qualify for the last 16. Landon Donovan provided the dramatic moment in injury time, sending his team to the top of the group. When Germany, as expected, beat Ghana in Johannesburg later that evening to confirm themselves as England's next opponents, the news caught the imagination, as evidenced by Winter in the *Daily Telegraph*:

'It's the Germans again. It's history and hysteria again, hopes and fears rolled into one heaving, epic confrontation again. At 3pm on Sunday, the nation will stop, tune in and watch nervously the pictures of the drama unfolding in Bloemfontein. The streets will be empty, the front rooms full because it's England versus Germany, the fixture that fixates.'

On the other end of the spectrum of taste was the *Daily Star*'s headline, 'Job done … now for the hun'. The *Nationalmannschaft* had made a dream start in Durban with a 4-0 win over Australia, but that was followed by a surprise defeat to Serbia in Port Elizabeth, where Milan Jovanović scored the only goal of the game immediately after Klose was sent off for a second bookable offence. For the match against Ghana, Löw introduced Boateng at left-back, joining the other under-21 European champions Neuer, Khedira and Özil in a settled side. The young Werder Bremen playmaker was the standout player of the group stage, and Karlheinz Wild explained why Özil was of such importance to Löw, 'The *Bundestrainer* sees this player as an enormously important mediator of his "conception of football, how we want to play": with skill and control, with dominance and speed going forward. Attractive, aesthetically valuable offensive football.'

Özil declared himself most comfortable in the number ten role behind the lone striker in Löw's 4-2-3-1 system, citing Günter Netzer and Wolfgang Overath as the German icons he wished to follow.

One other young player in this Germany team who was not part of the under-21 squad in Sweden was the 20-year-old FC Bayern forward Thomas Müller, a native Bavarian who had been with the Munich club since the age of ten and had signed his first professional contract at the start of 2009. Müller had given an impressive goalscoring display against Australia but then subsequently disappointed the high expectations he set for himself in the games against Serbia and Ghana. In the knockout stages in South Africa, he would light up the world stage.

27 June 2010
FIFA World Cup round of 16
Germany 4-1 England
Free State Stadium, Bloemfontein

Roger Boyes, the long-time Berlin correspondent of *The Times*, provided a useful insight into the confident mood of the German press ahead of this latest meeting with old rivals:

'Rarely is the German press quite so stridently confident before an England game. Partly this is down to the yo-yo effect. The German press talked the national team down before the cup began, promptly considered itself to be a potential world champion after beating Australia 4-0, self-flagellated after losing to Serbia 0-1 and now it's on the up again ... England v Germany has always been a metaphor for our relative standing in the world, and this time the Germans want it to be known that they are not ashamed of wanting to win.'

For England, meanwhile, the pressure to prevail in Bloemfontein was immense. Their first knockout international match since defeat in Gelsenkirchen in 2006 came in the first era of Premier League dominance in European club football, even if it was the Bayern side of Lahm, Schweinsteiger and Müller who had reached the most recent UEFA Champions League Final. English football provided six finalists in Europe's top competition between 2005 and 2009, with Liverpool and Manchester United winning in 2005 and 2008, respectively.

The national team now had a manager of the utmost international standing, with prestigious titles in Italy and Spain to his name. Captain Steven Gerrard, Frank Lampard and Ashley Cole had all won more than 80 caps, John Terry and Gareth Barry over 100 between them. Although still without a World Cup goal and affected by injury, Wayne Rooney was coming off the best season of his Manchester United career, in which he scored 34 goals in 44 games in all competitions and was voted the Football Writers' Association Player of the Year. If all that were not enough, the opposition was perceived by some to be a team of greenhorns, incapable of replicating past German achievements. 'It suits the morale of a nation to see renewal but, today, the callow openness of Joachim Löw's *Kinder* might be a disadvantage,' wrote Jonathan Northcroft in the *Sunday Times*. For all these reasons and more, the English fans and press called on the 'golden generation' to deliver. 'For England's players it *has* to be about now because their future is not guaranteed,' continued Northcroft. 'The golden generation have one last chance to do something deserving of their hype. Their cult began with a 5-1 win over Germany in 2001; now 0-0 and winning on penalties is all they need to go down in history.'

Elsewhere, verbal sparring between old legends of the fixture generated more heat. After Franz Beckenbauer had denigrated England's 'kick and rush' playing style earlier in the tournament, he now used his *Bild* column to call Capello's side 'stupid' for finishing second in their group, commenting that the players looked 'burnt out'. In the *Sunday Telegraph*, 1966 World Cup winner Martin Peters offered a robust response:

'One thing that has really disappointed me in the build-up is some of the comments by Beckenbauer. He has kept putting us down and I just wish he would keep his mouth shut. He was quite nasty about England and there was no need to come out with some of that rubbish. I saw that he tried to make a joke of it and I am glad that he has at least apologised.'

Understandably, penalties were at the forefront of English minds coming into the match, but the many column inches devoted to the psychodrama of the shoot-out proved to be redundant on this occasion as Germany ran out 4-1 winners in 90 minutes. The opening goal came via what is known in English football as 'route one', when Terry misjudged a goal kick from Neuer and then watched Klose wrestle free from Matthew Upson to poke the ball past veteran goalkeeper David James, the replacement for Robert Green after his howler against the USA. Twelve minutes later, it was 2-0. A neat passing triad on the right side between Özil, Klose and Müller took three English players out of the game and released Müller on goal with only full-back Glen Johnson rushing across to cover. The young Bayern star effortlessly set up Podolski, who arrived from his customary left-sided position and finished coolly through the legs of James.

The game looked to be heading only one way at this point, but on 37 minutes England found an equaliser from a set piece, exposing one of Germany's clear weaknesses. Adding to his goal in Berlin with a strong header from Gerrard's cross, Upson earned himself the distinction of scoring twice for England against Germany, a feat hitherto achieved by just nine other men since 1930. England were buoyed by the goal and pushed forward again. Not even 60 seconds had elapsed since Upson's goal when Lampard struck a dipping half-volley that beat Neuer, hit the underside of the crossbar, and bounced well over the line for a sensational equaliser. Incredibly, inexplicably, Uruguayan referee Jorge Larrionda waved play on. Where there had been doubt and confusion at Wembley in 1966, there was only outrage and embarrassment in Bloemfontein, as everybody, from Lampard himself to the television commentators, to the fans in the stadium, had witnessed a certain goal. The incident would generate endless debate, but about what England might have done from a position of parity, rather than about the decision itself. Notably, Lampard's *Wembley-Tor* also effectively ended debates around the implementation in football of goal-line technology, which was firmly in place by the next World Cup.

Six minutes after half-time, Lampard again hit the crossbar, this time with a thunderous free kick from 35 yards out. From another, closer, Lampard dead-ball attempt 15 minutes later, with everybody but Ashley Cole pushed up, England lost possession and chased helplessly as Schweinsteiger, Özil and Müller broke at pace. The swift counter attack culminated just inside England's penalty area at the feet of Müller, who smashed a right-footed finish past James at his near post. England's World Cup ambitions were then dismantled entirely within three more minutes, when Özil left Barry in his wake on the left and just had to square the ball for Müller to score his second. Both goals were stylish and ruthless counter attacks that punished England's inability to retain possession, and their propensity to leave themselves exposed at attacking set pieces.

The reaction in Germany was euphoric. The 4-1 result was Germany's record win over England, and it was also England's heaviest World Cup defeat. Oliver Bierhoff congratulated his colleague Löw on a 'tactical masterclass', while World Cup winner and columnist Thomas Berthold added, 'Löw has a philosophy, he demands both the right playing style and team spirit, he is a true coach who is not dependent on personalities and individuals. Löw was the key man in 2006 too!' The

Frankfurter Allgemeine Zeitung was similarly effusive about the impressive display, 'This unexpectedly decisive and attractive victory over the masters of the Premier League with Rooney, Lampard, and Gerrard was marked by excellent moments of play enriched with wonderful combinations, in a manner we have rarely seen from a German national team at a World Cup.'

For England, there was a dizzying array of factors to blame, although the scale of the defeat meant that the manager's post-match focus on the referee's grievous error found little sympathy. 'Don't be fooled by Fabio Capello's smokescreen over Frank Lampard's "goal",' wrote Henry Winter. 'Even if the midfielder's exceptional shot had stood, as it should have, England cannot escape the brutal reality that Germany were superior in every department.' For Michael Owen, it had been a tactical failure to persist with 4-4-2 in the face of an opposition that played two midfielders, Khedira and Schweinsteiger, behind a playmaker of Özil's versatility, 'It hurts me to say it as a striker who needs to play up front with another, but the days of 4-4-2 against a good team are going.' This was borne out by Löw's own assessment of his tactics, 'We knew Gerrard and Lampard would go up front and that the midfield would be open. Our goal was to pull Terry out of defence with Klose, because the defenders play quite wide. We wanted to expose the defence in this way, and we managed it.'

* * *

Six days after Bloemfontein, the *Nationalmannschaft* produced another stunning display to beat Argentina 4-0 in Cape Town and reach its 12th World Cup semi-final. A 1-0 defeat to the still-superior Spaniards followed in Durban on 7 July, and Germany had to settle for third place as they had at home in 2006. Yet the performances in South Africa had confirmed Löw's team as 'one of the world's most potent and attractive sides'. The average age of the starting XI was just 25, remarkably young for a successful team at a World Cup. What is more, there was one key player of the future, still 20 years old, who had only made four substitute appearances at this tournament. With FC Bayern's Toni Kroos in midfield alongside Khedira and Schweinsteiger in Brazil four years later, the picture was complete. In the latter stages, this triumvirate played ahead of Neuer and a four-man defence composed of captain Lahm, centre-backs Boateng and Hummels, and left-back Höwedes. Veteran striker Klose, who became the finals' all-time top goalscorer in history with 16 goals, played ahead of Özil and Müller. Backed by other squad players, most notably the young scorer of the dramatic extra-time winner in the final, Mario Götze, this team won Germany's fourth World Cup in the Maracanã Stadium in Rio de Janeiro on 13 July 2014.

Meanwhile, with three members of the so-called golden generation still in the squad in Lampard, Gerrard and Rooney, England, under manager Roy Hodgson, were eliminated from the tournament before Germany even kicked off their second match. The words of the veteran football writer Patrick Barclay after England's Bloemfontein defeat had pointed the way to this state of affairs. Noting the DFB's diligent and strategic reforms after the failures of the early 2000s, Barclay wrote, 'Germany is rewarded for doing painstakingly what the FA tries to do by throwing its money around.' While in 2010 the *Nationalmannschaft* under Löw had clearly exhibited a *Teamgeist* and a long-term vision, Capello's England were 'bound together by nothing. No philosophy except self-regard and a confidence that the FA will find the best manager money can buy.' Four years later in Brazil, the gulf was bigger than it had ever been, and England and Germany were worlds apart.

13

Touching Me, Touching You
2016–2022

In July 2014, Germany as a nation enjoyed the high point of its international reputation, adorned by the World Cup win in Brazil. Angela Merkel was halfway through her 16-year chancellorship of the Federal Republic when her party won its best result since 1990 at the 2013 election, although the collapse in the vote share of the liberal FDP party occasioned the third CDU-SDP grand coalition in the country's history.

Merkel had faced down major political challenges with 'a characteristic combination of firm moral principles, intellectual command of details and astute pragmatism', and her reputation in Germany was enhanced by her handling of the Eurozone crisis after 2009, even if she was fiercely criticised elsewhere, most notably in Greece. It was no coincidence, however, that her domestic approval rating reached its astonishing peak of 86 per cent in mid-2014, at the time of Germany's sporting triumph.

The chancellor flew to Rio de Janeiro alongside *Bundespräsident* Joachim Gauck and attended the World Cup Final, having already greeted the *Nationalmannschaft* in person at its first match of the tournament, against Portugal in Salvador, Bahia. Merkel was occasionally referred to as *Mutti* on account of her perceived maternal qualities, and after the impressive opening 4-0 win, Lukas Podolski coined a new phrase when he published a selfie with Merkel and thanked her for her *Muttivation*. A month later in the Maracanã dressing room, Merkel and Gauck were pictured among the squad, with the newly won World Cup trophy prominently in view.

In the business newspaper *Handelsblatt*, Thomas Sigmund wrote about the positive political impact of Merkel's relationship with her national football team, pointing out that, as clearly evidenced by the photographs from the Maracanã, her visit was no chore for the players, who respected her and welcomed her support. Indeed, Sönke Wortmann's film documentary on the 2006 World Cup had shown Merkel greeting the squad behind closed doors ahead of their historic campaign on home soil. She had accompanied this journey from the very beginning, and not always with her public image in mind.

Across German media and society, parallels were drawn between Merkel's government and Löw's world champions, as for example in Sigmund's analysis:

'If the chancellor had her way, Germany would adopt the national team as its role model to sustain its current success. After all, Löw's team plays exactly how the chancellor would like to do politics. Everyone stands up for everyone. Goal and success orientated. The exact opposite of egotists like Gerhard Schröder or [opposition leader] Peer Steinbrück, who are self-absorbed and like to have the political stage and the power that comes with it for themselves.'

In poignant juxtaposition, I find myself translating these words during the week that Prime Minister Boris Johnson, in the face of overwhelming criticism from almost all sectors of British public life, announced that he would resign as Conservative party leader and, at length, clear the path for his successor in 10 Downing Street. Johnson's protracted downfall has been so wrought with outrage, incompetence and mendacity that a national newspaper in its leading article is able to offer the following words, unimaginable in connection with a British prime minister just a few years ago, in response to his resignation:

'He claimed to understand the British people but, as the past torrid weeks have shown, he never shared or understood their moral decency. He behaved like a president, not a parliamentary leader. He governed by campaigning, not through collective deliberation and delivery. He abused his office by rewarding cronies and doing deals with donors. To the last, he was incapable of giving a straight answer to a straight question. He has now destroyed three Conservative governments in six years and done much to damage Britain's international reputation. The party, and the British people, are well rid of him.'

* * *

England faced Germany twice during the four-year tenure of Fabio Capello's successor, Roy Hodgson. Capello had quit suddenly and unexpectedly in February 2012, when John Terry, reinstated the year before, was stripped of the captaincy for a second time on the authority of FA chairman David Bernstein and without Capello's approval. Terry was facing trial on charges of racially abusing Anton Ferdinand, Rio's younger brother, during a Premier League match in October 2011, and with legal proceedings adjourned until after the 2012 European Championship, Bernstein placed the 'FA's wider role as regulator above the short-term interests of the coach'.

The FA subsequently ignored clamours from the public and especially the press for Tottenham Hotspur manager Harry Redknapp, cleared in court of tax evasion on the same day as Capello's resignation, to be installed as manager, opting instead for the internationally experienced and urbane Hodgson.

At the tournament in Poland and Ukraine, England showed that lessons had been learned from the public relations disaster of Rustenburg. Players were at ease in public outside their team base in Kraków, and delegations of players and staff visited Auschwitz-Birkenau and Oskar Schindler's former factory. On the pitch, the team were once again eliminated by means of a penalty shoot-out, against Italy in the quarter-final in Kyiv. England had now lost six times in seven shoot-outs across the FIFA World Cup and the UEFA European Championship, the worst record of any international team.

After subsequently securing qualification to the 2014 World Cup, England welcomed Germany to Wembley on 19 November 2013 to mark the 150th anniversary of the FA. Of Joachim Löw's first-choice XI in Brazil six months later, only Jérôme Boateng and Toni Kroos started this match, in which veteran Borussia Dortmund goalkeeper Roman Weidenfeller was handed an international debut. The German line-up was also notable for featuring twins playing together in midfield, Lars and Sven Bender of Bayer Leverkusen and Borussia Dortmund, respectively. Hodgson's team was undergoing a transition from 4-4-2 at Euro 2012 to the 4-2-3-1 system he would adopt at the 2014 World Cup, with captain Steven Gerrard, now aged 33, at the base of the midfield, on this occasion alongside Tom Cleverley. Ashley Cole and Wayne Rooney were the other experienced heads in the team, complemented by younger players such as Daniel Sturridge (24), Kyle Walker (23) and Andros Townsend (22).

Germany's winning goal came shortly before half-time from Per Mertesacker, the tall centre-back nicknamed 'the BFG', after Roald Dahl's *Big Friendly Giant*, at his English club, Arsenal. When a clearance found its way to corner-taker Kroos on the right, the FC Bayern midfielder played an accurate first-time cross back in to the penalty area, where Mertesacker rose above Manchester United defender Chris Smalling to head past goalkeeper Joe Hart. The 1-0 result gave the *Nationalmannschaft* its seventh win over England at Wembley in eight attempts since 1966.

26 March 2016
Germany 2-3 England
Olympiastadion, Berlin

Less than three months before the start of the UEFA European Championship in France, for which England had qualified with a perfect record of ten victories, Hodgson's team faced the world champions in Berlin. Rooney, who had surpassed Bobby Charlton's England goalscoring record in 2015, was missing due to injury, while Gerrard and Frank Lampard had both retired from international football after the 2014 World Cup. A young and inexperienced side represented the new generation at the Olympiastadion. Four of the starting XI – debutant defender Danny Rose (25), striker Harry Kane (22), and midfielders Eric Dier (22) and Dele Alli (19) – represented Mauricio Pochettino's Tottenham Hotspur side that was chasing Leicester City for an unlikely Premier League title that season, while Leicester's Jamie Vardy scored just two minutes after coming on as a second-half substitute.

Löw's team was significantly more experienced, with Kroos and Sami Khedira, now of Real Madrid and Juventus, respectively, together in midfield, and Mesut Özil, Thomas Müller and Borussia Dortmund's injury-plagued talisman Marco Reus playing behind Mario Gómez. The on-loan Beşiktaş striker thought he had given the home side the lead midway through the first half, but his goal was incorrectly ruled out for offside. An encouraging and committed opening period from England nonetheless ended in disappointment when Kroos scored from distance past goalkeeper Jack Butland, who was limping with an injured ankle and was withdrawn immediately afterwards. On 56 minutes, Khedira played a delicately chipped pass behind the defence, and Gómez headed in past substitute goalkeeper Fraser Forster to double Germany's lead.

Hodgson's young players would not give up England's unbeaten record in Berlin that easily, however, and began a spirited comeback with a magnificent goal on the hour. Two days after the sad death of the legendary Johan Cruyff at the age of 68, Kane – on just his ninth senior England appearance – beat both Müller and Özil with a Cruyff turn in the penalty area, before drilling a low right-footed shot through the legs of Emre Can and into the bottom corner. Then came Vardy's moment, an audacious back-heeled flick to divert Nathaniel Clyne's cross past Neuer at his near post. These were heady times among the visiting supporters in Berlin, who dreamed of a comeback victory and duly had those dreams fulfilled in dramatic fashion. From Jordan Henderson's injury-time corner, Dier rose high above substitute André Schürrle and headed in the winning goal. Hodgson called it his 'best night yet' after four years in charge. This was the auspicious high point from which England's fall on a balmy night in the south of France just three months later would seem all the more precipitous.

* * *

England's ill-fated match against Iceland in the last 16 of the 2016 European Championship came just three days after the United Kingdom woke to the news that the nationwide referendum of 23 June had resulted in 51.9 per cent of the votes cast favouring Britain's exit from the European Union, or Brexit. This was a political earthquake from which the aftershocks remain severe in 2022. The referendum resulted from the Conservatives' achievement of a parliamentary majority at the 2015 general election, where Prime Minister David Cameron had famously promised voters, 'A simple and inescapable choice – stability and strong Government with me, or chaos with [Labour leader] Ed Miliband.' Cameron's victory was immediately followed by the necessary legal measures to honour a Conservative manifesto pledge to hold the EU referendum with which he sought to resolve the enduringly vexatious issue of Euroscepticism within his parliamentary party.

The widespread suspicions that there were no plans in place for the eventuality of Brexit were soon substantiated. A month after the surprising result of the vote, a report from the House of Commons Foreign Affairs Committee stated that Cameron, who promptly resigned the day after the vote, had 'committed an act of gross negligence and deepened the uncertainty surrounding the impact of Brexit by instructing Whitehall not to make any contingency plans for a vote to leave the EU'. Cameron had also asked other European leaders not to involve themselves in campaigning ahead of the vote, for fear of arousing anti-European sentiment in Britain.

Upon hearing the result, Merkel gave a disappointed but acquiescent response, 'We take note of the British people's decision with regret. There is no doubt that this is a blow to Europe and to the European unification process.' In the German press, it had been a different story, with impassioned pleas for the British people to vote to remain in the EU published in many influential outlets.

Weekly news magazine *Der Spiegel* printed a union flag on its front page with the words 'Please don't go! Why Germany needs the British', while *Bild* on the day of the referendum published a list of humorous pledges under the headline, 'Dear Brits, if you stay in the EU …' The promises ranged from reserving poolside chairs for the British in the morning, to setting clocks back an hour to 'tick like you', but most prominent of all, illustrated with a photograph of the famous moment in 1966, was the commitment that 'even we will acknowledge *das Wembley-Tor!*'

2016 UEFA European Championship
France

England's humiliating 2-1 defeat to Iceland in the second round of Euro 2016 on 27 June was widely acknowledged as one of the national team's worst performances, certainly in the modern era, and was greeted in *The Times* with zero ratings out of ten for every single one of their players. Ever since finding themselves unexpectedly in arrears after 18 minutes, Hodgson's men were bereft of composure and struggled to create meaningful opportunities. It was a defeat that cut deeply not only because of the stature of the opposition, but particularly because England were afforded the perfect start and failed utterly to capitalise.

It looked early on as though Hodgson's loyalty to the players who had underwhelmed during the group stage might be vindicated, when Daniel Sturridge's accurate long pass found Raheem Sterling on a clever run behind the defence, and the Manchester City winger was brought down by goalkeeper Hannes Halldórsson for a penalty. Captain Wayne Rooney scored from the spot to give his side the lead just four minutes in. England had ostensibly overcome the major obstacle of the evening, which was to break the deadlock against obdurate, defensive opponents who were limited in attack, something they had failed to do against Slovakia in Saint-Étienne a week before. Yet, despite Iceland's obvious limitations, they proved too much for England in the minutes following Rooney's opener.

Parity was restored almost immediately, when Ragnar Sigurðsson scored from a long throw on the right flank, a predictable carbon copy of Iceland's opener against Austria in the group stage. 'England's centre-backs watched with all the rapt detachment of theatregoers,' wrote the *Daily Telegraph*'s Paul Hayward. Twelve minutes later England were behind, succumbing to a neat passing move on the edge of the penalty area. All Icelandic players involved were afforded time and space to pick out a pass, and Chelsea defender Gary Cahill stood off Kolbeinn Sigþórsson as he shaped to shoot from 16 yards. Nonetheless, the effort should have been saved by Hart.

It was all the more galling as Iceland's simple and honest approach, which relied on collective effort and physicality, ought to have been meat and drink for an England side so often maligned for lacking the subtlety and ball-playing technique of their continental counterparts. Here, England were essentially faced with organised and dedicated exponents of the traditional English game, and it inexcusably caught them off guard. England were shell-shocked, and needed to regroup by making positive, attacking changes at the interval, much in the way that Didier Deschamps had done for France on several occasions in the tournament. But Hodgson's only response was the introduction of Jack Wilshere, who was clearly short of match fitness and had already failed to impress in a 56-minute stint against Slovakia. Hodgson then inexcusably dithered until three minutes from full time before introducing the promising teenager Marcus Rashford, who duly ran at Iceland's defence and looked to create last-minute opportunities for an equaliser. It was too late, and an abject second half where England simply lacked the composure to string basic passes together ended with desperate attempts to score from range or from set pieces.

It all played out to a backdrop of disenchanted, enraged supporters witnessing one of England's most ignominious footballing defeats. Much like Cameron three days before, Hodgson's position was untenable and he quit with immediate effect.

On a night of high drama and utmost tension in the Bordeaux quarter-final on 2 July, Germany finally overcame *Angstgegner* Italy by means of a tortuous penalty shoot-out of 18 spot kicks. Left-back Jonas Hector of 1. FC Köln scored the winning penalty after an unprecedented seven attempts were saved, skied, shanked, or stopped by the goal frame. The match itself was one of heightened tactical intrigue, particularly as favourites Germany had adapted their formation to match Antonio Conte's system. Löw sprung a surprise with a back three, deploying erstwhile full-backs Hector and Joshua Kimmich as wing-backs higher up the pitch. The change allowed Germany to press Italy's wing-backs Mattia de Sciglio and Alessandro Florenzi, who had impressed in the *Azzurri*'s last-16 win over Spain.

In the cauldron of the Marseille semi-final five days later, Löw reverted to 4-2-3-1 but the hosts started fast and played with an intensity that had been lacking in the early matches of their campaign. Germany soon grew into the game and dominated possession as expected, with full-backs Hector and Kimmich playing high up the pitch and providing plenty of width. Emre Can replaced the injured Khedira in defensive midfield, while Müller led the line for the first time at these championships in the absence of Gómez. At a corner just before the interval, Schweinsteiger raised both arms when challenging for the ball with Patrice Evra, and referee Nicola Rizzoli belatedly awarded a penalty for handball. Antoine Griezmann scored with ease, and it was a crushing blow right on half-time for Germany, who had otherwise come to command the game.

Yet any feelings of injustice at the first goal were negated by the self-inflicted nature of the second. Schweinsteiger made the initial error of passing across his own penalty area to attempt to play his side out of trouble, and Benedikt Höwedes could only look for Kimmich with a similarly risky ball as the French pressed eagerly. Harried by Blaise Matuidi, a mistake from the young FC Bayern defender was as good as inevitable, and his poor touch allowed Paul Pogba to steal the ball on the left edge of the six-yard box. Pogba's trickery made a mockery of substitute defender Shkodran Mustafi, and his subsequent cross was palmed by Neuer only to the feet of Griezmann, who was waiting on the penalty spot to double France's lead with a simple finish. It was a night for France to savour as *Les Bleus'* first competitive win over Germany in 58 years helped to ease memories of semi-final heartache in 1982 and 1986, as well as the World Cup quarter-final in 2014.

* * *

On 22 July 2016, the FA appointed Sam Allardyce as the new England manager, following 'a comprehensive and structured process'. Allardyce had guided Sunderland to Premier League safety in the 2015/16 season, and he was hired on the basis of his track record for getting results from underperforming teams and his 'strong reputation as a forward-thinker with progressive ideas'. His immediate priority was to secure qualification for the 2018 FIFA World Cup in Russia, and in his first match in charge, on 4 September, England narrowly beat ten-man Slovakia thanks to a goal deep into injury time from Liverpool midfielder Adam Lallana.

Later that same month, the *Daily Telegraph* published a front-page story entitled 'England manager for sale', which revealed details of a sting operation in which Allardyce allegedly agreed a fee with undercover reporters for insider knowledge on football business. Yet again, unwelcome questions of probity swirled around the FA and the England manager's position, and Allardyce was relieved of his duties the following day, after just 67 days and one match in charge.

England faced four more games in the calendar year, including a high-profile World Cup qualification match against Gordon Strachan's Scotland, and the FA turned to under-21 manager Gareth Southgate, then aged 46, temporarily to steady the ship. England's 3-0 win over their oldest rivals at Wembley, their biggest against Scotland in 41 years, confirmed Southgate as the leading candidate for the permanent job in the English press. When he signed a four-year contract on 30 November, much was made of Southgate's prospective ability to form a bond with the players and improve the squad's psychological resilience, in view of his own experience as the unsuccessful penalty taker against Germany at Euro '96.

The nature of England's elimination from recent tournaments, particularly against Iceland that summer, had brought the issue of mentality to the forefront of discussion around the national team. 'This is not quite "year zero",' wrote the *Daily Telegraph*'s Jason Burt, 'but has to be pretty close in terms of England's standing in world football and the mental "brittleness" … that FA chief executive Martin Glenn correctly identified in the immediate aftermath of the humiliating Euro 2016 exit that remains at the heart of the problem.' Burt also cited the DFB's incumbent national team manager as an encouraging example for Southgate, 'Löw … shows the importance of backing a coach who fits what the country is trying to achieve. The fact he did not succeed at club level, an accusation levelled at Southgate, was immaterial because he was and has proven to be the right man for Germany.'

2017 internationals
Dortmund and Wembley

For only the third time since 1908, two England v Germany internationals took place within the same calendar year, in

2017. On England's first visit to Dortmund on 22 March, the occasion belonged to Lukas Podolski in every sense. As the last remaining link to the Klinsmann revolution, besides Löw of course, Podolski said farewell to the *Nationalmannschaft* as captain on his 130th senior appearance. In the 69th minute he received the ball from Schürrle around 25 yards out and hit a technically perfect left-footed drive into the top corner of Joe Hart's net to score the only goal of the game. Podolski thus finished his international career with 49 goals, including nine at World Cup or European Championship finals.

This was also England's first match since Southgate was appointed on a permanent basis. He handed a debut to Burnley defender Michael Keane, who gave an assured display alongside Smalling and Cahill in a 3-4-3 formation. As in Berlin a year before, England produced an encouraging performance, with Alli again full of energy and promise in attack. The young Tottenham midfielder was recognised as England's best player in both his first two appearances against Germany. The BBC's Phil McNulty observed, 'Alli showed some sublime touches in a system that suited him and brought the best out of his natural creative instincts, making chances and also acting as a goal threat as Southgate looks to find the new way forward for England.' Yet Alli's inability to take his chances on this occasion ensured that the evening ended with Germany's first victory over England on home soil in nearly 30 years, the 3-1 win in Düsseldorf on 9 September 1987 having been followed by England's 5-1 win in Munich in 2001 and the two successes in Berlin in 2008 and 2016.

This match also took place on the same day as the Westminster terrorist attack in which six people died, including the attacker, and this context intensified the obloquy of England fans' cross behaviour in Dortmund. In *The Times*, Henry Winter noted that local fans 'looked almost with pity at their unreconstructed guests', whose wartime songs and disrespect for the German national anthem were a cause of great frustration:

'Many fans seemed imprisoned by history, singing more about the RAF than Alli and Lallana. The "island mentality" that Southgate wants to escape may take the fans longer than the players. Their passion is admirable, their willingness to turn up in numbers around the globe commendable, but the offensive, Neanderthal grunts have to stop.'

At least at the next meeting between the sides, at Wembley on 10 November, the eve of Remembrance Day, Winter was able to report that there was 'strong applause for the German national anthem, which was respectfully observed by England fans'. For this first non-competitive international of the World Cup season, and with numerous squad withdrawals to account for, Southgate fielded a highly experimental and inexperienced side. The starting XI included three debutants, and two substitutes also earned their first cap. Tottenham Hotspur wing-backs Danny Rose and Kieran Trippier played outside a back three of Harry Maguire, John Stones and Phil Jones, but the latter, due to an early injury, was replaced by Liverpool's Joe Gomez. In midfield, Eric Dier played alongside Jake Livermore and debutant Ruben Loftus-Cheek, on loan from Chelsea at Crystal Palace. Another Chelsea loanee, Swansea City's Tammy Abraham, made his first international appearance in attack alongside Jamie Vardy. Everton goalkeeper Jordan Pickford was also wearing the England number one shirt for the first time, staking his claim in the wake of Joe Hart's rejection by Pep Guardiola at Manchester City.

Kicker selected Pickford as man of the match for his two saves in one-on-one situations with Timo Werner, but it was Loftus-Cheek who most impressed members of the English media. The midfielder's 'strength, skill and composure ... was a snap-shot of modern football in England, home-grown talent craving a chance', wrote Winter, before criticising the short-termism and 'flawed thinking' of Chelsea, where Loftus-Cheek was given few opportunities to break into the first team.

Germany's brightest player on the night was Leroy Sané, who started on the left but intermittently switched flanks with Julian Draxler. From the right, the Manchester City winger hit the crossbar with a dipping left-footed shot early in the game. Voted Young Player of the Year by the Professional Footballers' Association for 2017/18, Sané was surprisingly omitted from Löw's World Cup squad.

For England, this goalless draw, which averted a seventh consecutive Wembley defeat to Germany since 1975, was an encouraging result, but it could so easily have been converted into a win at the very end. When Rashford's injury-time set piece was headed back into the six-yard box by Maguire, the ball fell for substitute Jesse Lingard to score with the last kick of the game, but he skewed his finish over the crossbar. It was only the third goalless draw in the history of the England v Germany rivalry, and the match was also notable for being the first official game in the UK to feature a video assistant referee, or VAR.

* * *

It is easy in light of Germany's subsequent failure in Russia to forget that at this point the *Nationalmannschaft* was coming off an unbeaten series of 22 matches which included a perfect World Cup qualification campaign of ten wins from ten. In a notable 48 hours for German football, moreover, the under-21 team managed by Stefan Kuntz overcame a talented Spain side to win the UEFA Under-21 European Championship in Kraków on 30 June 2017, and a second-string senior team then beat Chile in Saint Petersburg on 2 July to win the last edition of the now defunct Confederations Cup. Southgate was present at both these finals.

A remarkable year for English and German youth football also saw England win the FIFA U-20 World Cup in South Korea in June 2017, with the likes of Fikayo Tomori and Dominic Calvert-Lewin in the team, while Chelsea youngster Dominic Solanke won the Golden Ball award for the tournament's best player. England then won the FIFA U-17 World Cup in India, beating Spain 5-2 in the final in Kolkata on 28 October. Manchester City prodigy Phil Foden, who scored twice in the final, won the Golden Ball, and Liverpool's Rhian Brewster claimed the Golden Boot for his eight goals across the tournament. Future England senior internationals Marc Guéhi, Callum Hudson-Odoi, Emile Smith Rowe and Conor Gallagher were also in this squad of world champions. These were England's first titles in the respective competitions, and the trophies were the first tangible returns from the Premier League's Elite Player Performance Plan, implemented in 2011, and the FA's multimillion-pound investment in the National Football Centre. Opened in 2012 at St George's Park, Burton upon Trent, the site oversees the development of all England men's and women's national teams.

2018 FIFA World Cup
Russia

Germany's group-stage exit from the 2018 World Cup was a seismic shock to the international football landscape. The last-gasp free kick from Toni Kroos which rescued the points from the second match, against Sweden in Sochi, had given hope that a misfiring campaign was on track after a poor start with defeat to Mexico in Moscow. In the final match against South Korea, however, an impotent German team was humiliated by two injury-time goals that confirmed the nation's earliest elimination from a World Cup since 1938. *The Guardian*'s Jonathan Wilson memorably conveyed the feeble nature of Germany's capitulation in the city of Kazan:

'This, then, is how the world ends, not with a bang but with a whimper. There are certain events so apocalyptic that it feels they cannot just happen. They should be signalled beneath thunderous skies as owls catch falcons and horses turn and eat themselves. At the very least there should be a sense of fury, of thwarted effort, of energies exhausted. And yet Germany went out of the World Cup in the first round for the first time in 80 years on a pleasantly sunny afternoon with barely a flicker of resistance. There was no Sturm. There was no Drang.'

For the gleeful *Sun*, meanwhile, it sufficed merely to print a definition of the word *Schadenfreude* on its front page, above a picture of the dejected German players. At home, the shock was so great that *Bild* ironically reprised its front-page layout from the 7-1 win over Brazil in 2014, in which the result was heralded by the headline '*Ohne Worte!*' – 'No words!' – and a full-page picture of Kroos. Löw and his staff had a lot to answer for, having failed for the first time in six tournaments to create an effective team spirit and settled side in time for kick-off.

In early analyses, the malaise was traced back eight months to the warm-up matches at the end of 2017, after qualification had been emphatically secured. Suggested reasons for failure included the choice of team base in Russia, the DFB's poor crisis management in response to Özil's photo opportunity with Turkish President Recep Tayyip Erdoğan, the failure to incorporate members of the Confederations Cup side into the World Cup starting XI, and even the excessive use of social media hashtags and marketing slogans which built an image of a team that was no longer reflected in reality. At a lengthy press conference two months after the event, the self-critical *Bundestrainer* conceded that it was 'almost arrogant' to believe that the team could progress past the group stage with a dominant, high-risk possession game, before then adjusting for knockout football. Löw also admitted that team spirit and enthusiasm were lacking in Russia, 'We approached things very strategically and neglected other things.'

News of Germany's defeat to South Korea emerged during England's press conference ahead of their own final group game, against Belgium in Kaliningrad. 'We've learned an enormous amount from studying Germany, not least last summer, and implemented that,' said Southgate. 'Indirectly, they've had a big bearing on what we're doing now.' These were no mere platitudes. In an interview with Keir Radnedge that was published in *Kicker* ahead of the World Cup, Southgate spoke of his admiration for German football:

'We studied Germany at the 2014 World Cup and their development in the youth teams. They have such self-confidence that they can pretty much send a youth team to the Confederations Cup and an even younger team to the under-21 Euros. That could have gone wrong, but it didn't. They modify their system and are constantly evolving … I have great admiration for Germany. As I said, we're looking at what we can learn from this nation, but we also have to find our own path.'

With Germany now eliminated and Sweden confirmed as winners of Group F, an ongoing, hubristic debate in the English media as to whether it would be more prudent to avoid Brazil or Germany in the draw was resolved. England stood top of their group with six points from a narrow opening victory against Tunisia in Volgograd and a 6-1 win over Panama in Nizhny Novgorod, and although it was impossible for Southgate to admit, his nine changes for the match against Belgium indicated an inclination, shall we say, to finish second in Group G. England otherwise benefited from a settled side at the tournament, with ten players starting every game other than the group match versus Belgium and the third-place play-off against the same opponent. Pickford and Stones started all seven matches, and the Manchester City centre-back was joined in a back three by Walker and Maguire. The wing-backs were Trippier and Ashley Young, the oldest member of the squad at 32, while Alli and Lingard played ahead of Henderson in the midfield three. Sterling and Kane, now the captain, played up front, with the Tottenham Hotspur striker scoring five goals in the first two matches. He added a penalty in the last-16 match against Colombia to finish on six goals and claim the Golden Boot award, emulating Gary Lineker's achievement in 1986. England exorcised their penalty shoot-out demons against the South Americans, prevailing after Carlos Bacca saw his penalty saved by Pickford.

An uncommonly comfortable 2-0 win over Sweden in Samara on 7 July then set up a semi-final against Croatia in Moscow four days later, England's biggest game in 28 years. Trippier's sensational free-kick goal after just four minutes had the nation dreaming, and for the best part of an hour England were firmly in control. After Ivan Perišić equalised on 68 minutes, however, Luka Modrić began to take charge of the midfield and Croatia continued to grow in stature. In the second half of extra time, Juventus striker Mario Mandžukić was too quick for Stones and Maguire in reacting to a Perišić header behind the defence and then provided a lethal finish to send his country to a first World Cup Final. Crucially, however, England had fallen back in love with its national team, and there was a stark contrast between this experience and the many tournaments that preceded it, as recognised by Winter:

'Everyone can see how different this tournament departure feels from previous ones – a world of difference. There will be no recrimination, only celebration of how well Southgate's young players did in reaching the last four. There will be no inquest, only renewed belief in the pathway that Southgate, England and the FA are on. Let's keep calm and carry on. Let's look forward hopefully to 2020 and 2022. Let's not look back in anger.'

* * *

A difficult year for Germany continued in the newly minted UEFA Nations League at the start of the 2018/19 season. The *Nationalmannschaft* failed to win a game in a three-team group with France and the Netherlands, and were beaten 3-0 in Amsterdam to make matters worse. Germany were only spared relegation to League B for the following edition of the competition because of a revamp which saw the top division expanded from 12 to 16 teams for 2020/21.

England, meanwhile, recovered from a poor start to win their group with Spain and Croatia, thereby progressing to the inaugural Nations League finals in Portugal in June 2019. The undoubted highlight of the campaign was a 3-2 win over Spain at Estadio Benito Villamarín, the home of Real Betis in Seville, on 15 October 2018. For Winter, writing in *The Times*, the first half, in which England stormed to a 3-0 lead through two goals from Sterling and one from Rashford, 'bore legitimate comparison with the second period of the famous triumph in Munich in 2001'. It may have been Seville and not Madrid, but this was another famous England win on Spanish soil to follow those of 1965, 1968 and 1987.

Southgate's men ultimately finished third in the competition via a morale-boosting penalty shoot-out win over Switzerland in the third-place play-off, following defeat to Ronald Koeman's Netherlands side in extra time of the semi-final in Guimarães. During 2019, England and Germany qualified with near-identical records for the 2020 UEFA European Championship, to be staged in 12 cities across the continent in celebration of the 60th anniversary of the competition. Before either team could fulfil an international fixture in 2020, however, the Covid-19 pandemic caused all football to be suspended, and on 17 March UEFA announced its decision to postpone the tournament by 12 months.

International football resumed in mostly empty stadia at the start of the 2020/21 season with the second edition of the UEFA Nations League, which visited abject humiliation on the *Nationalmannschaft* in the form of a 6-0 defeat to Spain, also in Seville, although at Estadio La Cartuja. This result was the joint-heaviest defeat recognised by FIFA in the history of the German national team, and it was followed by further ignominy on 31 March 2021 in Duisburg, where North Macedonia became only the third team in history to beat Germany in World Cup qualification. It now seemed clear to German observers that the Löw era was not to be revived, and there were grave concerns as to how the team would fare in a European Championship 'group of death', with matches on home soil in Munich against world champions France, Portugal and Hungary.

29 June 2021
UEFA European Championship last 16
England 2-0 Germany
Wembley Stadium

A tortuous 2-2 draw with Hungary at the Allianz Arena on 23 June at length confirmed that Germany would travel to Wembley to renew the rivalry with England in the first knockout round of the delayed Euro 2020 finals. Löw's side had lost the opening group-stage match to France after a Mats Hummels own goal but then responded by convincingly beating defending champions Portugal under immense pressure in the second game. The 3-4-3 system was particularly effective in this match, with Robin Gosens, of Atalanta in Italy, and Kimmich playing with great attacking endeavour in the wing-back positions. The fourth goal, a Gosens header from a Kimmich cross, was a perfect representation of the two players' impact on the game.

Against Hungary in the driving rain in Munich, Germany were shocked by Ádám Szalai's excellent early header and took the best part of an hour to find a response. When it came, from Chelsea's Kai Havertz on 66 minutes, a lapse of concentration allowed András Schäfer immediately to restore Hungary's lead at the other end, and with France and Portugal drawing elsewhere, Germany were heading for another unthinkable exit from the group stage. With five substitutions now permitted in the wake of the Covid-19 pandemic, Löw introduced a wealth of attacking talent, not least the Stuttgart-born teenager Jamal Musiala, a former England under-21 international. With just seven minutes remaining, Musiala played the key pass for fellow substitute Leon Goretzka which resulted in Germany's equaliser and, by extension, a date with England at Wembley.

Southgate's side had topped Group D with 1-0 wins over Croatia and the Czech Republic, and a disappointing, hard-fought goalless draw with Scotland. In all three matches, England played in a 4-2-3-1 formation, with Leeds United's Kalvin Phillips (25) and West Ham United's Declan Rice (22) forming the new midfield engine. The three players behind Kane were initially Sterling, Foden and Chelsea's Mason Mount, but Mount and his club-mate Ben Chilwell tested positive for Covid-19 after the Scotland game, necessitating a change for the final group-stage match against the Czech Republic. This enabled Southgate to start Aston Villa's Jack Grealish, a fans' favourite who was seen by many to be the answer to England's lack of expression in attacking play. England had won their group, but their style was beginning to alienate some observers, as noted by Oliver Brown in the *Daily Telegraph*, 'England have inched forward so tentatively at this tournament as to attract some scattered booing, an acrid reception befitting a team playing in third gear with the handbrake on.'

Against Germany, Southgate resolved to switch formation to match his opponent, much as Löw had done against Conte in Bordeaux five years earlier. In England's 3-4-3, Kyle Walker moved inside to form a back three with John Stones and Harry Maguire, and Kieran Trippier and Luke Shaw played as wing-backs outside Phillips and Rice. Arsenal teenager Bukayo Saka retained his place after taking over from Foden against the Czechs, and Grealish was the man to miss out in order to accommodate the additional defensive player. Henry Winter in *The Times* thought this tactical gamble was 'as big a call as Kevin Keegan putting Southgate in midfield to shadow Mehmet Scholl at Wembley in 2000', adding, 'This bowing to Joachim Löw's approach hints of insecurity.'

Given the opponent, English insecurity inevitably impinged on psychological aspects of preparation as much as tactical considerations. The weight of history bearing on this match was impossible to ignore, and the statistics alone were suffocating. It had been 46 years since England had beaten Germany at Wembley, and 55 years of hurt since a win against Germany in knockout competition. Furthermore, England had never won a knockout game in the UEFA European Championship without recourse to a penalty shoot-out, and the experience against Colombia in Russia did little to assuage a collective, national dread at the prospect of penalties against the Germans. It was of course Southgate's job to deny that history would have any bearing on the match, and he did so by foregrounding that many of his players were in infancy or not yet born on the night he saw his spot kick saved by Andreas Köpke 25 years previously. Winter explained what lay beneath this placid surface:

'Southgate often says he is over Euro '96, but the experience defines him. That was confirmed when he took the job, in immediately committing the players to practise penalties, having a proper order, not hurrying the kick, working with sports psychologists and embracing a culture of leaving nothing to chance. That penalty still shapes England.'

As Winter remarked, this match against Germany would be another step on the road to redemption for Southgate, 'yet the country and the team's supporters also need closure'.

A cagey first half in which the teams were well matched and mostly unwilling to take risks ended with the best chance falling to Kane in injury time. As Sterling was brought down by a posse of opponents on the edge of the penalty area, the ball broke loose and fell at the feet of the Spurs striker with only Neuer to beat, but Kane's heavy first touch allowed Hummels to make a desperate recovering tackle. Germany's best chance of the first period fell on the half-hour to the recalled Timo Werner, who was thwarted by Pickford in a one-on-one situation, just as he had been in the 2017 friendly. Shortly after half-time, Pickford again saved England, when he diverted a fierce left-footed volley from Havertz over the bar.

As the second half wore on, an already disjointed game became increasingly fragmented, and there were lengthy stoppages for Kane and Trippier to receive treatment. After 68 minutes, Löw introduced Serge Gnabry for Werner, and Southgate withdrew Saka for Grealish, who was met with a rapturous welcome. Wembley was riven with tension as the clock ticked past 70 minutes in a game that was suggestive of extra time, so much so that BBC commentator Guy Mowbray was moved to remark that 'the flame has gone out' on what had been a slow burner. On 74 minutes, however, Sterling drove into midfield and passed forward to Kane. With his back to goal at the edge of the penalty area, the captain fed the ball to Grealish, who played in the overlapping Shaw on the left. The wing-back flashed a first-time cross through Kimmich's legs and in behind Matthias Ginter and Hummels, and Sterling was there to divert the ball past a helpless Neuer from five yards and break the deadlock.

The goal was met with jubilant scenes in the Wembley stands, but in terms of an expression of relief, it was outdone just six minutes later when Havertz released Müller between the England centre-backs to advance on goal from fully 40 yards out. To the incredulous delight of England fans everywhere, the veteran of 105 international caps dragged his shot just wide of the post. If a signal was still needed that this was indeed England's time to change the narrative, this moment left no doubt. Müller subsequently posted a photo on social media of his crestfallen reaction, commenting, 'There it was, that one moment that you remember at the end, which keeps you awake at night. The one you work, train, and live for as a footballer. That moment when it's all in your hands to bring your team back into a tight knockout game and send an entire football nation into ecstasy. To get that opportunity and miss it really hurts.'

Five minutes later, Shaw returned the favour for Grealish, slipping him in on the left to enable him to provide another dangerous cross behind the German back line. This time it was Kane who met the ball, in the same position as Sterling ten minutes prior, and the England captain headed in to double his team's lead and settle the contest. Closure had been achieved.

* * *

Ahead of the match, the *Financial Times* published an article by the author Simon Kuper entitled 'England's one-sided football rivalry with Germany loses its bite'. Kuper claimed that the rivalry had 'lost what teeth it had' after a '30-year heyday' between 1966 and 1996. Confusing the admiration for Merkel's Germany among 'the UK's liberal left' with a 'dimming of passions' in the football rivalry, he predicted that at Wembley on 29 June 'emotions will be less primal than before'. Another England defeat, another extension to those intolerable statistics might just have lent this argument a sheen of accuracy as home supporters streamed away from Wembley with glum faces and disappointed hopes once more. The lifting of that immense historical burden, however, revealed the true depth of feeling beneath the pain of failure.

Kuper's thesis that 'the Germans have gone from bogeymen to guests trapped in the middle of an embarrassing domestic row' about Brexit and cultural politics was summarily disproved by the wildly jubilant scenes which greeted this result at Wembley and around the country. Unquestionably, the predominant unifying force was the slaying of a ghost in victory over Germany, but the context of the Covid-19 pandemic was another significant factor. Amid the celebrations of Sterling's opening goal, Mowbray commented, 'We haven't seen scenes like this in a football ground for a long, long time.' It was indeed an extraordinary twist of fate that caused England's long-overdue deliverance from suffering against Germany on the football field to coincide with the return of fans to stadia after a 15-month hiatus. England's group games at Wembley were each seen by crowds of around 20,000, and UEFA then sanctioned an attendance of 40,000 for the second-round match. Still less than half-full, Wembley generated an atmosphere of utmost euphoria, a unique and unrepeatable coalescence of liberation from public health restrictions and sporting triumph. In *The Guardian*, Barney Ronay wrote, 'It was hard to shake the feeling of people emerging from a dream into some strange new light.' For Henry Winter in *The Times*, the occasion was 'about hope, such a rare commodity in the history of the national team, and especially important after the year that the country has suffered'.

The national sentiment was aptly harnessed by the Wembley DJ Tony Perry, who opted to play Neil Diamond's 1969 classic 'Sweet Caroline' after the final whistle. The lyric 'reaching out, touching me, touching you' proved especially pertinent after so many months of social distancing, and with England's win satisfying a long-suppressed yearning for a positive collective experience. In this heady mixture of circumstances for England fans, there was a ring of truth to the idea that 'good times never seemed so good'.

Some months after the wave of euphoria around Euro 2020 had abated, I travelled to Germany and spoke with Jonathan

Harding, an English football journalist and author living in Bonn. I asked him how it had felt to cover the German national team as an Englishman on that day at Wembley, and his reflections are indicative of the profound personal significance that the game held for many people.

As a child growing up abroad, Harding developed an otherwise undernourished emotional link to his home country through the ritual of watching England matches with his father and brother, a ritual of disappointment where the team's performances were concerned. Harding has observed German football with a keen interest for over a decade, and in 2014 he began covering the Bundesliga and the *Nationalmannschaft* professionally. In 2018 he had the privilege of following the national team at the World Cup in Russia, but he told me that the opportunity to cover the match at Wembley represented the culmination of his years of hard work. On that day, the professional and the personal intermingled as he watched Germany take on a young and successful England side that not only stirred memories of childhood, before his parents' later divorce, but also gave rise to new feelings of pride. 'It felt good to be proud of this team and what they were standing for beyond the way they were playing,' explained Harding.

'You felt that something different was happening with England and the conversations were different. This was a conversation about inclusivity and about recognising different cultural roots and the multicultural nature of the team, and being proud that we were all playing together – that was something that really resonated with me on top of the emotional connection.'

As Southgate wrote in his open letter to the nation ahead of the tournament, 'You remember where you were watching England games. And who you were watching with. And who *you* were at the time.' It is this deeply personal connection that made England's win so cathartic an experience for Harding and many others like him. The pride that many English people felt in watching Southgate's team overcome Germany and then progress to a first major final for 55 years is also profoundly individuated, but for many like Harding, it originated in the values expressed in the manager's own words:

'I have never believed that we should just *stick to football*. I know my voice carries weight, not because of who I am but because of the position that I hold … I have a responsibility to the wider community to use my voice, and so do the players. It's their duty to continue to interact with the public on matters such as equality, inclusivity and racial injustice, while using the power of their voices to help put debates on the table, raise awareness and educate.'

* * *

Russia's invasion of Ukraine, commencing on 24 February 2022, precipitated an epochal shift in Germany's foreign policy. Chancellor Olaf Scholz, who succeeded Merkel in December 2021, gave a speech to the Bundestag on 27 February that is now known by a single word, *Zeitenwende*, or 'turning point in history'. Scholz pledged to send weapons to Ukraine and announced a €100bn increase in defence spending, representing a momentous U-turn in Germany's stance towards Russia and militarism in general. As we have seen, Scholz's SPD party in particular had long favoured diplomacy and inclusion in relations with Moscow, but now Vladimir Putin's aggression necessitated a change in course.

The events also sharpened scrutiny on former chancellor Gerhard Schröder, who ratified the Nord Stream gas pipeline in the Baltic Sea in 2005, shortly before joining the board of the company Nord Stream AG. As Philip Oltermann explained in *The Observer* in March 2022, 'The resultant increase in Germany's reliance on Russian energy, politicians in Berlin now concede, may have led Putin to believe Germany would be too hamstrung to support concerted economic sanctions.' The issue of Russian energy dependence has also raised questions around Merkel's legacy, since she unveiled the first pipeline in 2011 and supported its expansion, insisting that it was an 'economic project'. The CDU's Roderich Kiesewetter was quoted as saying, 'With Nord Stream, it is now apparent that Germany was simply tricked by the Russian side: this was always a political and not a commercial project.'

In June 2022, in her first public appearance since leaving office, Merkel defended her handling of Putin, 'I would feel very bad if I had said: "There's no point talking to that man."'" She said that while she never believed that Putin 'could be changed through trade', it was important to her to sustain economic relations with Moscow. 'It's a great tragedy that it didn't work,' said Merkel, 'but I don't blame myself for trying.'

7 June 2022
UEFA Nations League group stage
Germany 1-1 England
Allianz Arena, Munich

England's Euro 2020 campaign saw the team reach its first major final in 55 years, but it ended in yet more penalty shoot-out heartbreak with defeat to Italy at Wembley on 11 July 2021. A year later, and only five months before the 2022 FIFA World Cup in Qatar, England and Germany met in the third edition of the UEFA Nations League. The four-team group also included Italy and Hungary, and Germany's campaign began with a trip to Bologna to face the European champions. The DFB had announced on 25 May 2021 that Joachim Löw would be succeeded by his former assistant Hansi Flick, who never appeared for the senior national team but played alongside the likes of Lothar Matthäus and Andreas Brehme in FC Bayern's defeat to Porto in the 1987 European Cup Final. As manager, he guided the club to a sensational treble in the 2019/20 season, a campaign which included the famous 8-2 win over Barcelona in the UEFA Champions League quarter-final behind closed doors in Lisbon. Flick's tenure as *Bundestrainer* formally began on 1 August 2021, and the year ended with seven straight wins in World Cup qualification.

In Italy, the hosts took the lead after 70 minutes but Germany hit back quickly through Kimmich to secure a 1-1 draw. Flick started with a 4-2-3-1 formation in each of his first ten games, and despite initial confusion at the seven changes made from the draw with the *Azzurri*, Germany adopted the same system against England. New Real Madrid signing Antonio Rüdiger, with 51 senior appearances, marshalled an otherwise inexperienced defence which featured Lukas Klostermann, David Raum, and recent Borussia Dortmund recruit Nico Schlotterbeck. The experienced trio of Kimmich, Müller and

Ilkay Gündoğan were complemented by Havertz, still aged 22, and FC Bayern starlet Musiala. Germany's goal came early in the second half from Gladbach midfielder Jonas Hofmann, who received a clever through ball from Kimmich with his back to goal just inside the penalty area, turned swiftly, and shot straight at Pickford. The England goalkeeper raised one hand and should certainly have made the save, but the ball unaccountably flew past him and into the net.

Ahead of the match, Southgate maintained that Germany remained 'the benchmark' to which England must aspire, 'Even when everyone will talk about the 5-1 here, they ended up in the World Cup Final off the back of that qualifying campaign. You have to respect what they've been and what they are as a country in footballing terms. That mentality is what we're trying to create.' Southgate again showed his respect for the opposition in opting to match Flick's formation when England had been expected to start with a back three. The personnel was much the same as for the Wembley win a year before, although with Mount alongside Saka and Sterling, and Trippier at left-back. The manager's apparent caution in playing Phillips ahead of the highly fancied Borussia Dortmund teenager Jude Bellingham was negated by an early injury to Phillips. The later introductions of Grealish and West Ham United's Jarrod Bowen, who made his debut in Budapest just three days earlier, gave England some much-needed attacking impetus at the end of the game, and only two minutes remained when a dubious penalty was awarded via VAR review for a trip by Schlotterbeck on Kane. The England captain converted the penalty to score his 50th international goal, passing Bobby Charlton in second place in the all-time ranking.

As noted in the *Kicker* match report, it was not so much in these closing stages that the home side squandered two points, but in Germany's strong period after the opening goal, when the victory ought to have been secured. For long periods, Flick's side looked more assured and more tactically proficient. Yet England's response in arrears was encouraging, as noted by Barney Ronay, 'Losing to a more fluent team, Southgate changed the game and England got better. This is significant, because it is also the thing he has previously failed at. It is a regular point in the rolling ledger of Southgate criticisms that England's manager fails to react in real time to the key tactical details.'

* * *

Those criticisms, surprising to some after Southgate's achievements at two tournaments, are in part the inevitable result of the same manager guiding the national team for nigh on six years. As I write at the end of the 2021/22 season, however, the doubts have turned into widespread calls for his sacking, and the four-game series in the Nations League in June has badly undermined preparations for the forthcoming World Cup. The *coup de grâce* came in the very last game, a 4-0 defeat to Hungary at Molineux. This was England's heaviest home loss since Scotland's 5-1 win at Wembley in 1928, all of 94 years previously. Southgate and his remaining supporters can only hope that the woeful result was caused by weariness at the end of a long and difficult season, but his team were brutally exposed and left rooted to the bottom of the Nations League group, threatened with relegation to League B.

At the same time that England suffered this ignominious, indelible defeat, Germany faced Italy in Mönchengladbach. An enthralling performance against the admittedly poor *Azzurri* ended in a 5-2 win, with goals from Kimmich, Gündoğan, Müller, and a brace from Werner. After 12 games without defeat, this was Flick's first win against a top side, and it came in emphatic style. Under his management, German football will look to reach the World Cup semi-final at a minimum before steering a course towards the European Championship title on home soil in 2024.

Just a week before these simultaneous results, England and Germany had seemed well matched in Munich, and of course Germany have yet to avenge their most recent encounter at Wembley. Yet it strikes me how in the space of one evening on 14 June, the fortunes of these two great football nations could diverge again so markedly. Such is the enduring enigma of the England v Germany football rivalry, and indeed Anglo-German relations in a wider sense: so close, yet so far.

Statistical Appendix

FIFA World Cup record

Year	Host	England	Germany/ West Germany
1930	Uruguay	Did not enter	Did not enter
1934	Italy	Did not enter	Third place
1938	France	Did not enter	First round
1950	Brazil	Group stage	Banned
1954	Switzerland	Quarter-finals	**Winners**
1958	Sweden	Group stage	Fourth place
1962	Chile	Quarter-finals	Quarter-finals
1966	England	**Winners**	Runners-up
1970	Mexico	Quarter-finals	Third place
1974	West Germany	Failed to qualify	**Winners**
1978	Argentina	Failed to qualify	Second group stage
1982	Spain	Second group stage	Runners-up
1986	Mexico	Quarter-finals	Runners-up
1990	Italy	Fourth place	**Winners**
1994	United States	Failed to qualify	Quarter-finals
1998	France	Round of 16	Quarter-finals
2002	Japan and South Korea	Quarter-finals	Runners-up
2006	Germany	Quarter-finals	Third place
2010	South Africa	Round of 16	Third place
2014	Brazil	Group stage	**Winners**
2018	Russia	Fourth place	Group stage
2022	Qatar	Qualified	Qualified

UEFA European Championship record

Year	Host	England	Germany/ West Germany
1960	France	Did not enter	Did not enter
1964	Spain	Failed to qualify	Did not enter
1968	Italy	Third place	Failed to qualify
1972	Belgium	Quarter-finals	**Winners**
1976	Yugoslavia	Failed to qualify	Runners-up
1980	Italy	Group stage	**Winners**
1984	France	Failed to qualify	Group stage
1988	West Germany	Group stage	Semi-finals
1992	Sweden	Group stage	Runners-up
1996	England	Semi-finals	**Winners**
2000	Belgium and Netherlands	Group stage	Group stage
2004	Portugal	Quarter-finals	Group stage
2008	Austria and Switzerland	Failed to qualify	Runners-up
2012	Poland and Ukraine	Quarter-finals	Semi-finals
2016	France	Round of 16	Semi-finals
2021	UEFA	Runners-up	Round of 16

List of England managers

Manager	From	To	Major honours
Walter Winterbottom	1946	1962	
Alf Ramsey	1963	1974	FIFA World Cup 1966
Don Revie	1974	1977	
Ron Greenwood	1977	1982	
Bobby Robson	1982	1990	
Graham Taylor	1990	1993	
Terry Venables	1994	1996	
Glenn Hoddle	1996	1999	
Kevin Keegan	1999	2000	
Sven-Göran Eriksson	2001	2006	
Steve McClaren	2006	2007	
Fabio Capello	2007	2012	
Roy Hodgson	2012	2016	
Sam Allardyce	2016	2016	
Gareth Southgate	2016	current	

List of Germany/West Germany managers

Manager	From	To	Major honours
Otto Nerz	1926	1936	
Sepp Herberger	1936	1942	
Sepp Herberger	1950	1964	FIFA World Cup 1954
Helmut Schön	1964	1978	UEFA European Championship 1972; FIFA World Cup 1974
Jupp Derwall	1978	1984	UEFA European Championship 1980
Franz Beckenbauer	1984	1990	FIFA World Cup 1990
Berti Vogts	1990	1998	UEFA European Championship 1996
Erich Ribbeck	1998	2000	
Rudi Völler	2000	2004	
Jürgen Klinsmann	2004	2006	
Joachim Löw	2006	2021	FIFA World Cup 2014
Hansi Flick	2021	current	

Ballon d'Or winners

Year	Player	Club
1956	Stanley Matthews	Blackpool
1966	Bobby Charlton	Manchester United
1970	Gerd Müller	FC Bayern
1972	Franz Beckenbauer	FC Bayern
1976	Franz Beckenbauer	FC Bayern
1978	Kevin Keegan	Hamburger SV
1979	Kevin Keegan	Hamburger SV
1980	Karl-Heinz Rummenigge	FC Bayern
1981	Karl-Heinz Rummenigge	FC Bayern
1990	Lothar Matthäus	Internazionale
1996	Matthias Sammer	Borussia Dortmund
2001	Michael Owen	Liverpool

Anglo-German finals in European club competition
UEFA European Cup/Champions League

1974/75	FC Bayern 2-0 Leeds United	Paris
1975/76	Liverpool 3-1 Borussia Mönchengladbach	Rome
1979/80	Nottingham Forest 1-0 Hamburger SV	Madrid
1981/82	Aston Villa 1-0 FC Bayern	Rotterdam
1998/99	Manchester United 2-1 FC Bayern	Barcelona
2011/12	Chelsea 1-1* FC Bayern	Munich
	(Chelsea won 4-3 on penalties)	

UEFA Cup/Europa League

1972/73	Liverpool 3-0 Borussia Mönchengladbach
	Borussia Mönchengladbach 2-0 Liverpool
	(Liverpool won 3-2 on aggregate)

UEFA Cup Winners' Cup

1964/65	West Ham United 2-0 TSV 1860 München	Wembley
1965/66	Borussia Dortmund 2-1* Liverpool	Glasgow
1997/98	Chelsea 1-0 VfB Stuttgart	Stockholm

Bibliography

Books and journal articles

Beck, Peter J. *Scoring for Britain: international football and international politics, 1900-1939*. London: Routledge, 1999.

---. 'The Relevance of the "Irrelevant": Football as a Missing Dimension in the Study of British Relations with Germany.' *International Affairs* 79.2 (2003): 389-411.

Bishop, Hywel, and Adam Jaworski. - '"We Beat 'Em": Nationalism and the Hegemony of Homogeneity in the British Press Reportage of Germany Versus England During Euro 2000.' *Discourse & Society* 14.3 (2003): 243–271.

Charlton, Bobby. *1966: My World Cup Story*. London: Yellow Jersey Press, 2016.

Charlton, Jack. *Jack Charlton: The Autobiography*. London: Corgi, 2020.

Chronik des deutschen Fußballs. 2nd ed. Munich: Chronik Verlag, 2007.

Davies, Pete. *One Night in Turin*. London: Yellow Jersey Press, 1990.

Dawson, Jeff. *Back Home: England and the 1970 World Cup*. London: Orion Books, 2001.

Donald, Michael. *Goal! Intimate portraits and interviews with every living FIFA World Cup Final scorer*. London: Hamlyn, 2017.

Downing, David. *The Best of Enemies: England v Germany, a century of football rivalry*. London: Bloomsbury, 2000.

Edgerton, David. 'The "White Heat" Revisited: The British Government and Technology in the 1960s.' *Twentieth Century British History* 7.1 (1996): 53-82.

Fischer, Gerhard, and Ulrich Lindner. *Stürmer für Hitler*. Göttingen: Verlag die Werkstatt, 1999.

Fullbrook, Mary. *A Concise History of Germany*. 1991. 3rd ed. Cambridge: Cambridge UP, 2019.

Gehler, Michael. *Deutschland. Von der Teilung zur Einigung. 1945 bis heute*. Vienna: Böhlau Verlag, 2010.

Gillmeister, Heiner. 'The First European Soccer Match.' *The Sports Historian* 17.2 (1997): 1-13.

Glanville, Brian. 'Britain against the rest.' In: M. Sissons and P. French, eds. *Age of Austerity*. Oxford: Oxford UP, 1986.

Goldblatt, David. *The Ball is Round: A Global History of Football*. London: Penguin Books, 2007.

Green, Geoffrey. *The History of the Football Association*. London: Naldrett Press, 1953.

Grix, Jonathan. 'Sport politics.' In: Sarah Colvin, ed. *The Routledge Handbook of German Politics & Culture*. Abingdon, Oxon.: Routledge, 2015: 441-456.

Haeussler, Mathias. *Helmut Schmidt and British-German Relations: A European Misunderstanding*. Cambridge: Cambridge UP, 2019.

Herbert, Ulrich. *A History of Twentieth-Century Germany*. Trans. Ben Fowkes. Oxford: Oxford UP, 2019.

Hesse, Uli. *Tor! The Story of German Football*. 2002. 4th ed. Edinburgh: Polaris, 2022.

Hilmes, Oliver. *Berlin 1936: Sixteen Days in August*. Trans. Jefferson Chase. London: The Bodley Head, 2018.

Hughson, John. *England and the 1966 World Cup: A Cultural History*. Manchester: Manchester UP, 2016.

Hurst, Geoff. *1966 and all that: My Autobiography*. 2001. 40th anniversary ed. London: Headline, 2005.

Jacobs, Norman. *Vivian Woodward: Football's Gentleman*. Stroud, Glos.: Tempus, 2005.

Koppehel, Karl. *Geschichte des deutschen Fussballsports*. Frankfurt am Main: Wilhelm Limpert-Verlag, 1954.

Krämer, Gerd. *Im Dress Der Elf Besten*. Munich: Bassermann, 1961.

Le Carré, John. *Absolute Friends*. London: Penguin Books, 2003.

Leighton, James. *Duncan Edwards: The Greatest*. London: Simon & Schuster, 2012.

Leinemann, Jürgen. *Sepp Herberger: Ein Leben, Eine Legende*. Berlin: Rohwolt, 1997.

MacMillan, Margaret. *The War That Ended Peace*. London: Profile Books, 2013.

Marcuse, Harold. 'The Revival of Holocaust Awareness in West Germany, Israel, and the United States.' In: Carole Fink, Philipp Gassert, and Detlef Junker, eds. *1968: The World Transformed*. Cambridge: Cambridge UP, 1998: 421-438.

Matthews, Stanley. *The Way It Was: My Autobiography*. London: Headline, 2000.

McKinstry, Leo. *Sir Alf: a major reappraisal of the life and times of England's greatest football manager*. London: HarperSport, 2006.

Morgan, Kenneth, 'Britain in the Seventies – Our Unfinest Hour?' *French Journal of British Studies* [Online]. XXII-Hors Série (2017): 1-17.

Otto, Wolfgang. *Träume, Tränen und Triumphe – 100 Jahre Jahn-Fußball*. Regensburg: Forum-Verlag, 2007.

Paschalidis, Gregory. 'Cultural outreach: Overcoming the past?' In: Sarah Colvin, ed. *The Routledge Handbook of German Politics & Culture*. Abingdon, Oxon.: Routledge, 2015: 457-471.

Pyta, Wolfram. *Der Lange Weg zur Bundesliga*. Litverlag, Münster: 2004.

Reid, I., and Zisserman, A. (1996). Goal-directed video metrology. In: Buxton, B., Cipolla, R., eds. *Computer Vision — ECCV '96*. ECCV 1996. Lecture Notes in Computer Science, vol. 1065. Berlin: Springer, 1996.

Riddoch, Andrew, and John Kemp. *When the Whistle Blows*. Yeovil, Somerset: Haynes, 2008.

Robson, Bobby. *Farewell But Not Goodbye: My Autobiography*. London: Hodder and Stoughton, 2005.

Sandbrook, Dominic. *Never Had It So Good: A History of Britain from Suez to the Beatles*. London: Little, Brown, 2005.

Schulze-Marmeling, Dietrich. 'Der DFB nach 1945. In: Gerhard Fischer and Ulrich Lindner, eds. *Stürmer für Hitler*. Göttingen: Verlag die Werkstatt, 1999: 265-276.

Schiller, Kay. '"Siegen für Deutschland?" Patriotism, Nationalism and the German National Football Team, 1954-2014.' *Historical Social Research* 40.2 (2015): 176-196.

Sutcliffe, Richard. *Revie: Revered and Reviled*. Ilkley, Yorks.: Great Northern Books, 2010.

Tilkowski, Hans. *Und ewig fällt das Wembley-Tor: Die Geschichte meines Lebens*. Göttingen: Verlag die Werkstatt, 2006.

Urbanek, Gerhard. *Österreichs Deutschland-Komplex*. Vienna: LIT Verlag, 2012.

Wagner, Christoph. 'Thirty Years of Hurt: The Anglo-German Football Rivalry in the Sports Press 1966 and 1996.' In: Frank Jacob and Alexander Friedmann, eds. *Fußball: Identitätskurse, Politik, Skandale*. Stuttgart: Kohlhammer, 2020: 81-104.

Weintraub, Stanley. *Silent Night: The Remarkable Christmas Truce of 1914*. London: Simon & Schuster, 2001.

Wilson, Jonathan. *Inverting the Pyramid: The History of Football Tactics*. 2008. 10th anniversary ed. London: Weidenfeld & Nicolson, 2018.

Winter, Henry. *Fifty Years of Hurt*. London: Bantam Press, 2016.

Index

INDEX